ACCLAIM FOR
BUILT TO WIN

"What they've done is more than impressive. If they were to give a Pulitzer Prize in baseball, Bobby Cox and John Schuerholz and that whole organization deserve the Pulitzer Prize."
—Omar Minaya

"It's almost unbelievable. I don't know if you'll ever see that again. Just to be able to play that well that long, to be that consistent . . . It says a lot about their management, to put a team out there like that every year. They've had some good fortune, too, avoiding injuries, that kind of thing. But it's just an incredible accomplishment."
—Derrek Lee

"It's unbelievable, to have the run that they've had for so long, to constantly be chased and to win. Every year it was Atlanta. When I was in Philly, and before that when I was in Houston, we knew we were going to play Atlanta in the playoffs. They established that tradition, and that's what every organization wants to achieve."
—Billy Wagner

"Fourteen division titles—that's incredible. They've never gone in as a wild card. They're winning division titles every year."
—Michael Tucker

more . . .

"Together [Bobby Cox and John Schuerholz] found, located, and developed championship-caliber talent with the annual success never enjoyed by any other manager/general manager combination."

—Mark Bowman, MLB.com

"Fourteen straight titles. Only Russian pairs skaters and Tiger Woods are supposed to have runs like that."

—Mike Lopresti, *USA Today*

"When John Schuerholz first became a general manager in 1981, he was the Kansas City kid, the forty-one-year-old rookie among GM veterans like Paul Owens, Hank Peters, and Dick Wagner, names that defined how to run a club in the '70s. But a new day was dawning. Those who couldn't juggle bottom lines with batting lines fell away, leaving baseball's new world to a newer breed. And now, twenty-one years later, Schuerholz not only has mastered that juggling act, he has accomplished even more than those old luminaries—and staked out a rare claim to the Hall of Fame."

—Alan Schwarz, ESPN.com

BUILT TO WIN

INSIDE STORIES AND LEADERSHIP STRATEGIES FROM BASEBALL'S WINNINGEST GENERAL MANAGER

JOHN SCHUERHOLZ

WITH LARRY GUEST

WARNER BOOKS

NEW YORK   BOSTON

All photos are from the author's personal collection.

Warner Books
Hachette Book Group USA
237 Park Avenue
New York, NY 10169

Visit our Web site at www.HachetteBookGroupUSA.com.

Printed in the United States of America

Originally published in hardcover by Warner Books, an imprint of Warner Books, Inc.

First Trade Edition: April 2007
10 9 8 7 6 5 4 3 2 1

Warner Books and the "W" logo are trademarks of Time Warner Inc. or an affiliated company. Used under license by Hachette Book Group USA, which is not affiliated with Time Warner Inc.

The Library of Congress has cataloged the hardcover edition as follows:
Schuerholz, John.
   Built to win : inside stories and leadership strategies from baseball's winningest GM / John Schuerholz with Larry Guest.— 1st ed.
        p. cm.
   ISBN-13: 978-0-446-57868-4
   ISBN-10: 0-446-57868-1
   1. Atlanta Braves (Baseball team)—Management. 2. Schuerholz, John. I. Guest, Larry, 1942–   II. Title.
   GV875.A8S34 2006
   796.357'6409758231—dc22   2005035342

Book design by Charles Sutherland

ISBN-13: 978-0-446-69653-1 (pbk.)
ISBN-10: 0-446-69653-6 (pbk.)

In honor and in memory of my dad, John, a special athlete, a true gentleman, a kind and caring father, and my life's mentor. To my mother, Maryne, the sweetest person, my wonderful "Mud." And most especially to my loving wife, Karen, my constant bedrock of support and the real General Manager of our family and home. To our children, Gina, a caring daughter and dedicated teacher, and Jonathan, professional baseball player, a remarkable young man, and great son. They make me proud to be their son, husband, and father. They have made this journey joyful.

ACKNOWLEDGMENTS

Larry Guest: Friend and author who first suggested this book idea to me in 1991 and whose collaboration helped me turn forty years of baseball memories and leadership values into these words. Thanks to his tireless efforts and literary guiding hand throughout our partnership in this project, Larry helped make this writing challenge a labor of love.

Larry Kirshbaum, Time Warner Book Group: Without your vision and strong belief in this book, it wouldn't have happened. Thank you.

Rick Wolff: My editor, whose knowledge, understanding, and appreciation of baseball's unique twists and turns and his attention to excellence in editing detail kept this project on track and always aimed high.

Karen: My loving wife, at-home collaborator, and editor. Her understanding of my thoughts and the core-deep instincts of my ideas helped me keep those values on these pages expressed in an appropriate style and fashion. Your support in this project was special.

Lou Gorman: Thanks so much. You gave me my start in baseball and, most importantly, a greater appreciation of our most precious asset in life: good people.

Frank Cashen, former president of the Baltimore Orioles: For answering my letter of hope to the Baltimore Orioles in 1966 and opening the door to my baseball career and lifetime dream.

Pastor Dr. Robert Sims, senior pastor, Lutheran Church of the Redeemer: Your spiritual inspiration and intellectual stimulation have not only greatly strengthened my personal values but have enhanced and inspired my professional leadership principles. Your words and your spirit have not only lifted me but found their way in my thoughts and words in this book.

Terry McGuirk, chairman and president of the Atlanta Braves: Your unbridled confidence and ongoing support continue to give me the encouragement and drive to lead this proud Braves franchise and the spirit to work and perpetuate its greatness.

Stan Kasten, former president of the Atlanta Braves: What an exhilarating and exciting time we had as we partnered in the remarkable transformation of the Braves. Ideas and sparks flew wildly—and now the championship pennants fly proudly. What a great ride we had. Thanks.

Bobby Cox, Braves manager: Our future Hall of Fame manager and my constant partner in this remarkable, unprecedented, proud run of success. It has been my great personal and professionl pleasure to serve as GM with one of baseball's all-time great managers.

Frank Wren, Dean Taylor, and Chuck LaMar: My assistant GMs in whose judgment I relied and on whose commitment, hard work, and loyalty I have always depended.

Paul Snyder and Dayton Moore: Paul, for your lifetime of passion and dedicated work in scouting on behalf of the Atlanta Braves and the honor and dignity you've added to baseball; and Dayton, for perpetuating those same values and the work ethic that keeps the Atlanta Braves' talent pipeline filled with quality.

Melissa Stone: My executive assistant who not only manages my office but so willingly gave her time to coordinate the many aspects of this book project and still managed to give birth to her first child, Bradley. What a gal.

June Cornillaud: My first executive assistant with the Braves, who was so invaluable in guiding me through the organization's infrastructure in those early, crazy days, and always offered her strong opinions and even stronger loyalty.

Bob Costas: A man who's earned considerable accolades in sports journalism and whose remarkable knowledge of baseball is only exceeded by his passion for it. I am so honored that you were gracious enough to write the foreword for this book.

Jerry and Larry Schuerholz: My brothers, who always bring to mind the unmatched joy of a wonderful family life and the beautiful memories we share from it.

Bob Barnett: My literary agent, who marked the trail for my first steps along this challenging and exciting journey. Your guidance and assistance in this project started me in the right direction.

The Sand Iron 5: My good friends Nick Trigony, Bob O'Leary, Bud Wright, Ed Mellett, and Mike Franke, for their constant friendship, golfing camaraderie, always honest opinions, and creative suggestions for the title of this book.

Rich Levin, Brad Hainje, and Dean Vogelaar: Three public relations pros, from Major League Baseball, the Atlanta Braves, and the Kansas City Royals, whose research and confirmation of facts were of great help.

CONTENTS

Ten
Giving Back 243

FOREWORD

BY BOB COSTAS

In the fall of 1990, the Atlanta Braves were concluding a seventh straight losing year and a third consecutive last-place finish in their division. After the season John Schuerholz took over as the team's general manager, displacing Bobby Cox, who returned to field managing. Schuerholz got to work quickly, making a flurry of off-season moves. Every October since, when baseball has been played, the Braves have been playing it as a first-place team. Really, the story is that simple, and that extraordinary.

That year, you wouldn't have thought that a thirty-year-old accomplished, but not superstar, third baseman named Terry Pendleton would have an MVP season, but then again, you're not John Schuerholz. Pendleton was just the first in a long line of veteran free agents or trade acquisitions to restart or jump-start their careers in Atlanta: Marquis Grissom, Fred McGriff, Brian Jordan, Denny Neagle, John Burkett. Alongside them would be a never-ending stream of talented young players from the Braves system: Tom Glavine, David Justice, Chipper Jones, Javy Lopez, Andruw Jones, the list goes on. The pattern continues today. Who but Schuerholz and the Braves would continue to get good use out of forty-seven-year-old Julio Franco at the very same time that Jeff Francoeur makes the leap from Double-A to big league rookie sensation? These are but a few examples, and they are not isolated. Any team will catch lightning in a bottle with player moves now and then. But for Schuerholz and the Braves, this is an unending pattern, a pattern of shrewd and resourceful player evaluation and consistently effective cost-benefit analysis. This perennial first-place team has in many ways taken on the identity of its GM, universally admired for an excellence that is reliable and hard earned, as well as largely understated.

It's the sustained nature of that success that best defines the Schuerholz era in Atlanta. In a time of upheaval and constant change in sports in general, and baseball in particular, one of the precious few consistent things has been the uninterrupted excellence of the Braves. Now, certainly the club is not among baseball's have-nots, but the front office most definitely operates under a defined budget that has actually become significantly tighter in recent years. So they can't go off the deep end, and they have had to let the Glavines, Madduxes, Millwoods, Sheffields, and others go. Yet Schuerholz and the Braves always seem to find the replacement parts, either through an advantageous deal, well-considered free-agent acquisition, or the always well-stocked farm system. And then there's the Schuerholz application of the Branch Rickey philosophy of addition by subtraction. Few teams have displayed such a well-developed knack of getting a decent season or two out of a guy and then unloading him, just as his price was about to go up and his performance about to go down. This often frees up the payroll space the Braves need to keep their run going.

The other team that has had uninterrupted success over a long period of time is the Yankees. But there are significant differences betweeen the clubs. First, of course, there's seemingly no limit to what New York will spend on new players each off-season. Schuerholz doesn't have the same margin of error with decisions that the Yankees do—mistakes cost more dearly. And second, although as of this writing Joe Torre has weathered whatever storms he's faced, the storms happen nonetheless. Since the Braves have known October disappointment, it's fair to ask how many times over the past fourteen years Schuerholz, Cox, or pitching guru Leo Mazzone would have had their heads on the chopping block had they worn pinstripes instead of tomahawks on their uniforms. Luckily, sanity prevails in Atlanta, as does an appreciation for the long-haul test that is a baseball season, and now season upon season upon season.

Baseball's new three-division-plus-wild-card format has its plusses, but one undeniable drawback is an insufficient respect for the regular season. A wild card qualifier or weak division winner enters the best-of-five first round crapshoot at no significant disadvantage when taking on a team that has proven its true worth over 162 games. And the truth is that baseball—unlike football or basketball, where specific personnel advantages can be pressed moment to moment, game to game—

is a game of small incremental differences where even great teams can lose three of four, and the worst team that ever played a season could theoretically sweep a doubleheader from the '27 Yankees. This may make baseball's modern postseason in some ways exciting, but as the primary measure of an organization's success, it's misleading. Exhibit A: the Florida Marlins, who, coming out of the same division as the Braves, have never finished first in any season but have won two world championships since Atlanta's world title in 1995. While some respect should be accorded the September and October runs that produced Florida's titles, only a short-attention–span world—dominated by SportsCenter highlights and instant analysis (or lack thereof) on sports talk radio—would value those achievements above Atlanta's.

Have the Braves' postseason defeats stung? Sure they have, especially because some were so close that a single pitch or play could have produced another championship or an advance to the next round. But my point here is that we're in a world where a team that wins one Super Bowl gets more credit than the Buffalo Bills for making it to four straight title games. For my money, what the Braves have done, without an over-whelming economic advantage over their competitors, is one of the most remarkable achievements in the history of American team sports. And it's all been achieved without histrionics—when they've lost, there has been no excuse making, no irrational reassessments, knee-jerk house-cleanings, or crazed personnel changes. Rather, the Braves and Schuerholz have con-tinued on the same course, undaunted, and each year, they come back again and again, doing all the little things on the field and in the front of-fice that make a difference over the course of a long baseball season.

John Updike once wrote of Ted Williams that he was "the classic ballplayer of the game on a hot August weekday, before a small crowd, when the only thing at stake is the tissue-thin difference between a thing done well and a thing done ill." It is a commentary on the virtue, particulary in this game, of doing things the right way, not just for the outcome, but out of genuine respect for one's craft and appreciation for excellence for its own sake. If Updike is still paying attention to base-ball, I'll bet he admires Schuerholz and the Braves.

My own admiration for Schuerholz stems not just from his baseball track record—which includes, by the way, a world championship with the '85 KC Royals and apprenticeships under some of the sharpest baseball minds ever, Harry Dalton and Frank Cashen in Baltimore and Joe Burke in Kansas City. Beyond that, I have always been struck by the man's demeanor. He's a leader not just because of his baseball acumen, but because of his insight into people, which allows him to assemble, maintain, and motivate a consistently effective organization. He's a well-read man, with many interests outside the game. In a time of bombast and self-promotion, Schuerholz is unfailingly thoughtful, gracious, and self-effacing. But listen to others if you want the real story. Jim Bowden, who has been the GM at Cincinnati and now Washington: "John Schuerholz is the best general manager of our time. The GM award should be named the 'John Schuerholz Award.'" Prior to the '05 season, John Donovan of *Sports Illustrated* wrote: "Maybe someday, they'll find out that John Schuerholz was just really, really good at cooking the books. Or that he had a knack for blackmail. Or hypnosis. But until then, all we can do is bow down to one of the best general managers in any sport, at any time, a man who somehow has kept alive a string of unmatched division titles. Somehow, Schuerholz has found the right players, come up with just the right amount of money when he needed it, plugged the holes and put out the fires, and his Braves have responded by winning their division thirteen straight times."

Schuerholz would be the first person to give much of the credit for the Braves' run of success to Bobby Cox, an elite manager with an obvious talent for dealing with players old and young; and to Leo Mazzone, the former Atlanta pitching coach who's resuscitated and breathed life into so many careers that we've all lost count. But the Braves, more than anything else in this modern age, are a GM's team. Each spring, the baseball world looks at Atlanta, and notices that pieces of the puzzle at Turner Field have been switched out, rearranged, often in subtle yet significant ways. And each fall, the baseball world looks at the standings, and sees the Braves at the top of the heap. In so many ways, John Schuerholz is right there with them.

1

Barry Bonds a Brave—Briefly

BASEBALL'S SPRING TRAINING, IT HAS BEEN SAID, IS THAT time of year when everyone wins the pennant. Hope and optimism reign supreme. The pundits wax poetic about the mystical potential of this young phenom just up from the minors, or that solid veteran acquired to fill a pressing need. Rosters that were altered or tinkered with over the winter are gushingly introduced as cohesive, winning machines.

In Florida and Arizona, the warm sunrises bring each new day's glowing expectations as the teams renew themselves weeks ahead of, for many, the grim reality that eventually will set in sooner or later during the long baseball season to follow. Indeed, those expectations were never higher in the Braves' camp than in 1992 in our spring training in West Palm Beach. Those of us in the loop at the highest level of Atlanta's management were charged with the excitement that was about to be unveiled to the sports public shortly before noon on that fateful spring day.

There was a palpable adrenaline rush throughout our little mobile-home administrative office as we scurried about making last-second preparations to officially herald what would certainly be a pivotal, history-making trade.

Stellar, All-Star outfielder Barry Bonds had been acquired by the Atlanta Braves!

The deal had been closed late the previous afternoon. The Pittsburgh Pirates had agreed to take pitcher Alejandro Pena, young outfielder Keith Mitchell, and a prospect-to-be-named later for *the* Barry Bonds.

I had negotiated the trade over several days with Pirates GM Ted Simmons, the former standout catcher who had a solid playing career, primarily with the St. Louis Cardinals. As the talks progressed and Pena became a fixture in the potential deal, we had to seek Pena's permission to include him in the trade. Because of his stature as a newly signed free agent, we had to have him sign a trade release. I had to talk to Alejandro and explain the situation. After a brief time to consider, he was willing to accept a trade and signed the waiver.

So Ted Simmons and I agreed to the deal over the phone. Ted, forerunner of the modern thinkers, is a big, strong, ruddy guy. When his playing career was over, he worked his way into scouting and special assistant jobs in administration and, ultimately, into the general manager seat for the Pirates.

I was euphoric. Barry Bonds was a Brave! We had already won our division the previous season, my first as Braves GM. Now we were adding a high-caliber star to our already successful roster. There seemed no limits to what we could achieve over the approaching several seasons.

Stan Kasten, then-president of the Braves, recalls a pang of concern the next morning when he read a story critical of the Pirates for dumping salaries. Little did the media realize the salary-dumping mode had continued the previous evening, the Pirates dealing away Bonds, who had one season left on his contract. I rushed into my office early that day at the West Palm ballpark to prepare for a number of things that go with announcing a trade of this magnitude. About an hour before the announcement, I decided to call Ted Simmons just to coordinate the timing of the release.

"We have a problem," Ted said.

"What do mean, a problem? Don't want to release it just yet? What?"

"I can't do the deal," he said.

"You can't do the deal? You *did* the deal! Ted, we agreed over the phone, general manager to general manager. We *made* the deal!"

In baseball, that's about as sacrosanct as anything gets. That had never happened to me, nor has it since, where there was a total reneging of a trade. I did have a situation much later where a club went back on one of the financial terms of a trade, but we still made the trade. (I'll get more into that situation in a minute.)

Bailing out after two GMs have verbally cemented a deal very rarely happens. Especially in a deal of this caliber and this magnitude.

I said, "Ted, we have all the mechanisms in place here. We've told the involved players and our manager. I've told our owner. We're getting ready to announce this deal this morning that you and I agreed to make yesterday. We've been through all these steps."

He said, "Well, when I let Leyland know about the trade, he blew up."

Jim Leyland was the manager of the Pirates at that time. When informed of the trade, Jim went barging into Pirates president Carl Barger's office and, according to Ted, went absolutely haywire. He said Barger came back to him and said it was a situation so troublesome to the manager and this and that, they couldn't do the deal. And ultimately, it was called off.

I guess we can say Barry Bonds was a Brave for fifteen hours. At that time in his career, he didn't have the right to approve a deal, so I'm not even sure he is aware this happened. If he had had the right of trade approval and they had to discuss it with him, I'm sure Barry would have said something to somebody and this story would have come out long ago. So I doubt Barry knows he was a Brave for one night.

But he will when he reads this book.

I had kept our manager, Bobby Cox, and Stan Kasten abreast of the deal as it developed. We were thrilled that we were going to get, arguably, the best player in baseball for, essentially, two prospects. Making it even sweeter was our confidence that we would be able to sign Barry to a long-term extension. We were flying high back then and our payroll was beginning to grow. We had room to sign Bonds to an extension, though it would mean we wouldn't have had the money to sign Greg Maddux the next year. (Ironically, at the winter meetings the next year at the Galt House hotel in Louisville, the Giants signed Bonds, we signed Maddux, and poor Carl Barger collapsed during an owners meeting and died.)

As for the fallout, I didn't come away from this with a distrust of Ted Simmons, or a notion that I'd never engage in trade talks with him again. He is a bright guy, very intellectual, and I had no reason to doubt his integrity, and still don't. He just got caught in a whipsaw. But I was a little gun-shy about doing any deals with Pittsburgh for a period of time after that. You have to let some scar tissue grow over feelings like that. There's a lot of work that goes into making a deal of this size and this was a very complex deal.

That fiasco made me further appreciate my situation in Atlanta and before that in Kansas City as general manager, with regard to autonomy and ownership support. I've never had to worry about being overruled. What I have to worry about is to be certain that I advise my boss, the president of the team, and that information goes up the chain of command before it becomes public—not before I made a decision. Not before I do something. Because their assumption is that what I do will be right and beneficial to the team. They just want to know about it before the public does. That's my responsibility.

Does that have something to do with how efficient and how successful we've been and how consistent we've operated? I think so. I think the fact that part of leadership, as it relates to the level of president and the level of ownership, is to find someone in whom they have trust and confidence. Find someone they respect to do the work that needs to be done. Give that person all the support and encouragement possible and let that person do his job. Now, if that person proves to be ineffective or inept, then obviously he shouldn't have that authority or freedom or power any longer. In my case, whether at Kansas City or Atlanta, I have been permitted the latitude to do what I thought best for the club, always. But I've always recognized that I have to be held accountable for my decisions.

THE OTHER TRADE THAT HAD A HICCUP WAS A DEAL INVOLVING A player that was traded from one club to another, which in turn passed him and his contract to us. The contract came to us with a clear understanding how much of a financial obligation we would have.

What wasn't made clear to us, however, was that subsequent to our trade, there was a clause in the contract that called for additional payments to the player's charitable foundation of $200,000 per year. Now the player was due that money, so we had to pay the $200,000 to keep from voiding the contract. Somebody had to pay it, so we paid it and protested to the Commissioner's Office. Ultimately, it was ruled in our favor; the money was paid, but the Braves were not obligated to pay it and we were reimbursed for the $400,000 we had paid on this clause during the player's first two years with us.

I am hesitant to identify the player or the club because I don't want to impugn the general manager involved. He's a young guy and he's done good work and I'm not sure how much of this matter was his doing.

But back to the Bonds trade. Had the Pirates not done a 180 on us, this was a deal that might have changed the course of baseball history in a number of ways. Though Barry couldn't have produced more division titles for us, might he have powered us to another World Series title or two? Would he have developed into the same prolific home run hitter he became in San Francisco after his move to the Giants? Would his public image be the same? How would we have fared *with* Bonds, but *without* Maddux?

Those questions would be open to far-reaching conjecture by the

Hot-Stovers, the bloggers, and others who feverishly thrive on debating baseball's twists and turns.

But I can say with a considerable degree of confidence that if Barry would have been a Brave, he would have quickly accepted our long-standing team rules regarding issues such as not wearing jewelry while in uniform and not being allowed a recliner at his locker instead of the simple, canvas captain's chair our other players have. Nor would he have been accorded any other special star perk that might set him apart and above his teammates. The same rules as applied to John Smoltz, Chipper Jones, Greg Maddux, Tommy Glavine, Gary Sheffield, and all of the other star-caliber players we have had.

History is on my side on this one. With rare exception, the players who have pulled on a Braves uniform during my time in Atlanta or a Royals uniform when I was in Kansas City have accepted the rules and disciplines we keep in place to promote a team aura and suppress any individualism that might erode that concept.

I strongly believe one of the key ingredients in building a winning team or business is the creation and enhancement of the team concept. Whether it's in baseball or business. Whether you are in management or sales or administration, a parent or a partner.

You assure yourself and your business of succeeding more if you create the strongest team possible. You do that by selecting the right people, then investing in them, improving them, and leading them. While it is obvious that baseball and successful corporations demand great individual skills, they also require an effective and committed team focus—either on the playing field, in the boardroom, or throughout the organization.

We are very exacting in our selection of people to come into this organization, whether administrative staff, uniformed field personnel—managers, coaches, instructors—or players. And we take great pride in that selection process. Do we make mistakes? Sure. We have made a few. But as soon as we find out that we've made a mistake, we address the issue. Quite often, that person is soon excused.

Each of us, I tell our employees, no matter what our individual responsibilities to the company or in our personal lives might be, must create, promote, and strengthen our team concept by our actions, our words, and our attitudes. As responsible and committed leaders, we assume considerable responsibility for creating and nurturing an environment in which the winning team concept will not only survive, but flourish. We must all see to it that we and others in our organization understand how to work effectively and cooperatively, displaying a working harmony, a common purpose, and a support system for one another.

At the staff level, we foster that camaraderie in many ways. Two of the many small, but important, examples:

Early in each spring training, we have a golf outing with Bobby Cox, his coaches, our minor league personnel, scouts, and other baseball-side staffers. It's an informal, jocular scramble event that has come to be known as the SWT (Schuerholz Wins Tournament) Classic. Bill Acree, our director of team travel, organizes the tournament and has been darkly accused of stacking my team each year. For the 2005 event, we returned to Orlando's Orange Tree Golf Club, where I typically reside in a golf villa each spring and where the Tony Wisne ownership family has been generously hospitable to us for many years. Aside from the usual good-natured ribbing and hoots, the '05 event produced a couple of surprises.

First, Pat Kelly, manager of our Triple-A Richmond club, stepped back on a bulkhead alongside the first green to line up a putt, lost his footing, and fell into the lake. Second, four of the five teams finished tied for first. An Orange Tree club staffer rushed home to fetch a child's snorkel and flippers, which we presented to Pat Kelly as the tournament's very first "Jacques Cousteau Award" winner. As for the fact that sixteen of the twenty players tied for first? We could only take that as an omen that we have a lot of winners in that group.

Jose Martinez, who works as a special assistant on baseball matters to me, produces a meaningful bonding event each spring for our office personnel. An excellent chef specializing in his native Cuban cuisine, Jose brings all of his cookers and warmers and pots to the park two or three times each spring and prepares sumptuous and much anticipated lunches of black beans and pork or paella or some other Spanish delicacy.

In the clubhouse, we concentrate on promoting pride and warding off the kind of individualism that can become rampant among high-profile athletes. In addition to banning earrings and limiting other jewelry during games, we ask our guys to wear their uniforms in a manner that we think is proper and which projects pride in our organization.

Some clubs allow their batting helmets to become covered in pine tar. We don't allow that. We don't ban facial hair, but our policy is neat and trimmed. Neat and trimmed occasionally gets challenged and pushed beyond the limits. Bobby is usually the first to notice and a little word from him quickly solves the problem.

Before I came to Atlanta, Bobby had many of the same rules in effect, so we are in lockstep on the team concept. Says Bobby: "I've never had a problem with that. It's funny on rules. You try to make the players part of your selection of the rules. 'Hey, if this is too tough, step in.' Any player who has had a history of doing all that stuff, hasn't had a problem with it here."

If our acquisition of Barry Bonds had stuck, I suppose we would have had to ban another famous earring. But it would have been easy. That's just the way we operate. Those are our guidelines and it makes it easier when you have a manager who feels the same.

It's like when we made the deal for Gary Sheffield after he had his controversies with the Dodgers' owner and general manager. I spoke with Gary on the phone with his agent, Scott Boras, who was in the room with him. Stan Kasten and Frank Wren, the assistant general manager, were in my office, listening in as well. I explained to Sheffield, "Gary, we have a deal made with the Dodgers and we're going to acquire you in a big trade. But I need to say some things to you and get your response to them."

I went into how we operate as a team and how we operate as an organization and what we would put up with and what we would not put up with and how we expect our team members to act, and our earring policy, and so on. And he said, "I have no problem with that."

Despite all the baggage that has been associated with Gary Sheffield, there was not one issue in the two years he was here. And talking about that in terms of leadership is clearly communicating guidelines, clearly communicating expectations, clearly communicating the rules and regulations and the philosophy of your operation. And *clearly* communicating the expectation of that player abiding by those items.

Gary gave his word and lived up to his word.

He had two years remaining on his contract when we acquired him, plus an option year we could have exercised for a certain amount of money. But he had the right to demand a trade because he was in the midst of a multiyear deal. We offered a compromise. We would drop the option clause from the contract in return for his agreeing not to exercise his right to demand a trade after the first year. So it was going to be a two-year relationship.

And if it became more if we reached an agreement to sign him beyond that, so be it. But he was absolutely perfect as a member of our team and as a member of our community, did everything we asked of him, handled himself in perfect fashion, comported himself in a first-class manner, was engaged in all of our community efforts—schools, hospitals, and so forth—and was an absolutely sensational teammate.

The closest he came to causing a stir was near the end of his two years with us and this could be chalked up to his intense competitive nature, not to misbehaving. He mildly opined that our recent postseason disappointments could be traced to what he considered a laissez-faire attitude in the clubhouse. He said we were laid-back. But what he saw as laid-back is in reality a calm and consistent and even-keeled environment that allows a baseball team to play naturally and without extraordinary stress over 162 games. Bobby Cox creates that kind of environment. If a guy has a brutal week he is not going to be lambasted, chastised, called out, made fun of, made an issue of in the newspaper. If a guy has great success and contributes to the team, he is praised, celebrated, and complimented. That's Bobby's style. A real players' manager.

And that so-called laissez-faire attitude is an outgrowth of that even-keeled, evenhanded, calm-water environment that Bobby creates so these guys can come to work every day relaxed, natural, and normal in their approach to the difficult and demanding game of baseball. Teams with more of an uneven, rah-rah environment tend to find themselves at a precipice time after time during the long season. Then it becomes a roll of the dice whether such a team will be on one of those emotional highs at playoff time. Assuming that team even makes the playoffs.

If you create an environment of professional, competitive intensity in an even-keeled manner, which is what we do every season, your chances of making the postseason are much greater. And while I have respect for Gary and his opinion, what he saw as a shortcoming, I see as the constant strength of our ball club.

Obviously, there are players who don't agree with our rules, but most seem transformed once they become exposed to our environment and the team-oriented persona of the vast majority of our veteran players. They quickly sense that self-serving attitudes don't play well in the Atlanta clubhouse.

HERE IS AN EXAMPLE OF THINKING OUTSIDE THE BOX AND HOW FAR WE go to determine if a prospective acquisition will fit into that clubhouse: When our needs following the 2004 season included a power-hitting outfielder at a modest salary, our attention turned to much-traveled Dominican vet Raul Mondesi. There was reason to think it might have been a worthwhile gamble that Raul had sufficiently overcome some injuries to regain something close to his former All-Star productivity with the Dodgers. However, there were widespread concerns about his overall attitude, stemming from his sudden and acrimonious departure from his most recent three teams. He angrily left the Yankees' clubhouse early after being lifted for a pinch-hitter and missed the team charter, prompting his 2003 release. Then he was released twice in 2004—first by Pittsburgh, then by Anaheim—for going absent due to what he felt was a personal problem endangering his family's safety.

With a little investigation, we determined the family safety issue had been resolved. But we needed to find out about the man, about his personality, about his problems, about his character, about his commitment, about his physical conditioning, about all those things. I received some glowing e-mails from Fred Claire, the former Dodgers GM, about Raul's time in L.A. in the '90s. Claire said he liked Raul and had a strong appreciation for him.

So I turned to Jose Martinez, with whom I have worked for more than twenty years in Kansas City and Atlanta. Jose, who was smuggled out of Cuba as a youngster by his parents to escape the Castro regime, still speaks English with a very thick Cuban accent. He honored me when he named me godfather to his son, Juan Carlos, when the lad was born in 1993. Jose and I were separated for a while when he was a coach with the Cubs. But he rejoined me in Atlanta before the 1995 season and has been a vital cog in our continued success. There is no one who knows the game better, who works harder, whom you can rely on more than Jose Martinez. I always want people like Jose in my foxhole.

While we were considering Mondesi, I knew that Jose was going to the Dominican Republic to visit our training academy where we work with all of our young Latin players.

I asked him to make it a point during his visit to set up a meeting with Mondesi, who lives in the capital city of Santo Domingo. Our academy is about an hour away in the town of San Francisco de Macorís in the lush Cibao Valley. I said, "Jose, I want you to sit across from him and look him in the eye and find out what kind of guy he is and whether or not you think we should sign him."

He said to me, "No, boss. You don't want to sign him. I know too many things and what people have said about him."

I asked where this information came from. He said it was information he had gathered. I asked how old the information was and he said four or five years.

"Okay," I said. "Since it's been four or five years, I want to give ourselves a chance to get some updated information. I want you to go down there. I want you to sit across the table from Raul Mondesi and ask him every question you think you should ask. You tell him what kind of environment we have here. You tell him what the expectations for players are here and see how he reacts to that. Then I want you to tell me at the end of that conversation if he's the kind of guy we want to add to this team."

Jose called Raul and set up a meeting for November 11 in San Francisco de Macorís to "personally deliver a message from the Braves organization and particularly from John Schuerholz."

Raul was punctual and they went up to Jose's room on the second floor of the Hotel Las Caobas. Jose didn't want to hold the meeting at the academy and attract a lot of attention because he had heard that another club, Kansas City, also was considering Mondesi.

Jose was impressed with the way Raul, clad in a snug T-shirt, looked to be trim, alert, and in good physical condition. Raul took a seat on a couch near the window looking out to the Cordillera central mountains in the distance. Jose, remembering my instructions, dutifully pulled a chair directly in front of Raul to have a clear view of his eyes. "I wanted to see his face when we talked," Jose would say later. "I've been in baseball a long time and I know how a player can fool you. But I saw him clear."

Speaking Spanish, they talked about Raul's personal problems. They talked about his past interactions with teammates and managements. They talked about Raul's desire to regain his high performance level. They talked about his conditioning.

For more than a half-hour, Jose listened and looked into Raul's eyes. He saw what he felt was sincerity, resolve, and a scrubbed-up attitude.

"We have a high interest in you being a part of the Braves," Jose said, winding down the session. "We want you to be a part of the Braves organization. This is a special organization. We don't want problems. If you're going to have problems, you're going to cause me problems. And I don't think you want to do that to me because we've known each other for so many years."

Raul reached over and tapped Jose on the arm.

"I won't embarrass you," Raul said firmly. "And I won't embarrass the Braves."

They shook hands and Mondesi headed back to Santo Domingo.

Jose called me immediately and announced: "I just met with Raul Mondesi. I was wrong."

And Jose doesn't say that. Jose very seldom in his life ever says the words "I was wrong." But he said it. He said, "This guy would be a good guy for us. This guy we should add to our team. This guy will help us."

"Jose," I said in teasing tones, "you were so strong about not wanting him."

"I know, I know, I know. I met with him and I am telling you we should sign this guy."

Quite candidly, our $1 million salary offer was the sort of deal that a player like Raul had to be saying, "Look, I'm doing this because I know in my heart I can play again and I'm taking this deal which is substantially less than I should make, substantially below the level of income I should generate, based on what I've done in my career despite my recent problems. But I'm going to do it because I want to be with the Braves and I want to show you and the rest of the world that I can still play baseball."

We let him know this is the perfect environment for that. This could be a new platform for him to play well for us, help us win a world championship, and demonstrate to the rest of the baseball world that Raul Mondesi had cleaned up his personal dossier.

The renewed Raul checked into our spring training five days early. His conditioning, exemplary attitude, and play in 2005 spring games inspired more than one baseball writer to predict Comeback Player of the Year honors for Raul.

Alas, by late May, it became apparent that the gamble on Raul's on-field production would not pan out. We let him go after he struggled to keep his batting average above .200 through the first two months of the season. But off the field and in the clubhouse, he was exemplary. In fact, when we had to deliver the disappointing news, he apologized for not doing more to help us win, shook my hand, and even hugged me. As I turned to walk away, Raul said, "John, one more thing." He went on to say how impressed he was with young Ryan Langerhans, with whom he had been sharing outfield playing time, and suggested Ryan playing on a more regular basis would be a boon both to Ryan and the Braves. Classy.

Obviously, our due diligence on his character/attitude issues to preserve our clubhouse environment was right on target.

BEFORE WE SIGNED THE REMARKABLE TWO-SPORT ATHLETE BO JACKson in Kansas City, Bo had always worn an earring. He didn't like the earring rule. But he complied.

I regard that rule as an example of one of the guidelines that help our team to function as one, rather than as a collection of individuals doing individual things and making individual decisions about how they wear their uniform, how they wear their jewelry, how they present our organization to the world, how much a part of our team they want to engage in. We don't give them any options. You engage in all parts of our team.

My relationship with Bo now is good and I have great admiration for him. But when Bo mentioned me in the book he wrote, he said

"John Schuerholz' crackers don't float in my soup." Meaning he didn't agree with some of my policies during our Kansas City days.

Bo was the greatest pure athlete I've ever seen in a baseball uniform. Second was Deion Sanders. But Bo was clearly the best athlete. However, that was the only similarity between them. Bo could hit a ball farther than anyone I'd ever seen, run faster than anyone I've ever seen in a baseball uniform, and throw a ball better than anyone I've ever seen in a baseball uniform.

And what a coup for us to draft and sign him away from the NFL Tampa Bay Bucs. We drafted him in the fourth round. He should have gone much earlier, but most teams assumed he would sign with football. A relatively young scout of ours, Kenny Gonzalez, had the territory in Alabama where Bo played football and baseball at Auburn. Kenny became friends with Bo and Bo's mother, who was a maid in the Holiday Inn where Kenny stayed when he was in that area. Kenny gets full credit for us drafting and signing him.

Bo quickly became a legend of folkloric proportions in a baseball uniform. We sent him to the minor leagues and he was hitting balls over the roofs of buildings beyond the outfield fence in Memphis and jumping over chain link fences that were chest-high down the right field line. He would come over to the fence on a foul ball and, from a standing start, would jump flat-footed over the fence to try to catch the ball. We persuaded him not to do that, but he had that capability.

Maybe it's part of his legend, but there are people who swear his hands were so quick he could catch a house fly buzzing around his head while talking to you. What I have seen him do is this: Outside the clubhouse in Royals Stadium beneath the stands there were huge concrete support pillars. As part of the demonstration of his athleticism, he'd pull on sneakers and run full speed toward the pillar and run *up* the pillar, flip over backward, and land on his feet.

He would tell of the time as a kid when he would come home later than his curfew, and would get a running start and run up the side of the house and pull himself into a *second-story* window. Superman-like.

Bo could have been a Hall of Famer. I'll never forget this phone call. I'm lying on an X-ray table at St. Luke's Hospital in Kansas City, having dye injected in my arm and getting ready to have a rotator cuff examination. I'm on this table, flat on my back, and someone came bursting through the examination room double doors and exclaimed: "You have an urgent phone call."

I thought something truly horrible must have happened.

It was Royals co-owner Avron Fogelman, who needed to speak to me immediately. So I got up from the table, hospital gown flapping, to take the call. "John! Bo Jackson has decided to play football! What are we going to do about that? I need to talk to you."

I mean, that was devastating. It was such a turn from what Bo had told us and the commitment he had made. It was so urgent and so important and so unsettling to Avron that he had to talk to me right then no matter where I was or what I was doing.

I can only assume if they were actually operating on me, he would have waited for me to regain consciousness.

Bo had made that fateful decision to play football. The rest is history. He was carrying the ball on a pretty routine play down the sideline. A defender tackled him but Bo tried to pull away. The guy had a grip on his ankle and Bo separated his hip. And the bleeding and bruising and trauma that occurred with that hip injury eventually caused him to have a hip replacement.

We had terminated our contract with him when he chose to jump to football because of a lot of significant financial obligations built into the contract if he stayed with our club. We obviously couldn't commit ourselves to that kind of financial involvement with a guy who (a) decided to play football, which was in violation of our agreement with him, and (b) would be exposing himself to a career-ending injury. Sadly, the latter more or less happened. It was in Bo's mind to play both sports, but it was not something we were comfortable with.

He did come back to play baseball for a short stint with the White Sox on that artificial hip—a remarkable feat likely possible only for someone of Bo's extraordinary physical gifts—though he was not the same player.

Bo was a sportsman, an expert with the bow-and-arrow. What he would do to practice and keep his bow-and-arrow accuracy honed was stand at one end inside the Kansas City clubhouse and fire at a target at the other end of the clubhouse. Obviously, there was no one there at the time, but it was my great concern that a clubhouse attendant or someone from the front office might decide to walk through the door at the target end of Bo's makeshift archery range. I had to tell him it was an inappropriate activity and it had to stop.

However, Bo was exemplary and in no way did I ever consider him a risk to our team-oriented philosophy.

Sometimes you *do* take chances. We took a chance on the speed and athleticism of Deion Sanders, who stands as one of the very few who, sadly, was unaffected by the environment in our clubhouse.

Bobby Cox: "We like them to be team-minded, civic-minded. If we have to show up at banquets, we want them there. Through the years, some people just don't want to be part of the team and they're better off being somewhere else."

Years earlier, when I was in Kansas City, we drafted Deion out of his Fort Myers high school. A fifth-round draft choice. We knew he was a football star and Florida State had a football scholarship for him. But we tried to entice him to be a baseball player. During our spring training camp at Terry Park in Fort Myers, Deion showed up at our invitation to participate in a casual workout. Brian Murphy was one of our scouts and was primarily responsible for our drafting Deion. Other members of our scouting and player development staff were there. We wanted to expose him to baseball and our team to coax him into signing a contract with us.

Little did I know, Dick Howser, our manager, Florida State grad and icon, a close friend and admirer of Florida State coach Bobby Bowden, was convincing Deion to go to Florida State. My friend, our manager!

That was the one time that Dick and I clashed swords. I had to remind Dick who he worked for, who signed his paycheck, and that it was in our best interest to get this player to Kansas City, not Florida State. I told Dick I didn't want Deion around there anymore if Dick was going to be talking to him about FSU. We were not going to be using our Kansas City Royals facility and environment to convince him to reject us and take someone else's offer.

Obviously, we didn't sign him and Deion went to Florida State where he became a two-time All-American cornerback. But he injured his foot about a year or two into his time at Florida State. I looked out on the field during spring training one day and was shocked to see Deion Sanders standing by the batting cage, on crutches. I was livid. I simply didn't think it appropriate for a guy who had rejected us to play football to be at our batting cage. I got word down to the field immediately that Deion was not authorized to be there and he was to be excused.

So that was the last interaction I had with Deion until he became a Brave on January 30, 1991, some four years into his pro career as a full-time NFL player and sometimes baseball player. He had been signed by the Yankees originally, was released, and we signed him. Still playing cornerback for the Atlanta Falcons, Deion's four seasons as a Brave were an adventure. We were willing to do a two-sport deal considering it was two teams here in town. We felt like we could work that out and signed him to a contract stipulating that he would join the Falcons only after our season was over.

Then he got sideways with the Falcons over his contract and decided to become a full-time baseball player. He was a talented player and played the game with a lot of ability and intensity, especially for a guy who hadn't played that much baseball.

As I said earlier, Deion was just a great natural athlete, the second-best I had been around, behind Bo Jackson. He was intimidating on the base paths and could fly. That was his game—he could flat-out run. He made himself into a decent hitter and decent outfielder. Playing in

97 games in 1992, Deion batted .304, stole 26 bases, hit eight homers, and led the league with 14 triples. In 95 games the next season, he dropped off only slightly with a .276 average, 19 stolen bases, and six homers. When he appeared in our '92 World Series, he became the first athlete to play in both a World Series and a Super Bowl.

But he always seemed to exert extraordinary effort to narrow the focus of the spotlight on him. It seemed to everyone with the club that it was more important to him that the attention was directed his way and that it was all about him.

Bobby Cox again: "Deion was for one thing—himself. He couldn't care less about the team. He was into promoting himself as that football-baseball combination—the first guy to ever do this or do that. It was all about Deion. And he didn't want to participate in our duties off the field—going to luncheons, fan photo days, things like that, responsibilities that come with being a Braves team member."

I had to laugh when I read the way *College Football News* chose to lead off an assessment of Deion when naming him No. 8 among its 100 greatest college players of all time: "Deion Sanders was an obnoxious, self-promoting egomaniacal prima donna who rarely tackled anyone with any consistency. He elevated the art of trash talk to a nuclear level, firing on everyone within earshot and always bragging about how great he was."

Keep in mind that was the opening burst in a *tribute* to him!

The Braves were just a platform of sorts for him to demonstrate his athletic prowess. A lot of people in our clubhouse felt that way and didn't sense he was committed to this team. He liked to promote "Prime Time" as his nickname. Around our offices, he was more often referred to as "Ego Man." Then when he decided to leave the team during the '93 playoffs to play in a football game, that was more or less the final straw.

Without consulting any of us, he just announced that that was what he was going to do. It was a pretty clear indication that all this was about Deion, not about contributing to a team that was trying to win a playoff series. He didn't miss any games for us. He played in our game, then left and played for the Falcons, then flew back in time for our next game.

At this late date, with our roster in place, we would have cut off our nose to spite our face and would have diminished our team talent if we benched or suspended him for running off to a football game. He aggravated the situation when he became miffed at something television analyst Tim McCarver said during one of the postseason telecasts about Deion being self-absorbed. When McCarver came down to the clubhouse to conduct postgame interviews, Deion slipped in behind him and dumped a large plastic pan of ice water on him. Childish. Stupid. Unprofessional.

We tried to make it work with Deion again the next spring, but things kept building up. A month into the '94 season we traded him to Cincinnati for outfielder Roberto Kelly and pitcher Roger Etheridge. Good player. Good riddance.

After the '97 season, we similarly threw in the towel on center fielder Kenny Lofton, who also could never embrace our environment or ideals.

"Deion and Kenny weren't bad guys," Bobby Cox recalled. "But you like them to be more part of the team, part of the city, part of the organization. We all like to fit into one. Both of them were kind of quiet in the dugout. In fact, some of the writers had trouble with them, refusing to talk. I don't know what they were trying to prove. Wasn't good."

When Johnny Carson died recently, Orlando columnist David Whitley wrote a tribute suggesting a lot of star athletes could learn from Carson's great knack of making guests on his show look good. Whitley pointed out that Carson's gift was being comfortable as a contributing part of an effectively woven team that succeeds, as opposed to standing out as an individual whose ideas, the person thinks, are brighter than everyone else's and won't commit to teaming up with anyone else.

Whitley concluded his column with this: "Then he died on Sunday and we were reminded of Carson's simple lesson for success. The best teams usually win because the star doesn't act like one."

Pardon me if Deion came to mind.

MY LEADERSHIP CREDO IS "WE AND US." THAT LONG-STANDING management policy and philosophy are reflected in a poem I composed nearly thirty years ago:

> I and My are words oft used.
> By those who are themselves confused;
> Why won't their super egos trust,
> The use of words like We and Us?

I often recite that poem at public presentations and staff meetings, stressing to everyone that it embodies how I feel about the job that I do and the people I work with. It really captures my leadership and operating philosophies.

The inspiration for the poem came at one spring training, early in my career with the Royals. It was 1969 and as a young administrative assistant, I was assigned the duty of driving around Jack McKeon, then a manager in our farm system. He managed our Carolina League team at High Point/Thomasville, Georgia.

In those days, Jack had a very healthy ego. I spent the better part of a day with Jack, hearing him bombard me with the personal pronouns "I" and "my." It was so much against the grain of my philosophy as a leader, as a worker, as an administrative team member, that I was inspired to pen "I and My."

Jack is a different man now. The grandfatherly skipper has gone on to manage in the majors at several stops, most notably leading the Florida Marlins to a World Series title in 2003. He was more cocky and aggravating in his younger days. He and I have both grown older and somewhat more mellow. He is a delightful guy and his management style has certainly been effective. Players respond well to him. But in those earlier days, it was irritating when he was so cocksure of himself and let everyone know it.

THE MOST IMPORTANT ATTITUDE AN ORGANIZATION NEEDS TO create and foster is the winning attitude, either by assembling people who are already winners or coaching your people on how to become winners. I am absolutely convinced that people associated with winning teams or successful companies expect to work harder and smarter than others—to do whatever it takes to be the best.

They expect—even *demand*—to be better prepared, more intensely committed to their tasks and responsibilities. They want to be the best in their industry. They have a passion to compete and excel. They are winners!

The most readily identifiable quality of a total winner is an overall attitude of personal optimism and enthusiasm. They know life is a self-fulfilling prophecy. Things don't "just happen" in their lives; they make life happen by choosing a goal or destination worthy of their effort and commit to reaching it.

As I repeatedly say: Winners make commitments. Losers make excuses.

How to tell a winner from a loser:

A winner says, "Let's find out." A loser says, "Nobody knows."

When a winner makes a mistake, he says, "I was wrong." When a loser makes a mistake, he says, "It wasn't my fault."

A winner says, "I'm good, but not as good as I ought to be." A loser says, "I'm not as bad as a lot of other people."

A winner tries to learn from those who are superior to him. A loser tries to tear down those who are superior to him.

A winner says, "There ought to be a better way to do it." A loser says, "That's the way it's always been done here."

Winners encourage innovations, creativity, and passion for their work, for their life.

There's a wonderful story that illustrates what I mean by a winning attitude. A man was walking home one time by a park where kids were playing a Little League game. He walked over to the sideline and asked a boy, "What's the score?"

The boy, with a beaming smile on his face, said, "We're behind, 14 to nothing."

"You don't seem to be very discouraged about it," the man noted.

"Discouraged? Why would I be discouraged?" the boy countered. "We haven't even come to bat yet!"

We must give people a chance to come to bat. Don't tell them they can't do it if they haven't been to bat yet. Give them an opportunity. I've seen lots of baseball games and, except for those shortened by rain, I never saw a team win a game that did not make at least twenty-four outs.

Life for winners is not about making outs. It's about scoring runs. It's about having opportunities and people believing in you. It's about making progress and never quitting.

Bob Brenly, the manager for the 2001 world champion Arizona Diamondbacks, caught and played third base for the San Francisco Giants. In 1986, in the fourth inning of a game against the Braves, Brenly booted a routine groundball. A few moments later, he kicked away another grounder and, in his anxiety to pick up the ball, threw wild to home plate. Two errors on the same play. Moments later, Brenly booted yet another grounder to become the first major league player in the twentieth century to make four errors in one inning.

We can only imagine how he felt when he made that long walk from third base to the dugout. How he hung his head and felt awful inside. How he must have felt like a failure for having let his team down. We understand and relate. There have been times in all of our lives, and in our business, when the fourth inning seemed like four years and it seemed like we made four *hundred* errors.

But the story doesn't end there. In the fifth inning of that game, Bob Brenly hit a home run. In the seventh, he ripped a bases-loaded single to drive in two more runs. Finally, with the score tied and two out in the ninth, who should come to bat but Bob Brenly. On a 3-2 count, he launched another home run into the left field stands that won the game.

It ain't over till it's over. For Bob Brenly or anyone else in determined pursuit of their success. As a wise sage once said, "The glory is not in never falling, but in rising every time you fall."

2

Gentlemen, Start Your *Moneyball* Arguments

Aside from politics, there can be no more fertile area for debate than baseball. The arguments and the second-guessing have long been as much a part of the game as doubleknits and double steals. The relative merits of players, game strategies, managerial decisions, trades, umpiring calls, batting orders, pitching rotations, equipment, and even concession menus are dissected, analyzed, argued, appealed, and mediated right down to a dry pulp. Those of us in baseball know this, accept this, and embrace it.

Into this conundrum of hyper-disagreement stepped a gifted writer named Michael Lewis to exploit baseball's penchant for spirited discourse. In his best-selling 2003 book called *Moneyball,* Lewis, who was originally trained as a Wall Street bond salesman, advances a theory that the exotic use of player statistics is becoming the new wave cure-all for baseball clubs to jettison the game's long-accepted, scout-based manner of player selection.

For two years, the enduring debate over the *Moneyball* premise has produced enough heat to thaw the hearts of even certain player agents. Well, almost.

The title is catchy, though terribly misleading. At first glance, one might assume it to be an examination of the deep-pocketed New York Yankees, whose payroll is perennially so far ahead of the pack that whatever team is in second place is but a speck in the pinstripers' rearview mirror. Checkbook baseball at its zenith. However, the Yankees are not an example of a *Moneyball* team, but rather the true antithesis of one as seen through the prism of Lewis's sabermetric panacea.

Perhaps a more apropos title would have been *Statsball*. Or maybe *Lackofmoneyball*.

Lewis used the recent success of the Oakland A's and their bright young general manager Billy Beane as a vehicle to advance the author's thrust that choosing one's roster almost solely on the basis of certain individual statistics trumps us dopey old traditionalists who cling to the long-standing model that relies on the combination of conventional stats *and* input from human scouts. *Moneyball* contends that the low-budget A's, forced to play *little* checkbook baseball, were able to win their division in 2003 and contend during recent seasons by primarily cobbling together an economy roster of inexpensive kids and scrap heap vets on the basis of some trendy statistical analysis. This "revolutionary" formula virtually discards not only the trained eye of seasoned scouts, bunting and base stealing, but brands as meaningless the value of an effective closer.

Your Honor, I offer spirited—and, I might add, *proven*—testimony that good teams are built, structured, and allowed to win consistently because of talented people, a process, a program, and an environment within an organization.

The *Moneyball* premise is about statistical analysis vs. traditional judgment and instinctive evaluation. As portrayed in that book, it is a bogus concept because I know you can't make baseball judgments entirely on statistical analysis to build a team.

The Red Sox are the best example of that. They and a couple of other teams were characterized as Moneyball teams. But Boston has the second-highest payroll in baseball and tried to create a bullpen-by-committee because that's the way the Moneyball formula was originally written. That didn't work; they became world champions only when they acquired a true closer and bolstered their defense—which is not a big part of the Moneyball blueprint. The basic Moneyball theory is, substantially, on-base percentage for position players and groundball outs for pitchers—a pure statistical way to put a team together.

In addition, to suggest that there are only four or five teams that look at statistics and value them for what information they provide is inaccurate. Very inaccurate.

In my twenty-four years as a major league general manager, I have never made a deal—*ever*—for a player without a dossier of information on that player. That dossier is a compilation of all scouting reports on that player as well as a thorough review of his stats—from both a cumulative career perspective, recent stats, and trends those numbers reveal. We analyze and utilize all of that.

The author of *Moneyball*—and not Billy Beane—made it read as if there are only a few people on this earth in this game of baseball who actually utilize that process. Well, that's also not true.

Now, the real differentiation that is accurate and true is that an organization like Oakland, with a relatively low operating budget, has an even greater challenge than those of us who have a $75–$80 million payroll. And far greater challenges than those who have $180–$200 million payroll. And quite honestly, Oakland was a good team to represent as the poster child of *Moneyball* because the A's won. But I think they won mostly because Billy Beane is a smart guy and makes good decisions about players and has good instincts. And I also respect that Billy was a high draft pick, has played the game both at the minor and major league levels, and knows what it's like to go 0-for-4 and then get on a bus for eight hours to the next town, to think about how difficult the game of baseball is to play. Human experience and lively intellect are a valuable combination.

There might be somebody running stats that are unique or more in-depth. But the lingering characterization introduced by Michael Lewis was that everyone else in baseball who doesn't understand and use these new statistical concepts are a bunch of dolts. And that's not true, as I think the Braves have proved. I also don't think anybody thinks Walt Jocketty of St. Louis or Terry Ryan of Minnesota or any of my colleagues or myself are dolts because we don't engage in sabermetrics to the extent that Lewis suggested is the golden way—the path of enlightenment. ("Sabermetrics," a word that had furrowed itself into contemporary baseball lingo, is an acronym of Society for American Baseball Research–metrics. In large part, this is a group of numbers crunchers who see the game of baseball as merely a mathematical exercise.)

But neither am I saying the Braves are even *semi*-Moneyball. We're "winning-ball." That's what we are about. I don't normally ascribe labels to anything. That's unnecessary. That was an author selling books. He did a good job; he assigned a label and he sold a lot of books.

Quite simply, we do our *job*. In order to win 14 consecutive division championships and five National League championships and a World Series, you have to do all facets of your work well. You have to analyze your scouting reports. You have to listen to scouts. You have to hear what they say and see their expressions. You have to hear them pitch a player and know the ability of that scout. Of course, you also have to have a basis of reliability on a player's productivity—statistics.

In my very first year as a general manager in the winter of 1981, I was talking to my No. 1 confidant in Kansas City, major league scout Tom Ferrick, who pitched in the big leagues for the Yankees. Long before Michael Lewis even dreamed of Moneyball, Tom said this to me: "Stats don't lie."

This was my very first year as a general manager! Every player I've ever traded for or every acquisition I've made to this day, I would have somebody in our organization prepare a dossier that included all the scouting reports and all the statistics for his entire career. Day games, night games, artificial turf, grass, home games, road games, before the All-Star Game, after the All-Star Game, against right-handers, against left-handers, against amphibious mammals.

Tom Ferrick was right: Stats don't lie. But they also don't tell the complete story.

Not that I didn't know it before because as director of player personnel and a scouting director, we always used stats as a verification or substantiation of a player's true ability. I would assure you that if a GM gave his word and promised to acquire players based only on his review of statistics—only based on that, and didn't counsel with scouts or look at scouting reports—I'd take my chances playing against that team every day and twice on holidays.

I contend there is no general manager who has built a consistently winning team that made judgments solely and purely and only on statistics or sabermetrics.

Even those clubs characterized as Moneyball organizations have blended—to one degree or another—judgment, instincts, and intuition. Either their own, or a scout they trust, or someone who made a human judgment about the player they are considering. It wasn't a roomful of sabermetricians with green visors and rubber bands around their sleeves and pocket guards with pens and calculators in their shirt pockets, crunching numbers on their computers until they declare: "This is the guy who ought to be our shortstop."

Or, "This is the guy who ought to be our No. 1 pitcher."

No one can tell me that has ever happened, or that it could happen.

Now, do some organizations use and rely on statistics more than others? Yes. Have some organizations taken statistical analysis to a more finite level? Yes. Have some organizations hired sabermetricians to search through numbers to find trends of players that, in their opinion, they would recommend for consideration to a team? Absolutely.

But I go back to my premise: There is not a general manager who has built a winning, championship-caliber team who has ever solely and purely and exclusively looked at a pageful of numbers and said, "I want this guy on our team as our shortstop." "I want this guy on our team as our catcher." "I want this guy on our team as the center fielder."

They will use those statistics and they may dig more deeply into them and see what the ninth and tenth and eleventh layer down might say about a trend by the player. But they will combine that with many other factors. Human, subjective factors. *Scouting!*

My view and contention is there has not been one championship team that has been built by someone who even espouses to be characterized as a true Moneyball team, who has built his team based on that process alone. Championship team, I'm talking about. Winning team. A team that wins, consistently.

The perception that was presented is that this is a better way. An enlightened way. A rounder wheel. A better mousetrap. A faster, more efficient rocket. And I simply don't believe it is.

But I have no problem with it. What I have a problem with was the suggestion—perhaps not even by the teams that were being written about, but was simply the author's view and presentation—that the value of baseball traditionalists, whether they are scouts, player development guys, minor league staffers, or executives, seemed to be diminished in the presentation in his book. In praising and lauding and placing on a pedestal the intellect that Lewis ascribed to Billy Beane, the A's, and any other alleged Moneyball team, he diminished and trivialized and mischaracterized the real value of the traditional baseball man.

That was the exception I took to it, and I still do.

IT DOESN'T BOTHER ME IF A GUY WANTS TO BUILD A TEAM BASED ONLY on statistics. Because we're going to use statistics, too. But we're also going to use the judgment and the intuition and the knowledge and the gut feel of the Paul Snyders and Jim Fregosis and Chuck

McMichaels and the Frank Wrens and the Dean Taylors. And the Chuck LaMars and Dayton Moores and Roy Clarks and Tyrone Brookses. Our scouts and executives.

I'm going to use their passion about a player. When Roy Clark, our scouting director, stands up in a group discussion about a potential trade and says with emphasis that he would not trade a certain minor league player because of this and this and this, I admire that conviction, that passion. I think that's healthy. And Roy typically will add: "Obviously, John, whatever decision you make we're behind you. But I want you to know how I feel about this guy."

(Actually, Roy likes to playfully say, "We're with you, boss, win or tie.")

Roy's passion bubbled up like this when we were prepping for the trade we made with Oakland to acquire star pitcher Tim Hudson. One of the players we discussed including in the deal was left-handed pitcher Dan Meyer, who had been impressive in 2004 stints for our Class AA Greenville and Class AAA Richmond farm teams. Roy, passionate, said, "Even for Tim Hudson, I wouldn't want to put Dan Meyer in a deal. He's close to the major leagues now, could even help us this coming season, and has a chance to become an outstanding major league pitcher."

We didn't offer Meyer initially, but we ultimately decided to include him in the deal due to the A's insistence, much to Roy's dismay but always with his understanding and support.

I get a lot of comfort out of listening to that kind of intellectual, intuitive, and heartfelt input from our scouts. Some would say they're not as intellectual as they should be and more emotional than they ought to be, but I trust the balance of the intellect and emotions of our people. We have a lot of smart people who know players very, very well. And who have studied them, talked to people that have worked with them, talked to people who have coached them, talked to trainers who have dealt with them, and, by the way, have looked into the statistical background of the player to be sure that there is some sense of validation in terms of productivity to what they believe in their gut that this guy can do. And they tell me that. One may tell me this thing about the player. Another may tell me that thing about the player. And all the shades of gray.

Ultimately, I serve as the final filter in this process—making the decision on who we decide to bring to this team. The buck stops with me, whether it is a trade we make, the signing of a free agent or the terms of a contract, or whether to include a minor-leaguer in a deal. I will say, for example, we're going for Tim Hudson and these are the players we will have to give up to do it—then listen to their opinions.

I am not the end-all and be-all from beginning to the end—the alpha and the omega. I am the conductor of the orchestra who knows when to point his baton to each individual in our organization. On one particular occasion, I'm going to point to the cellist because he knows this situation better. On another occasion, I'm going to point to the drummer to give me something. But I know when and whom to point to for their involvement, for their intuition, for their judgment, for their recommendation. Who knows pitchers best? Who's the best judge of infielders? Who judges competitive personalities best? After all, that's the characterization of the orchestra conductor so that together we play this beautiful music of winning.

The concert we give is winning. And if all the people in our organization whose instrument is scouting or player development or major league scouting or player knowledge—and all play well—we're going to have the most beautiful symphony of success. And I think we have.

BECAUSE I RELY SO HEAVILY UPON THE INPUT FROM OUR SCOUTING AND player development staffs before I reach a final decision on most any roster move, I put just as much emphasis and care in the formation of that staff roster as I do our player roster.

These are the key people on staff who contribute their judgments, evaluations and instincts and gut feelings and recommendations to me about players, about acquisitions, about decision-making in the best interest of the Atlanta Braves.

Scouts are, in a manner of speaking, like major league players. You bring players to your team because you think they have the ability to strengthen the team you're assembling. And it's no different with the scouting team. You make presumptions based on a guy's past record, based on his reputation in the industry, based on your personal knowledge of him, based on recommendations from people you trust. Just like you put together your baseball team, you put together your scouting team.

When the players on your team continue to produce, you continue to rely on them to help your team win. When your scouts continue to produce, you continue to rely on them and they help you win by finding good players. But when someone begins to demonstrate inability or a lack of work ethic, or whatever, scouts are no different from players who no longer produce. The player whose batting average sinks is soon no longer part of your team. And the same goes for scouts.

And just as we blend in new, young talent on our player roster, we do the same on our scouting and player development roster. We try regularly to bring a breath of fresh air into our player roster. Some of the changes are brought about by economic reasons, but some of them are planned because we think bringing good, young players adds a freshness to the team. Clubhouses respond better that way. A team is better able to go about their work with vigor and energy when you have an effective mix of veterans and new young guys with higher energy. The same is true for the scouting roster.

As for the total number of scouts we employ, we are not quite the largest scouting system in baseball, but certainly in the top third. But that's okay. That is consistent with our philosophy. Each time someone asks me how we have been able to win so consistently over the past fifteen years, I say principally because of our scouting and player development staff and the work they do. So if we're going to talk the talk, we'd better walk the walk. We'd better have a good, sound, robust scouting program and player development program. And we clearly do.

As we entered the 2005 season, we had more than 450 scouts under contract—thirty-seven full-time scouts, twenty-six part-time scouts, and some 400 associate scouts. The latter group consists of the high school coaches, the insurance salesmen, the barbers who do this primarily for the love of the game. If they recommend a player whom we ultimately draft and sign, they get a commission each time that player progresses up the ladder.

With respect to our international scouting, we concentrate more on the Latin American corridor than the Pacific Rim. We deploy three scouts in the Pacific—in Australia, Japan, and Korea—while we devote more manpower in the Hispanic countries. The latter has proven to be a more fertile and affordable talent source.

We've had full knowledge of the players who have come out of the Asian pipeline. We've had complete scouting reports. We knew who they were. We evaluated them and our evaluations, up against the cost of signing them, were so disparate, we had no chance to compete for the top guys. The players that have come to the U.S. out of the Japanese leagues are established stars with multimillion-dollar price tags. It doesn't mesh with our economics to have to pay so much money for one star Japanese player. Our preference is to spend our money on the deeper talent pool from Latin America.

We have to keep the pipeline of talent filled in this organization so that we always have good players matriculating to our major league roster from our own system. Players that we find and we train to play baseball the way the Atlanta Braves expect it to be played. Our scouts, from all around the world, help keep that pipeline filled for us. They have produced. Ours is regarded as one of the finest scouting organizations in baseball, and our farm system has constantly been flush with highly regarded prospects being groomed by our player development staff.

The 2005 season underscored this, often with seven or eight

"homegrowns" in our starting lineup. In an interleague game June 15 at Texas, we even had ten (including the DH) with this starting lineup:

Pete Orr, dh*
Marcus Giles, 2b
Kelly Johnson, lf*
Adam LaRoche, 1b
Andruw Jones, cf
Ryan Langerhans, rf*
Andy Marte, 3b*
Brian McCann, c*
Wilson Betemit, ss*
Kyle Davies, p*

This is unheard of, especially on a winning, contending team. Of those ten homegrowns, the seven with asterisks were rookies, most of whom had been called up from our minor league teams in Richmond and Pearl, Mississippi, to plug holes created by the uncommon string of injuries we incurred. Those rookies, reflecting the quality handiwork of our scouting and development staff, saved our bacon during that critical May–July period and kept us in the division pennant race.

That wealth of rising young talent not only allows us to keep home-grown talent flowing to our major league roster in Atlanta, but provides me with the playing talent capital to acquire proven major league players when the need or opportunity arises. We could not have obtained Tim Hudson from Oakland without our prized Triple-A pitcher, Dan Meyer, whom the A's demanded in return. We could not have made the very critical acquisition of cleanup hitter Fred McGriff in midseason 1993 if we hadn't had three highly regarded minor league prospects the Padres insisted upon.

Unlike many other clubs, we align our professional scouts not on a purely geographic basis, but more of a linear basis. Each man has a number of major league teams to follow and that includes most of that team's farm system. So a scout covering the Padres, for example, might routinely travel halfway across the country to see the Padres' Triple-A team and Double-A team. We feel it is important for each scout to have a feel for the vertical knowledge of the talent flow within an organization, providing that scout with a deeper understanding of that organization. That's why we align our scouts in that fashion.

But no matter the structure of one's scouting department or player development staff or special assistants to the GM, it gets back to the quality of those individuals. I'll mention a couple.

On our professional scouting staff roster, we have six men with that responsibility. Jim Fregosi, one of our major league scouts, has been an All-Star player, a major league manager, and later a special assistant to the general manager for a variety of teams. Prior to his time with us, Jim had worked last under Brian Sabean at the San Francisco Giants. The Giants decided to restructure their staff and when Jim became available, I quickly acted to hire him. I have always regarded him as one the best—if not *the very best*—judge of talent and information gatherer at the major league level. He has a network of people and sources from major league managers to coaches to trainers to players to scouts everywhere throughout major league baseball. He gets good information that assists him in his evaluations and recommendations.

Jim is also decisive in his evaluations of major league players. And his recommendations are clear and precise. For me, as the general manager, it is comforting and reassuring to have someone with this kind of information-gathering network, who has this abundance of inside knowledge of players through his conversations—some overt, some direct, some surreptitious—with a broad spectrum of well-placed and trusted sources. He, of course, makes his own observations and evaluations of a player and presents them to me in a strong fashion. I have developed great confidence in and reliability on what Jim and our other major league scouts recommend.

I could go right down our staff roster. But suffice it to say they are all important, trusted scouting staff members because I had personal knowledge of their talents, or someone we hired in turn recommended them to us because of their sound judgment and instincts.

That same staff excellence exists within our amateur scouting department as well. For example, Roy Clark, our scouting director, and Paul Snyder, formerly the longtime Braves scouting director and now a special assistant to me, recommended that we hire Dayton Moore, a young assistant college coach at George Mason University in Virginia, as a scout. Dayton has grown so quickly and remarkably that he has elevated himself to the position of assistant general manager/baseball operations, overseeing both scouting and player development. This arrangement gives great synergy to an organization where one person has direct responsibility, authority, and daily communication links to both departments. He deals with the scouts finding the raw marble and the artisans who wield the hammers and chisels of player development, creating the final major league product.

IN FAIRNESS, *MONEYBALL* MADE FOR A GOOD READ, EVEN THOUGH I feel the basic premise is terribly flawed.

I have no animosity toward any of the guys who happen to be the general managers of the teams who were designated Moneyball clubs, either by the author or by television pundits who carried it further into the public consciousness. (Although in fact some of the designees have disputed the designation.)

There has been a wave of prominent baseball people to go out of their way to offer counterpoints to the supposed sabermetrics magic advanced in the book. In a speech to an Orlando group, Ken "Hawk" Harrelson, the colorful former batting star and ex–general manager of the White Sox, debunked the theory in the strongest terms. Hawk argued that the A's were winning not because of statistical formulas but rather because they had three pitchers blossom into 20-game winners. He noted they had those pitchers before Billy Beane ratcheted up his dependence upon statistical profiles. As the team struggled at the start of 2005, many baseball observers continually pointed to the strength of Barry Zito, Tim Hudson, and Mark Mulder as the key to the A's previous success.

Respected Cardinals manager Tony LaRussa, in his 2005 collaboration with Buzz Bissinger, *Three Nights in August,* said he appreciated the information generated by computers and studied the rows and columns. But he also knew that could take you only so far in baseball, maybe even confuse you in a fog of overanalysis. LaRussa said he embraces the humanity of the players for whom he is responsible and asserted that they are more than just statistical sets to be plugged into the grand equation of the game.

Heck, even some of the principals with teams that were identified as Moneyball teams in the book came out publicly denying that was their modus operandi. Those principals proudly claimed membership among those who have constructed winners through more traditional methods. So do we. And we have the proof on display all along the upper-deck facade at Turner Field: a string of yellow banners representing our unprecedented run of division titles. And I can assure you they weren't put there by fancy logarithms or dancing digits.

To me, when we have notable visitors to Turner Field point up to those banners and compliment our success, I know the praise is for the work of many baseball people, not a handful of numbers crunchers. An example of that was during the postseason matchup against the San Francisco Giants at Turner Field in '02. Giants owner Peter Magowan, standing down on the field with me, shook his head at those banners and said: "Do you realize, John, how impossible that is to do? How remarkable that is? How it will never be repeated again in the history of Major League Baseball?" And that was after only eleven in a row.

Later, Andy McPhail of the Cubs visited and looked up at those banners. "Do you realize, Dick Clark," he said, using the nickname he gave me after the forever young-looking TV disc jockey, "what you've done here? How remarkable this is?"

Before our first spring game with the Yankees in 2005, Alex Rodriguez, Derek Jeter, Tino Martinez, and Don Mattingly all came up to me by the batting cage, shook their heads, and asked me how we keep doing this.

A couple of years earlier in Atlanta, I was talking with Cal Ripken, who was in for an interleague Braves-Orioles series. He pointed out there and said the same thing. Next, Curt Schilling was there on the field talking with me, and he looked up at those banners and said, "This is unbelievable what you guys have done. This can't be done in baseball. And you've done it."

Yes, we did. And with neither mirrors nor numbers.

NEVERTHELESS, THERE ARE THOSE WHO WANT TO DWELL ON THE FACT we haven't won more World Series titles despite making the playoffs every year. I keep getting asked why we have postseason "fadeouts." I don't think we've had any playoff fadeouts. We just haven't won as many as we could have, or should have. But we didn't fade out.

Football has a playoff system where the top teams in the regular season get a pass through the first round. In the old days, the two baseball teams that won the most games over the long regular season went directly to the World Series. You didn't have to pass Go. You didn't have to go to jail. You didn't have to land on Boardwalk or Park Place. And you surely didn't have to wade through a postseason tournament.

Then we went to the division format and you had to win your division, then the playoff against the other division winner. That was one step added, and then we added the wild card.

Now, you can win your division and separate yourself from the pack, as we did in '97. We beat the Marlins by nine games. That was the year that Eric Gregg's strike zone was as wide as a boardroom table in that one critical playoff game. It's tough now. It's a tournament, like an NCAA basketball tournament. And in those short series even one game is crucial. Some greater consideration should be given to the teams that won their division over a 162-game schedule.

For more than 100 years, Major League Baseball rewarded the teams that survived the regular season as champions, whether it was

128 games, 154 games, or, as it is now, 162 games. When you're the best team over 162 games, you ought to be able to hopscotch over one or two levels of the opening rounds. Let the wild card teams knock each other off and then start the tournament. And give a break to the teams who over 162 games passed the old traditional litmus test of baseball excellence. The No. 1 seed in our postseason tournament has no better chance and has no better opportunity to win it all than a team that just enters in as a wild card into a championship tournament like we now have.

Wild cards have advanced to the last four World Series, winning three—the Angels in '02, the Marlins in '03, and the Red Sox in '04.

My kidding remark now to those writers who ask pointed questions about why we haven't won more World Series is that I'm now trying to be "smart enough to construct a wild card team." Maybe that's the solution.

I'd like to win another World Series so that maybe—and I'm not sure it would do it even then—these negative observers who don't truly understand baseball would be stopped from continuing to refer to the "postseason flameouts of the Braves."

I AM CONSTANTLY PRESSING OUR PEOPLE TO THINK OUTSIDE THE BOX; the Moneyball concept *is* a player acquisition box. And there can be no better example of creative thinking than what we did in August 2001, searching for another solid hitter to bolster our playoff push. It would be safe to assume that no other major league team ever reached into the Mexican League for a forty-three-year-old first baseman/pinch-hitter, looking for help.

That's exactly what we did when we looked past Julio Franco's age. We relied more on the human judgments that assured us this transplanted Dominican's gaudy batting numbers for the Mexico City Tigres that year were not the mere result of feasting on some of that league's weaker pitchers. Frank Wren, my assistant GM, ignited our study of Julio after reading a *Baseball America* mention that the former major-leaguer was leading the Mexican League with a .427 batting average.

We then plugged into our network of sources and scouts for an assessment and began monitoring Julio's play daily as the Tigres were winding down their regular season. Although he had had earlier stints with seven different major league teams, there was not much fresh information readily available on Julio. He had been bouncing around the globe, playing one season in Japan and two in Mexico. Among those whose input we sought was one of the opposition managers in the Mexican League, Eddie Díaz, a friend and contact of Frank's. When asked how he did against the top pitchers in that league, Díaz said, "Julio hits *everybody*. He can still play. He's outstanding around first base and is in phenomenal condition."

The other recommendations were as strong, so we decided to go for it. However, we wanted him by August 31, which is the major league deadline for roster additions that would be eligible for postseason play. The Tigres made the Mexican League playoffs and had they advanced all the way would have played past the deadline. Fortunately for us, they were eliminated two days prior to the deadline and we rushed Julio to Atlanta.

At that time, the baseball world thought Julio had just turned forty. It was not until the heightened security checks following the 9/11 tragedy the next year did the fact surface that Julio was actually three years older. He had always danced around the question of his age, and for good reason. Would we have brought him aboard at forty-three instead of "only" forty? Good question.

It seemed dubious enough to some that we were resurrecting a forty-year-old from the Mexican League. After his name came up in several internal discussions, Bobby Cox gave us a funny look and said, "You guys are serious about this, aren't you?" Bobby conceded he envisioned a portly old guy waddling to the plate.

When Julio arrived on August 31 and began pulling on his Atlanta Braves uniform, Ned Yost, one of our coaches, walked into Bobby's office to advise that Franco was there and could be added to the lineup card. Bobby skeptically inquired about Julio's apparent condition and Ned brightened. "Well, he's not fat. In fact, he's a strong-looking dude and may be in better shape than anyone in there."

As we have come to appreciate, Julio out-works, out-lifts, out-prepares everyone and continues to improve. After hitting .300 for us the final month of that season, he has continued to defy Father Time with solid production. He vows his goal is to play major league baseball past his fiftieth birthday. And, with his spirit and determination, he just may do that.

MONEYBALL DISCIPLES DEMAND GROUNDBALL OUTS BY THE PITCHERS they acquire? When we picked up Jaret Wright off the waiver wire late in the 2003 season, he hadn't thrown many groundball outs the previous few seasons. Or much of any kind of outs. Jaret hadn't pitched more than about 50 big-league innings in any of the prior three seasons, the result of some arm problems. He was attempting to come back from major shoulder surgery and was tagged with a bloated 8.37 earned run average that season for the San Diego Padres, who placed him on the waiver wire.

Before he developed the shoulder problem, Jaret had been an exceptional young pitcher with the Cleveland Indians, headed for stardom.

Routinely, when a name comes over the waiver wire, we immediately send out a telephone message to all our major league scouts. If any of them have interest in the player, they are to call our office. They started calling in, one after another.

"I like this guy."

"His arm is coming back."

"His delivery looks free and easy, like he's almost all the way back from that shoulder surgery."

"He's throwing the ball with great velocity, but not getting good results out of it."

"In our environment, this guy could really be fixed and really be made into a productive pitcher again and ready to blossom again."

Four separate major league scouts on four separate looks at him that season talked about the same thing—the free and easy delivery, the velocity and life in his fastball. His command of his pitches wasn't good, which made him hittable, but he looked like his arm was back. Or almost so.

I called up on my computer the reports our scouts had filed on Jaret earlier in the season and noted that Jim Fregosi gave his fastball a rating of 70. In our 20-to-80 rating system, 70 is excellent. A 70 doesn't often come over the waiver wire.

But it wasn't so much the 70 in the rating; it was the velocity of his fastball and the notes that these guys included in their reports. He was being clocked in the mid-90s and occasionally in the high 90s. Jim had him once at 97. Al Kubski, one of our part-time scouts, had Jaret at 96. By our standards, that's a crackling, major-league-dominant fastball. When a pitcher with an exceptional fastball is available for nothing more than the waiver price of $20,000, I tend to get interested.

Here was a pitcher with a stratospheric earned run average with the last-place Padres, but four different scouts who had seen him that year said something positive that, collectively, tapped out the message that we needed to see him in a Braves uniform. The picture they painted was that his recovery from shoulder surgery was beginning to bear fruit. We were looking past the raw numbers and relying, instead, on the subjective judgment of our scouts.

No fewer than five of those scouts were telling me, "Get this guy."

We had the National League's best record at the time, meaning Wright would have to be bypassed by every other National League team on the waiver wire for us to take him. And that's exactly what happened. Over the final month of that 2003 season, we used him in spot relief, with encouraging results. He was scored upon just twice in 11 appearances, then allowed no hits and no runs in a total of four innings of work in the playoffs against the Cubs.

The next spring, we gave him a shot at earning a spot in our starting rotation. This economy waiver wire plum validated our scouting system by ringing up a a career-high 15-8 record in 2004 with a team-leading 3.28 earned run average in 32 starts and led the club with 159 strikeouts.

WOULD THE GREEN EYESHADE BOYS HAVE GONE AFTER OUTFIELDER J. D. Drew immediately following a 2003 season in which he missed 62 games with two different ailments, had a rather pedestrian .374 on-base percentage for a feature hitter, and coaxed just 36 walks? I think not.

We did, because we looked beyond the numbers. We looked deeply into his medical history and determined his ailments were not chronic. We looked into his personality and character and determined he would be a good fit in our clubhouse. Only then did we target J.D. as our preferred puzzle part to fill the role of departing Gary Sheffield and acquired him as the focus of a five-player swap with St. Louis.

That decision was rewarded by a 2004 performance in which J.D. had career highs in homers (31), RBI (93), runs (118), walks (118), and games (145).

Drew raised his on-base percentage to a lusty .436 and was a key factor in our second-half rocket ride up the NL East standings to yet another division title—and then caught the attention of the Moneyballers. When Drew became a free agent after that season, Dodgers GM Paul DePodesta signed him to a five-year, $55 million free agent contract.

When we acquired J.D., I predicted to our staff we would have him for only the one year remaining on his contract. He is represented by Scott Boras, who pushes his clients into free agency when at all possible and, if J.D. had the kind of productive season I fully expected, would demand far more than our budget would accommodate. The best offer we could, and did, make was a three-year, $25 million package. Boras laughed at it.

*   *   *

I ALSO FIND IT RATHER DOUBTFUL THAT A MONEYBALL GENERAL MAN-
ager would make his principal off-season free agent acquisition a guy
fresh off a 1990 season in which he missed 41 games with nagging injuries and hit just .230 with six homers and 58 runs batted in. In fact,
there were some who found it questionable that any general manager
would have gone out on a limb for Terry Pendleton that year. But in
addition to the numbers, I had the advantage of due diligence by our
scouts and other informed sources who convinced me that Terry's
physical problems had been resolved and that he could easily reclaim
the productivity he had enjoyed a few years earlier for the Cardinals.

Venerable Atlanta columnist Furman Bisher was the first and harsh-
est critic when I signed Terry that first year I was in Atlanta. Dumbest
thing he'd ever seen anyone do. Terry didn't play very well or very much
because he was hurt. St. Louis dumps him and Schuerholz signs him
to a three-year contract? Furman and I laugh about it now. Be reminded that Terry Pendleton was the National League MVP that first
year in Atlanta when he hit .319, 22 homers, scored 94 runs, and drove
in 86.

Furman let me have it on numerous other occasions, especially
when we had the distasteful, but unavoidable, task of trading pitcher
Kevin Millwood and his $10 million contract.

But I'll give Furman credit. He finally began to cut me some slack
after only thirteen straight division titles. After we defied all logic by
winning No. 13 in 2004 with replacements for several departed stars,
we were back at it the next winter, cobbling together another new roster for '05 after more stars bolted for big free agent bucks.

Furman wrote sneers about a projected lineup that would feature
acquisitions like oft-troubled Raul Mondesi and oft-injured Brian Jordan. But he covered his rump by adding the caveat: "But you always
keep this in mind: Never sell Schuerholz short, never." Although the
Mondesi experience didn't pan out, we were willing once again to be
creative with our roster reconstruction. Managing changes by thinking
outside the box.

Agents were the bane of my existence for the first half of my run as a general manager. Now certain factions of the media have become another burr under my saddle. We have people on staff who deal with agents, and do so effectively. We do our business and win championships while dealing with agents who represent players we want. I no longer interact much with them. But I have a responsibility, as the principal spokesman for the organization, to interact with the media every day. And they can color the opinions of fans and our sponsors and our supporters and our potential season ticket holders in ways that can reflect badly or well on us. Quite often, it is the former.

And I banter with and crack jokes with the guys who cover us on a regular basis all the time. I laugh with them. So I get along with them fairly well, but I know their job is to cast a critical eye. Maybe it's not their job, but it's certainly the inclination of the modern media in this increasingly in-your-face society.

Perhaps they just find it an irritation that we haven't screwed up enough in recent years to give them column fodder, as Atlanta writer Mark Bradley suggested in a wry 1997 piece:

"So now it's six years going on seven, and still this guy Schuerholz flies under the Rip Radar. This is tragic. The one thing a critic cannot appear is to be a homer; a cheerleader, a PR man. Otherwise your whole worldview gets skewed. You find yourself being optimistic. You extend the benefit of the doubt. Some days you wake up and, horror of horrors, feel like smiling.

"So here I sit, Mister Acerbic having turned into Mister Rogers. Soon I'll get the hankering to go watch college baseball. Soon I'll have fond memories of the run-and-shoot. This guy Schuerholz—he broke me. Darn him."

Maybe they would have been happier if I had gone Moneyball and handed over our player selection process to a bunch of sabermetricians with green visors and overheated calculators who would never have hired Pendleton or Wright or Drew or Franco.

I swear on my stack of suspenders—and a lot of people don't believe me when I say this—I don't allow media criticism to get under my skin too often. I really don't. Occasionally, somebody will bring it to my attention and I may go back and look at something and fume. I do appreciate the media's value in publicizing and (sometimes) romanticizing our sport. I appreciate the talent that is required. And I understand the deadline pressures they are under, particularly in a sport like baseball with so many night games.

You just wish they didn't have this ongoing compulsion to home in on the warts we all have, to be quite so critical.

Teddy Roosevelt had a great quote about critics that I keep at my desk as a reminder:

"It's not the critic who counts. It's not the man who points out where the grown man stumbles, or how the doer of deeds could have done them better. The credit belongs to the man who actually is in the arena, who strives violently, who errs and comes up short again and again, who knows the great enthusiasms, the great devotions, and spends himself in a worthy cause, who if he wins knows the triumph of high achievement; but who if he fails, fails while daring greatly, so his place will never be with those cold and timid souls who know neither victory nor defeat."

That's the quote I live by with regard to media criticism.

3

A Rotation for the Ages

Our classic starting rotation of John Smoltz, Greg Maddux, and Tom Glavine will long be remembered by most everyone in baseball as the game's most effective rotation in the '90s. They were the key to building on our string of division championships, year after year. Collectively, they won six National League Cy Young Awards and rang up seven 20-win seasons. The domination of that trio even stretched at times to a fourth man, first young Steve Avery, then Denny Neagle, and later Kevin Millwood.

Eventually, the ravages of time and injuries and the escalating cost of contracts took their toll. As much as we would have preferred to perpetuate that group, we were forced to make adjustments.

First to go was Avery, who is best remembered by Braves fans for his classic performance against the Pittsburgh Pirates in the 1991 NL championship series. The indelible image is Steve with his cap characteristically pulled down low to his eyebrows, staring and glaring into home plate and challenging every hitter that walked up there. He was MVP of that series, winning two games and allowing not a single run in his 16 innings of work. Alas, his arm went sour. Simply got sore. He tried to pitch through it with his mental toughness. But it just wasn't there anymore and his arm just kept getting worse.

Three arm surgeries yanked Smoltz out of the rotation in the late '90s when the trauma simply wouldn't allow his arm to hold up as a starter. He rebounded to become a sensational closer, virtually unhittable in his short, mostly one-inning bursts for us over four seasons. Through extremely hard work and competitive drive, John eventually regained the endurance to make an uncommon reincarnation as a starter for the 2005 season: He pitched 169 innings and posted a 14-7 record, with a 3.06 ERA.

Maddux, the peerless craftsman and certain Hall of Famer, simply became too expensive for our payroll management. We had to let him go to free agency after 11 great seasons for us. In 2004, his first season back in Chicago where he had pitched a decade earlier, he won 16 games for the Cubs. We knew Mad Dog could still pitch; we just couldn't afford him. The immortal Branch Rickey used to say a good general manager is one who moves a star player one year too early rather than one year too late.

Millwood came on to capably plug the rotation hole left by Smoltz's move to the bullpen. But baseball's new economics forced us to part with Kevin so we'd have the money to re-sign Maddux, who filed for arbitration prior to the 2003 season and forced us to trim $10 million off our payroll. Losing a future Hall of Famer like Greg and having to trade Kevin were bitter pills to swallow. But the departure of Tom Glavine turned out to be the toughest to deal with personally.

Tommy's long and glorious tenure with the Braves was punctuated by a heartfelt, soul-searching meeting I shared with him at his home late on a Saturday evening as he wrestled with the verbal commitment he had just given to sign with the New York Mets.

TOMMY GLAVINE WAS SELECTED BY THE BRAVES IN THE FREE AGENT draft of 1984 and was outstanding during his three-year rise up through the minors. He became a solid performer in his first three full seasons in Atlanta, then blossomed, luckily for me, into a 20-game winner and Cy Young Award winner in 1991, my first year as GM of the Braves. He followed that by winning 20 or more games the next two seasons.

Tommy continued to pitch effectively, year after year, with his style of change-up after change-up after change-up. Come and hit this pitch if you think you can. If you do, I'll make it even more difficult for you to hit it the next time. As a painter of corners, he was an absolute Michelangelo. And that's how he had success for us.

When he played out his contract and became a free agent after the 2002 season, we tried to keep him. We really wanted Tommy to stay. Our negotiations came to a head in one last, six-hour, heated meeting on Tuesday, December 3, in the conference room just off my office. It was me, Braves president Stan Kasten, Tommy and his agent, Greg Clifton, that evening, from four o'clock to ten. We were the last four people in the stadium, Tommy and Stan were yelling at each other like I had never heard. Previously, they had developed and enjoyed a strong relationship. Friendly, professional, and respectful.

We thought we had a proposal that made sense. We were trying to fend off the Mets with a salary offer of around $10 million a year. The Mets were trying to unseat us in our division, knock us off our perch. What better way to do that than to take away one of our key performers and add him to their lineup?

The contract proposal we made was unique, with what we call an "evergreen" clause. That provision is structured in such a way that if you pitch a certain number of innings in a season, your contract automatically rolls over, adding a year. The clause doesn't take into account won-lost percentage, earned run average, or anything other than simply the number of innings, which measures a starter's recovery, resiliency, and ability to pitch. If he isn't pitching well, you're not going to start him and he won't pitch as many innings. Or if he's getting banged around, he's not going to stay in a game very long.

We said to Tommy, "We are more than willing to pay you at this level of compensation provided you can pitch. That's all we're asking, so we can then manage our team's payroll. If we know you can pitch, we're prepared to pay you at this level. But we have to control the payroll." And we were adamant about that. We couldn't be tied down to a huge salary for a thirty-six-year-old guy who might become ineffective.

Tommy kept hammering on the fact that, a year earlier, we had signed John Smoltz to a four-year deal coming off an injury. And now he wanted the same thing. That was all the more reason we couldn't afford to get further strung out with huge, long-term contracts. We were already gambling on John. If something happened to Tommy, we would run the risk of having to eat two huge salaries. We would have been devastated, completely unable to manage our payroll or construct a team.

Plus, this was just when the market was changing. Had this been a year earlier, we might well have given him a four-year deal like John's.

Braves chairman Terry McGuirk called my cell phone near the end of the meeting to check the progress. As Terry recalls: "John told me how contentious it had become and that Tommy had begun lecturing them and wagging his finger at them. I told John to get out of the room. I felt it was over."

After the meeting, I told Stan there were times when I should have stepped in to cool things down. Other times I would have. But Stan reasoned—and I agree—that's why you have a second guy in there on both sides. The truth is I didn't really want him to calm down because we had already stretched the numbers beyond what we should have. We couldn't afford to be more conciliatory, and that's what would have happened.

We had all gone into the meeting on edge. There were times during the weeks before this meeting that Tommy said he would have his agent call and promised not to take what Stan called the "Glavine Across America Tour" to shop himself to several teams. But we went days at a time with no call from the agent and Tommy did take the tour.

Two days later in the paper, he referred to us as "unprofessional" and made several unfounded accusations, which really stung me and Stan. We have never negotiated in the paper. Ever! We had always called *him*. We had called his agent a number of times, but he wasn't returning our calls. They were putting all their offers in the newspaper. We kept everything quiet, professional, and confidential. But they decided to use the media to state their case. There were bad feelings created because of that tactic.

So bad, in fact, that on Thursday, Tommy called me and apologized for his "in the heat of the battle" comments.

That same day, the Mets announced that they had reached an agreement with Tommy, pending a physical. We had actually thought he might be going to Philadelphia, another division rival.

That Friday, December 6, we did the unthinkable. Stan and I sat down with the media in that same conference room and presented a blow-by-blow of the previous two months, every conversation we had with Tommy. Which basically refuted a lot of the allegations he was making. What about this call, Tommy, and this letter? We had never done that before and I think Tommy and his agent were counting on us to *not* call their hand and, instead, take our public lashing in silence. Because we negotiate in private. No exceptions. Well, sadly, we were forced to break our policy. We were left with no choice.

The press conference was instant fodder for the talk shows. The reaction of the fans was: *Hey, wait a minute! Who does Glavine think he is? The Braves DID make him an offer. They DID do this and that.*

According to Stan, Tommy told a media confidant about his anger at our press conference but expressed second thoughts about agreeing to join the Mets. The confidant told him, "If you feel bad, just go back to the Braves. Screw the Mets." Tommy, with his emotions in a swirl, purportedly told another close friend, "Screw it. I'm just going to play for one year and retire. I don't know why I did this."

A year later, Tommy ran into Stan at an Atlanta Hawks game and they had their first conversation in all that time. Tommy said, "I really don't know why you did that press conference. That really hurt."

"We did it," Stan explained, "because you were lying about us. And my franchise is more important than any individual player. We couldn't let you call us unprofessional after all the things we did."

As for length of contract, our offer was similar to that of the Mets— three years, plus an option year. But the Mets were offering $35 million over the three years plus a $3 million buyout for the fourth, and we were offering $30 million. We were resistant to committing a four-year guaranteed deal to a thirty-six-year-old pitcher, thus the evergreen provision.

Tommy had made his home in Atlanta and his family loved it here. It was a tough decision for him to make. We felt he really wanted to stay. But Tommy was a fierce competitor—a former hockey player, drafted by the NHL—and an equally fierce, competitive negotiator. Strong-willed. And that six-hour session was a negotiating bout where adamant positioning on both sides of the table and strong-willed positions on both sides caused the deal not to get done. The deal couldn't be made. Not right there, that day.

They wanted four years and no evergreen. Did his agent nudge him into being intractable on that? I don't know for sure, but I do know, from talking to both Tommy and Clifton much later, that his agent played a large role in Tommy's ultimate choice to leave. That's not saying that Clifton pushed Tommy into anything. I don't think anyone could push Tommy Glavine anywhere he didn't want to go. I think Tommy made his own decision. I think it was more the emotions around not being able to get a deal done that he thought was appropriate. No doubt the players union was suggesting the four-year deal was more appropriate for him and his agent was suggesting he deserved that.

Whatever the driving force, I can see where his competitive nature might have led him to think: "If they don't think enough of me to give me what I think is right and fair, then I'll show them. I'll go else-where."

However, we have long known the union has communicated with agents what they think contract terms should be. Usually higher!

So on Thursday, Tommy Glavine told the Mets he would take their offer. The plan was for him to fly to New York that Sunday night to take his physical, sign the contract, and be there for the public an-nouncement on Monday.

But during the few days in between, Tommy went through a pur-gatory of second thoughts. It was the same purgatory I had gone through when I was first lured to Atlanta from my beloved Kansas City eleven years earlier. That's the best parallel I can make.

I could empathize with Tommy because I, too, had wrestled with those demons of indecision—for a lot of the very same reasons.

He had spent his entire major league life in Atlanta. This is where his career as a professional baseball player was born. Where he was raised as a baseball player. Where he matured as a player, succeeded as a player, and where he was a world champion as a player. Perhaps even a Hall of Famer.

Tommy was part of this community. And yet he thought—or at least he and his agent thought—there was a better opportunity finan-cially elsewhere and he made his decision on that basis. And then he started to wonder: Is that all there is to life? How about how comfort-able my family is in Atlanta? How about how comfortable my kids are here? How about how much we love it here? How about my familiar-ity with Bobby Cox as a manager and my comfort with his handling of me? And our trainers and our team doctors and all of that?

I think that's natural.

He shared with some close friends and associates how terribly con-flicted he was, and that was relayed to me.

So with all of these second thoughts swirling around in his brain, Tommy called Bobby Cox at Bobby's farm at Adairsville, Georgia, that Saturday and, as Bobby related to us, said, "I made a mistake. I don't want to do this." Bobby called me, concerned about Tommy's well-being. He liked the guy. Tommy was like a son to him. Bobby said, "John, I think you should call him."

So I called him. Tommy invited me to come out to his house.

First, I called Stan. He said because he and Tommy had such heated exchanges in the six-hour negotiation meeting earlier that week, it was best that I go alone. Stan then called Terry McGuirk, his boss, who was just arriving at a private Christmas party. Terry recalls standing in the street getting this news on his cell phone while his wife went on into the party. "I would spend the whole evening," Terry remembers, "going in and out of the party to get cell phone updates."

I got in the car late that evening and drove there, a pretty good distance. Tommy lives out in Alpharetta, on the extreme northern outskirts of the Atlanta area, at the Country Club of the South. We shared a great bottle of Silver Oak cabernet wine. He and his wife, Chris, and I talked. The three of us talked and talked and talked. It was a tough visit. At times, we were all on the verge of tears. Tommy did most of the talking—about what was on his mind, which was about remaining a Brave. I related my similar experience when the Braves coaxed me into leaving Kansas City.

I said, "Tommy, we would be *happy* to have you remain with us if that's what you want. If that's how you feel, I give you my word that we will do all that we can to make that happen."

I explained to him again about the parameters of our offer and the parameters of our capabilities. I did not renegotiate. I just said here are the facts. Here are the realities. In fact, before I went to Tommy's house, Stan and I agreed we had extended ourselves too far with the offer we had made. I suggested that if Tommy decides he wants to stay, we should offer him a two-year deal. No games, no incentives, no deferred money. Two years, here's your money, and we'll worry about whatever happens after that. Stan agreed.

After a lot of soul-searching, Tommy decided that he was going to stay.

Quite obviously, he was relieved. His wife was relieved. And I was bouncing their son on my knee. There was a sudden air of contentment. While I was still there, Tommy tried unsuccessfully to reach his agent, Greg Clifton, and left a phone message. (We had learned earlier how extremely difficult, if not impossible, it was to reach Clifton by phone.)

Stan alerted TBS that there could be a major news conference the next day. He also took care of one more complication. All of this was coming down on the same Saturday night that is annually the major league deadline for tendering a contract to your own unsigned players. The Mets would have been placed in an unfair position if Tommy stayed with us and the Mets nontendered some other player thinking they had Glavine coming.

In an effort to be fair to the Mets, at ten o'clock that night, two hours before the deadline, Stan tracked down Rob Manfred of the Commissioner's Office to explain the problem.

Meanwhile, I was driving home from Tommy's, thinking we might get to keep our pitcher and that Tommy would get to preserve his family happiness. While en route, I received a call on my cell phone from Clifton, who was livid. How *dare* we do what we did? His client had made his decision, had made his commitment and gave his word to the Mets that he would take their contract. He said he didn't look kindly upon what he felt was our continuing intrusion after Tommy's decision had been made.

In the strongest terms, I reminded him we hadn't done anything. It was *his* client who called *our* manager and said he wanted to change *his* mind. I said we owed it to him after all the loyal years of service he gave us to at least hear him and talk to him. Besides, I noted, Tommy invited *me* to *his* house. I wasn't intruding on anything.

Clifton angrily fired back that he could have me up on tampering charges, because Tommy was already someone else's property.

Could he? Tommy wasn't signed at that moment, but I'm not a lawyer. Stan is and was more combative about that: "Screw him! He's going to stand in the way of what his client wants? I'd like to see how he answers that one at the bar association!"

When Tommy hadn't called later that night or Sunday morning, I called him just before noon. He explained simply that he had decided to stick with the Mets deal. An hour later, Tommy and his family boarded a private plane and flew to New York's Westchester County Airport to begin his new life as a Met.

The issue ended with Clifton, and I suppose the union, persuading Tommy that it would be in everyone's best interest if he did not change his mind about the agreement he made with the Mets. I was later informed by a number of people that there was pressure applied to Tommy by outside sources. His agent was one of them and I suspect the union was another.

In the meantime, I was getting roasted in the media for allowing Glavine to get away. I thought we made a valiant effort—and creative, with the evergreen clause—to try to assuage his interest in making more money, and our interest in managing our payroll in a way that would permit us to maintain a championship team. We didn't want to risk being locked down with a contract for a guy if he could no longer perform and have $8 million or more in the deep black hole of no returns.

We thought that was a fair position to take. What we were asking, simply and purely, was that if we have to pay this kind of money, then the player has to assure us he will be able to perform to that level. In baseball today that has come to be regarded as a foreign concept. But it's the most fair-minded concept that exists—good pay for good performance. We thought the evergreen clause was a good bridging mechanism between his request and our offer.

My public thrashing was considerable over this. But there were also some voices on the other side due to Tom's high-profile involvement with the union during the 1994 strike. I can remember people writing in, referring to him as the "shop steward," and all that. He didn't endear himself to a lot of fans, particularly with some of his public comments on the matter.

One of his worst was: "Look, it's not about the money. I'd even work for $2 million." That wasn't received too well.

As I had mentioned, Stan and Tommy had a strong relationship and Stan publicly defended him for his union role. "What we love about him when he puts on our uniform," Stan was quoted at the time, "is what he exemplifies in his role with the union. He's a dogged, determined competitor."

During the strike talks in '94, they had been spokesmen for the opposite sides. They flew to meetings together and developed a strong mutual respect. Stan thinks at the end of the day, Tommy felt Stan would come through for him. But in the six-hour negotiating meeting, they became very animated and headstrong.

In their conversations, Stan and Tommy had always been animated, but without the rancor. In his previous contract, Tommy wanted Stan, who was also president of the NHL Atlanta Thrashers, to throw in a VIP box at the hockey games. "Hey!" Stan chortled. "I'm one of the few people in town who know what you are making and you're going to *buy* a bleeping box!"

They both laughed. And Tommy bought the box. They used to laugh a lot.

Looking back, Stan recently made this observation about Glavine: "I am an enormous Tommy Glavine fan. I like him personally as much as professionally. But we have had our moments."

Some think Tommy was naive, but I don't share that. I think he was heartfelt. I think he knew the circumstances, the details, and the issues. He knew them, and this was how he felt about it. Tom is a guy the union counted on a lot and he's a strong union supporter. But that does not change the kind of competitive, successful pitcher he has been—a guy who had a chance to win 300 games and be one of the finest pitchers ever to wear the Braves uniform.

If he had stayed, he would have owned Atlanta. Forever. The player who loved Atlanta so much he couldn't leave.

As I sat watching Tommy Glavine agonize that emotionally charged Saturday evening in his home, I saw myself. As I've said, I could empathize fully with his inner turmoil because I had gone through the same thing a dozen years earlier wrestling with the decision to leave Kansas City and take the GM job in Atlanta. There were so many parallels.

There's an old saying in the railroad industry that goes, "Off again, on again, gone again Finnegan." They'd use that phrase when a train derailed and they'd have to put it back on the tracks. That's how I felt going through the hiring process with the Braves. I made two trips to Atlanta—the last on October 2, 1990, the day after my fiftieth birthday—to discuss the situation with Stan and Terry McGuirk. Stan and I met both times in Stan's office in the impressive CNN Center. He didn't want me to go near the dreary Braves offices in the stadium for fear that might chase me away.

We negotiated the parameters of a deal and I returned to Kansas City after the second trip knowing in my heart that I was going to be a Brave. I had asked for certain things—in terms of compensation, in terms of length of contract, in terms of a commitment from them, in terms of certain levels of autonomy in the operation. All of that I had gotten. But just as pleasing as Stan's agreement to the terms during our negotiating session in his office in the CNN Center was his unexpected demeanor. At one point, he reached behind his desk and pulled out a rubber chicken and waved it about. He'd also press a button on a machine on his desk that played a rim shot—badda badda boom!—when he made a point in negotiations.

I could tell in the first five minutes that the working environment in Atlanta and with Stan Kasten would be stimulating and fun. And I was right.

"Outwardly, John has his stuffy side," Stan says. "People who don't know him think of him—to be charitable—as stuffy. That isn't what John is about, and I let him know that. At that time, we needed some stuffiness. We needed tightening up and buttoning down. But we all intend to have fun here and I demonstrated that by pulling out the rubber chicken. I needed a little of him. He needed a little of me. And that's how it worked out."

I came home from that meeting and told my wife, Karen, I had laughed more in those two hours than I had laughed in the last three years with the Royals. It was not a loose or fun environment for me in Kansas City any longer. It was serious, stoic, very businesslike, almost stodgy. And all of a sudden here's a guy who was the president of a club holding up a rubber chicken and making me laugh and walking around his desk swinging a bat *while we were negotiating my contract!*

At first I thought, "How bizarre!" Then I thought, "How much fun! How great is this?"

By then, I had come to know Stan much better since first interacting with him a few months earlier on an MLB committee. I quickly developed great admiration for his intellect. He's one of the sharpest guys I've ever known—still is. At the time, he was president of both the Braves and the NBA Atlanta Hawks—and later also the NHL Thrashers. It all seemed so very tempting, but also all of these nagging thoughts kept racing through my mind about Kansas City. *What am I thinking here? I'm leaving this beautiful place, a wonderful place to raise children, this great franchise, this marvelous place to live? What am I doing? I'm going to Atlanta, home of the last-place Braves? And yanking my family out of the only home they'd known?*

Leaving Kansas City was something I never thought I'd do. I constantly told my friends and family: "They're gonna carry me out of here in a pine box. I love it here so much. That's the only way I'm leaving KC."

This from a guy who had never lived anywhere but Baltimore before moving to Kansas City. And for twenty-two years from the first day I set foot in Kansas City in 1969 to the autumn of 1990, I thought of Kansas City as my personal heaven.

Karen was born in Detroit, but her family moved to Kansas City when she was just eight months old and she had lived her entire life there. Our children, Gina and Jonathan, were both born in Kansas City and had lived nowhere else. So the sudden and unexpected move from Kansas City would be no small thing to Karen or Gina or Jonathan. Just as it was no small thing for the Glavines to leave the Braves and Atlanta.

I gathered the family in my office at home in suburban Leawood, Kansas. I explained the circumstances fully, then asked for their opinions. Jonathan spoke first, blurting out: "I vote for Atlanta!" Gina quickly said the same. Karen, who didn't really want to leave Kansas City, said whatever I thought best to do, she was with me. She always is. Let's hear it for Karen.

We decided that if, indeed, I took the Atlanta job, they would remain in Kansas City until the spring so Gina could complete her senior year at Leawood's Blue Valley North High School. Jonathan was seven years younger, in the fourth grade, and we figured he would be resilient enough to handle the change. Gina is now an outstanding fifth-grade teacher in Atlanta. Jonathan is pursuing his dream, playing professionally as a second baseman in the Braves' organization. And Karen continues to be the "general manager" of our family, having created our new home in Atlanta.

I was so conflicted about whether to take the Atlanta job, in fact, that I sat down and tried to list all the pluses and minuses of both jobs in sort of a matrix. Once these sheets were done, it was obviously a virtual toss-up. I knew I had to make a major decision. And I did. It's somewhat like in a player deal, when I have a roomful of scouts telling me their opinions on a particular player that we're considering to acquire or trade. Half of the room says here are the reasons we should do it and the other half of the room is saying here are the reasons we shouldn't. The same instincts that allow me to listen to all those things and hopefully make the right decision on behalf of the roster construction are the same sort of juices that flowed in me that allowed me to weigh and balance and measure the gut-check decision that I made to leave Kansas City and come to Atlanta.

As it turned out my instincts led me to make the right decision. It was time for me to go and these past fifteen years in Atlanta have more than validated that. This was one of the many big decisions I had to make in my leadership life. Many more were to follow. Deciding to commit multiple millions to sign Greg Maddux. Deciding to trade for Fred McGriff to fill our cleanup hitter void. Trading David Justice and Marquis Grissom to free up the money to sign Tom Glavine and John Smoltz to contract extensions. Deciding to trade for recalcitrant Gary Sheffield. And, of late, deciding to allow Maddux, Glavine, Kevin Millwood, Javy Lopez, Gary Sheffield, J. D. Drew, Russ Ortiz, and Jaret Wright to leave, to manage our roster's payroll efficiently.

Decisions, decisions, decisions!

Stan knew I was conflicted, but kept calling to persuade me. One call came while I was in the shower. He and Terry McGuirk were on the phone and this was a funny moment, me stepping out to take the call, cold and dripping in the bathroom and bare-ass naked. It was time for me to make a decision, one way or the other. I was literally and figuratively naked before the world in this decision-making time.

Soon after I went in and told Royals president Joe Burke that I was leaning toward taking the Braves job. He said he was sorry to hear that, but agreed that I had to do what I thought was right. He, of course, reported this to Royals owner Ewing Kauffman, who summoned me to meet with him.

We met at the Kansas City Club, the beautiful, venerable old private club in downtown Kansas City. He obviously was a member and invited me to meet him there. It was just the two of us and I'll never forget this meeting. This was going to be a sad meeting.

It was a terribly difficult thing for me to do because I had such respect for Mr. K and loved working for him and was proud to be in his organization. Here I was talking to a man who by his determination and intellect became a billionaire in the pharmaceutical industry. There is a book about his life, *Prescription for Success*. He started Marion Laboratories on his own—sold pills during the day and did billing and administrative work at night.

He came out of the Navy and went to work for a pharmaceutical company. He was so aggressive and competent as a salesman that he made more money in one year than the president of the company. So the president said he couldn't have a salesman making more money than him and reduced Mr. K's territory by some substantial margin. But the next year, Mr. K made even more money selling in his newly confined territory. The owner and president of the company decided to restrict him further. Mr. K decided that wasn't right, quit and got a banker friend, Charlie Hughes, to bankroll him and started Marion Laboratories. That's the M in Mr. Kauffman's name. Ewing Marion Kauffman. He came upon some doctor who said ground-up oyster shells could produce the best calcium supplement possible and no one had produced that. So Os-cal was born at Marion Labs, and that was the product that made his company a huge success. Mr. K became a self-made billionaire. And a great philanthropist in Kansas City.

He had the most dynamic, crystal-clear, steel-blue eyes I've seen on a human being. He smoked a pipe, had a steel-trap mathematical mind, was a business genius, and was a compassionate, kind, caring human being who demanded excellence from you in the work you did and the effort you put forth. In turn, he did all he could for you, personally. He was great to me, from a personal and financial standpoint.

He said, "John, I am not going to let you come back. As hard as it is and as much as it pains me to say that, there is too much uncertainty in your heart and in your mind about where you want to be and how you feel about staying in Kansas City and what this opportunity is for you.

"You . . . *must* . . . go," he said, the pauses and emphasis his.

He made it clear he wasn't saying he didn't want me to stay, but there was too much uncertainty that he sensed in me for me to stay and do the kind of job I had done in the past. And he was crying. Tears were running down his cheeks. Mine, too. Because I felt so strongly about this good man.

I flash back to that meeting with Mr. K a lot. It was a poignant moment in my life, when I made a big decision—or a big decision was made for me—that was the right decision. He knew it. He understood that. And, instinctively, I did, too.

Both scared and exhilarated, I was formally announced in a press conference three days later, Wednesday, October 10, in old Fulton County Stadium.

So some twelve years later, I fully understood and appreciated what Tommy Glavine was going through. I had lived it myself.

GREG MADDUX BECAME PART OF OUR "BIG THREE" AFTER WE BECAME a late entry in the 1993 Maddux signing derby. By all reckoning, he was destined to become a Yankee. Everyone had written that. We had thought about making a run at Greg. We were debating between Greg and Barry Bonds, whom we had momentarily acquired in the aborted trade with Pittsburgh the previous year and was now a free agent.

It had always been my philosophy since I entered baseball in 1966 with the pitching-rich Orioles (who beat the Dodgers in four straight in the World Series of '66 with a great pitching staff) that it's all about building winning teams around pitching.

We finally focused in on Maddux and decided that's who we wanted to acquire. We thought it a long shot because he was so far down the road with the Yankees. He had already made his visit to New York. Greg and his wife were taken out to dinner and were on their way back home to Las Vegas when we made our first serious offer to his agent, Scott Boras.

So a few days later, at the winter meetings in Louisville in December 1993, we had two suites across the hall from each other at the Galt House. In one we had all of our scouts and other baseball operations guys. Anytime we talk about deals, I always discuss the components with that group and get their opinions. On the other side of the hall, we had Scott Boras, with whom Stan Kasten and I were negotiating potential contract terms for Greg Maddux.

As it became obvious to us that we had a good shot to sign Greg, Stan made it clear we couldn't do this without moving a lot of dollars off our payroll. Greg was seeking a five-year, $28 million contract.

The one player who had the kind of money we needed to move was pitcher Charlie Leibrandt. But there was only one team interested enough in Leibrandt for us to engage in any serious conversations. I'm in the suite on one side of the hall talking by phone to Dan O'Brien, Sr., of the Texas Rangers, who legitimately had interest in Leibrandt. And he should have because Charlie was a quality pitcher. But they were the only club interested. Thus, we had just one opportunity to pull this off. After some give-and-take—and quite a few apprehensive moments—we were able to make a deal with the Rangers, Leibrandt and pitcher Pat Gomez for third baseman Jose Oliva, a good offensive infielder, that would allow us to put the full-court press on Maddux.

I rushed back across the hall and rejoined Stan in the discussions with Boras. We were able to get the deal done. That was a unique contract situation, demonstrating our efforts to effectively manage our responsibilities to the roster while managing the payroll. Here we had a chance to sign a player whom we regarded as the finest free agent pitcher ever to come on the market. And for us to do it, even back in '93, the economic factor was in play and we had to manage our payroll, albeit at a higher level than a decade later. It had to be managed. We couldn't just add the Greg Maddux free agent salary.

In "recruiting" Maddux away from the Yankees, the one significant and most effective point we made was that it was Atlanta instead of New York. It was the quality of life that was more appealing to Greg and his wife. But we didn't have to put on a huge sell job. When he became involved, his interest piqued around us because he knew we had had success in our early goings in Atlanta. He said, "This is a team obviously committed to winning and that's what I want to do. And I love the quality of life we can have in Atlanta."

Although he still maintains his primary home in Las Vegas, he and his family clearly enjoyed their time in Atlanta.

Greg might be able to pitch until he's fifty because he's so smart. The most intelligent pitcher I've ever been around in my entire life. He would find a way to succeed. Greg went about pitching as if it were a chess match, crafting sequences of pitches and locations tailored for each hitter to set up an out pitch.

Former Atlanta pitching coach Leo Mazzone likes to relate the incident during an interleague game against the Yankees, when Greg had runners on second and third with personal nemesis Jorge Posada coming up. Bobby Cox went to the mound to ask Greg if he wanted to pitch to Posada or put him on and pitch to the next batter.

When Bobby returned to the dugout, he shook his head and told Leo, "Wait'll you hear this: He said, 'If I get behind 2-0, I'll go ahead and walk him. But I think I can get him to pop up to third on the second pitch.'" Greg felt he could set up Posada with a first pitch low and away, then come back with a cutter high and on the hands to induce the popup.

On the second pitch—that high, tight cutter—Posada popped up to third base.

Leo swore that Greg could hit the target more consistently than any pitcher he has ever seen and likes to cite another game against the Yankees when he allowed no walks, struck out 11, and threw fewer than 100 pitches. "Afterward," says Leo, "the umpire said, 'Well, Maddux is everything as advertised.'"

Greg's arm has always held up, which has been a wonderment to medical people about how he was able to do that.

Our appreciation and admiration for Greg continued even after he became a free agent and signed with the Cubs. Stan and I went to Chicago in anticipation of his 300th career win. He didn't get it that day, but did in his next start. Stan was there. I couldn't be. Greg sent me an autographed ticket from that game. What a joy and honor is was to have an association with a pitcher and professional of Greg's caliber. I definitely plan to be in attendance at Cooperstown when he is inducted into the Hall of Fame.

KEVIN MILLWOOD WAS THE THIRD MAJOR ATLANTA STARTER LOST TO another team. And while there was mixed reaction to Tom Glavine's departure a year earlier, the public seemed solidly united in its view of our trade of Millwood to Philadelphia for little-known minor league catcher Johnny Estrada: I was an idiot. In capital letters!

The Millwood trade was entirely an economic matter. We were in the process of reducing our overall payroll and we had his contract in place with a guaranteed $10 million salary for the approaching 2003 season. In an effort to make a trade that would help us manage our new payroll guidelines, I called virtually every general manager in baseball—the ones I felt had the financial wherewithal of assuming all or most of Kevin's contract. We needed to move him. Maddux was taking us through arbitration at that time and we knew that was going to have a huge impact on our payroll. Indeed, Greg's salary went from $13.1 million to $14.75 million. So we had to find a way within our payroll structure to make room for that impact. He didn't go the full route of that lovely process of arbitration, since we reached a settlement at that latter figure.

The only team willing to take Kevin Millwood's salary of $10 million was the Philadelphia Phillies. With the opening of their new stadium, they had the flexibility in their payroll to take him. With every other team, we would have had to pay some part of that salary and that would not have filled our need to trim our payroll to accommodate the new, industrial-size Maddux arbitration-caused salary.

Arbitration pushed Greg's pay to an unnatural level—at least in our minds—even for a great pitcher like Greg. I love Greg Maddux and admire and respect him more than anyone I've ever seen pitch. But we had to balance out the impact of that $14.75 million on our team payroll. If we were going to have to pay a boatload to one guy, then we had to off-load a substantial amount to make it work. The irony here is that both players are represented by the same agent, Scott Boras. Because we were taken to arbitration by him with Maddux, we were forced to trade another of his clients, Millwood, to clear financial room.

A similar situation had happened years earlier. We had to trade David Justice and Marquis Grissom in 1997 so that we would have the money available to re-sign Glavine and Maddux. We paid those two pitchers handsomely. At that time, we weren't being outmatched by people paying their players much more than we were paying. We were battling. We were spending money we didn't really have because we were, by nature, competitive people and a competitive organization. Each year, we thought our next World Series title was just around the corner. We rationalized that investing in these high-caliber players—and especially pitchers—was worthwhile because it may lead to our next world championship.

We had come so close in '91 and '92 and '93 and '96 and '97. Every year, it seems, we felt if we just have that one more guy and pay a little extra, our budget would be a bit out of whack, but if we win a world championship we might make it up in added revenue. Well, we never made it up.

But now we have moderated our payroll, sensibly, while some others have continued to catapult upward. So the separation in team payrolls has become greater.

With Millwood, we were not trying to trade the player. We really didn't want to trade Kevin Millwood. We were trying to eliminate the $10 million contract that happened to have Kevin attached to it.

I'll never forget this scene. I'm visiting my hometown Baltimore on a cold winter's December day with my wife, Karen, and we were taking my mother out to lunch at Bowman's Restaurant to have a couple of crab cakes and a cup of crab soup. My cell phone rings and it is Ed Wade, the Phillies' general manager.

I let Karen and my mother out of the car so they could go in and get a table. I'm sitting in the parking lot on this gray, cold, dreary day, talking about trading a stud right-handed pitcher who grew up a Brave, is a 220-innings-a-year guy and potential 20-game winner, breaking up our rotation—because *we can't afford him.*

Talk about losing your appetite. I had indigestion *before* lunch.

Ed and I had had some preliminary conversations, but right there, as I sat in the parking lot of Bowman's, I agreed to trade Kevin and his $10 million contract for catcher Johnny Estrada, who had spent most of that previous season with the Phillies' Triple-A farm team in Scranton, Pennsylvania.

The Millwood-for-Estrada trade was announced on December 20, 2002. Merry Christmas, Braves fans.

One of my more infamous quotes came out of that. For months, when asked about that trade, my whine was: "Baseball economics stink!"

I was angry and frustrated. I was really mad that we had to trade this guy. I wasn't mad at our organization because we had a new budget philosophy that said, "You know what? We don't want to keep spending $10 or $11 or $12 or $15 million more to operate this franchise than we earn. We don't need to keep doing that." We were tired of being economic fools.

I was just mad that players' salaries had risen to the point that they didn't make any economic sense and we had to trade good players because of their salaries, not their abilities.

Fortunately, we had done our homework on Estrada and knew him to be a bright prospect. And, indeed, two years later he had a terrific, clutch-hitting first full season for us in 2004 and was the National League All-Star catcher. But at the time of the trade, the media and the public only saw our trade being a proven starting pitcher for an unknown minor-leaguer.

At first, even Johnny was puzzled by the trade. When Ed Wade called Johnny at his North Carolina home, his first thought was to wonder who the "big name" from the Phillies was in the deal. "It couldn't have been just me for Millwood," Johnny recalls thinking that day. "Then I found out it *was* just me. I later found out about the economics that were involved. But I didn't care. I was going to a good organization and a winning organization. I knew Javy Lopez was coming off of a subpar season, so I might have a chance to move up.

"I never let the criticism of the trade get to me. I had to deal with that for two years—'Who is Johnny Estrada?' It bothered me. I just got over it and waited for my opportunity and hoped it would come. And it came."

It was like an early Christmas present to Johnny. Growing up in Fresno, California, he and his father were avid long-distance Braves fans, watching the TBS telecasts of Atlanta games almost nightly in the late '80s. "Back then, the Braves were terrible. They were like 'lovable losers' and I enjoyed watching them," Johnny recalled.

We went to great lengths to explain to our Atlanta media all the background to the trade including the Maddux salary, the inescapable need to keep some semblance of sanity in our payroll structure, and the absence of *any* team outside our own division interested in taking Millwood and his big contract. We really stepped outside the box to call press conferences, both with the Millwood situation and also Glavine, to lay out step by step what happened in negotiations and how aggressive we were in trying to keep this remarkable rotation together. We had never done that before. But we felt it necessary because we were getting blasted by some people who had agendas, and part of my responsibility as GM is to accurately and honestly communicate our organizational position and thinking.

After laying it all out, I felt good that the media seemed to understand. The next day, though, venerable columnist Furman Bisher of the *Atlanta Journal-Constitution* ripped me for trading Millwood. The peanut gallery was not far behind.

On a fans Web site, one loyal and compassionate supporter wrote this: "Unbelievably stupid. I won't watch another game until Schuerholz is fired or dead. I mean it. It's over."

Blogged another: "That incredible idiot just traded Kevin Millwood. To the Phillies! A division rival! For Johnny Estrada, a twenty-six-year-old AAA catcher! That's grounds for commitment, not just dismissal."

And another: "I'm going to throw up on John Schuerholz's suit."

Please understand that I don't sit around reading fan chat sites. Rest assured that I would not have been aware of the above comments if my co-author hadn't pointed them out. I can't be overly concerned about daily fan approval. I do care about running the club in a way that I think gives us the best chance for success both in the standings and with our bottom line.

In November each year, clubs must decide to offer or not to offer a new contract to any player who has just played out the final year of his existing contract. That offer cannot include a cut of more than 20 percent. Or the club must decide to nontender a contract, meaning you have chosen not to make an offer and the player becomes a free agent. You can then sign the player for whatever he will accept or he can shop himself around to anyone. That was the decision we had discussed on Millwood. We much preferred the idea of trying, instead, to make a trade for him and getting *something* in return rather than nontendering him and getting nothing.

By nontendering a player, you create a clean slate in salary negotiations with him. Because a guy's salary keeps building upward—especially if he has good productivity as Kevin had—the way you break that string is to nontender him. The danger, obviously, is you can lose the player and get nothing in return. So rather than doing that, it was in our best interest to trade him. But as I said, there wasn't much of a trade environment out there for Kevin with his $10 million salary. The Phillies were the one interested club because he fit their needs and new payroll.

This was on the heels of a contract offer we had made to Scott Boras. In Tucson, Arizona, at the general managers meeting a month earlier, my assistant GM, Frank Wren, and I met with Boras and offered a three-year, $25 million deal. Scott literally laughed at that offer and reminded me that Kevin wanted five years, not three, and the money didn't begin to interest him. So we signed him to the one-year, $10 million deal and traded him to Philadelphia for Estrada.

A FOOTNOTE TO THE KEVIN MILLWOOD TRADE. IRONICALLY, WE TRIED to sign Kevin again in the winter approaching the 2005 season. He had suffered some physical problems and the Phillies didn't re-sign him after the '04 season. So he became a free agent and word was sent to me that Kevin wanted to become a Brave again.

He and his wife, Rena, have continued to live in Atlanta, even after the trade to Philadelphia. They are delightful people and I like them both. One day I get a message to call Kevin and did. He said he was interested and wanted to talk to me about returning. I let Kevin know we'd be delighted to have him back and would offer him all that we could afford to pay him. He obviously told that to his agent, Scott Boras, who called.

"I understand that you have spoken to Kevin. I just want you to know that Kevin has interest in talking to you," said Boras.

I said fine and I called Kevin and told him what we could offer, which was $2.5 million. He said he wasn't sure about that and said he'd call me back. The next day, he called again and said it was going to cost $6.5 million for us to sign him on a one-year deal. We didn't have anywhere near that in our budget and said we would have to decline. Not long after that, he signed with Cleveland for $7 million.

My earlier whining period after the Millwood trade eventually subsided and I got over it. Now I am absolutely and completely comfortable in the new economics suit of baseball general manager that I wear. I am at ease attempting to sensibly create a roster that comes at least closer—not close—to balancing that time-tested economic standard that you should only spend as much as you make. And we're actually spending more than we make, even now. But it's a much closer balance than it was before we trimmed more than $20 million from our payroll. And I think it is responsible. I know we did the right thing. We didn't just decide to reduce our payroll and make ends meet no matter the quality of team on the field. Our ownership has never once mandated that we do that. Ever.

What they did say, in effect—and we think quite reasonably—that we'd like you to build a winning team and spend less money to do it. I thought that was a fair request since we had lost so much money over the years. And we did it.

Time Warner is our parent company and there is a direct link of operating impact and operating communication with our company headquarters in New York, in terms of dealing with the Braves' economics. We still lost money the first year of our downsized $80 million payroll, but we lost considerably less. We didn't lose double-digit millions as we had several years before.

We were now managing our payroll better, but with Glavine and Millwood gone, our team earned run average rose to 4.10 in 2003, the highest since I came to Atlanta. By then, that feared Big Three was down to a thirty-seven-year-old Greg Maddux and whatever starting staff we could construct. Lefty Mike Hampton was promising. Russ Ortiz came along to give us two terrific seasons. Exciting young Horacio Ramirez was incubating. Reclamation find Jaret Wright had a big '04. And well-traveled John Thomson turned out to be a solid hand.

But with a deep-rooted appreciation of starting pitching, my eye was on the goal of some way, somehow, assembling yet another classic rotation.

CONTRARY TO SOME CRITICS, MILLWOOD-ESTRADA WASN'T THE WORST trade I'd ever made. While I hate to bring it up, that dubious honor goes to a five-player deal I made with the Mets in 1987 while I was GM of the Royals. The principal parts of the trade were a promising young arm attached to a former Kansas City schoolboy star athlete named David Cone, and catcher Ed Hearn, whose arm was barely attached.

We needed a quarterback-type catcher, someone who could call a smart game, could set hitters up, knew how to work pitchers. In the judgment of our top major league scout, Tom Ferrick, Hearn was exactly the ticket. Cone was one of several young arms in our system, and the decision was made that swapping him for Hearn would be a wise move.

But as luck would have it, as soon as he joined us, Ed had a shoulder injury and couldn't throw. He wound up playing a total of 13 games for us. Cone, on the other hand, went on to a sterling, fifteen-year career highlighted by a Cy Young Award, five All-Star Game appearances, and a pair of 20-win seasons. Nice deal!

After his playing career ended prematurely, Ed Hearn had to endure three kidney transplants and successfully fought off a bout with cancer. Still living in the Kansas City area, Ed has become an exceptional motivational-inspirational speaker. He's a good man.

My son, Jonathan, added the definitive footnote to that trade: "Dad, the advantage of the David Cone trade," he said playfully, "is that whenever somebody asks you what was the worst trade you ever made in your life, you'll have no trouble remembering the answer to that quickly." Thanks a lot, son.

Fortunately—and thanks in large part to the sage advice and solid input from a legion of great scouts like Tom Ferrick—I have been able to more than balance the books with a lot of trades that have worked out a little better than the Cone-Hearn deal. But the best and most unique value-for-value swap of my career came with input not from professional scouts, but rather one of our former Braves catchers.

Greg Olson caught for us in the early '90s. He retired, went back home to Minneapolis, and became a real estate agent. But he kept his hand in baseball by managing a Minnesota independent, professional minor league team, the South Minny Stars.

Olly called me in 1996 and said there was a gifted young pitcher on his Stars, a University of Minnesota engineering graduate named Kerry Ligtenberg. "John, this kid can pitch in the big leagues and help you guys," he assured. I was skeptical, but said I knew he had caught enough big-league pitchers to recognize the species and trusted his judgment.

"Okay, Olly, we'll give him a shot. What do you want in a trade?"

"Well," he says, "we're an independent team without much money or equipment. We need equipment. Bats and balls."

"Okay. I'll trade you a couple dozen bats and six dozen balls for Ligtenberg."

"That's a deal," he said.

I've made a lot of deals, but this one stands alone. Kerry Ligtenberg has the distinction of being the only player I know of that was acquired by a major league baseball team for two dozen bats and six dozen balls.

That is a true story. We made the trade and Kerry was a more than serviceable relief pitcher for us for five seasons, then played another couple of years elsewhere before Toronto released him late in the spring of 2005. He joined the Diamondbacks after that. I don't know how long Olly's bats and balls lasted.

Another rather bizarre trade was made when we obtained pitcher Russ Ortiz from San Francisco in December 2002. One of the players the Giants wanted in the deal was a young pitcher who was a teammate of my son at our Class A Danville club. At the end of the '02 season, we learned this young pitcher wasn't who he said he was.

He was going by the name of Manuel Mateo and was one of the many Latin American kids who changed their name to shave a few years off their age. We advised the Giants that we actually did not know his name, but they insisted he be included under the name of Manuel Mateo. We later learned that his name is Merkin Valdez, who rocketed up the Giants' chain and made their major league roster.

But at the time of the trade, I told Giants executive Dick Tidrow that we would agree to include Mateo in the deal and he would truly be—drum roll, please—a player to be *named later*.

In any event, in the season after Mateo/Valdez joined the Giants organization, he happened to be pitching one night against our Rome,

Georgia, Braves and hit my son, Jonathan, in the back with a pitch. The story was that Mateo/Valdez was so upset with me for trading him that he allegedly retaliated by nailing Jonathan. I told my son, "If every player I've traded is mad enough to take it out on you, well, you'd better get a suit of armor."

Easily the most timely trade we made came in 1993 and probably started the charitable notion that I can pull the proverbial key rabbit out of the trade hat whenever needed. We were still in the NL West at the time and midway through that season, we were 9½ games behind the division-leading San Francisco Giants.

Our offense was sputtering and it was clear to me the one thing we needed was a legitimate cleanup hitter. A run-producing, power-hitting cleanup hitter to put in the middle of our lineup. Everybody in the batting order was trying to be one, whether it was the leadoff batter or Ron Gant or David Justice or whoever. The Pennsylvania Dutch had a saying—"The hurrier I go the behinder I get." Well, the harder our guys tried to be a cleanup hitter, the worse they became.

We did all our due diligence. We began our final filtering process to find this critical offensive piece. I had all our major league scouts give me their reports and we determined the guy we wanted was Fred McGriff of the San Diego Padres.

We were able to put a deal together July 18, 1993, to acquire Fred. The Padres were looking to get young and they liked several prospects coming up in our farm system. We traded minor league outfielders Melvin Nieves and Vince Moore, and pitcher Donnie Elliott for Fred (aka "Crime Dog") McGriff.

Fred arrived in Atlanta and put his Braves uniform on for the very first time on July 20, as our cleanup hitter. That was the very night a fire broke out in the press box level of Altanta-Fulton County Stadium, some two hours prior to game time. It started in a hospitality suite right next to my general manager's suite. A food-warming sterno container apparently tipped over. We were all down on the field during batting practice when the fire started and began spreading with awesome speed.

It burned much of the press box, destroying my suite and everything in it. It was such an intense fire that it literally melted the steel girder joints in the upper deck. You could hear them popping and exploding. We're on the field around second base watching all this unfold.

Ted Turner was standing out there with us and made two profound comments.

First: "We are going to play this game tonight." We were excited and anxious to launch the Fred McGriff era, but I didn't figure there was any way we would be playing that night. The stadium just caught on fire. There was smoldering matter falling down into the seats on the first level.

Then Ted added: "The stadium caught fire tonight and so are the Braves going to catch fire tonight."

Little did he know at that moment how prophetic he was. Remarkably, we did play the game. That night, in Fred McGriff's first game—after the fire was doused and the burned area cordoned off with yellow police tape—he hit not one, but two home runs and almost single-handedly wiped out a 5–0 deficit to beat the Cardinals, 8–5. In the 68 games after he joined us, we were a white-hot 51-17, Fred hit .310, belted 19 of his 37 homers that season, and we overcame the Giants to win our third straight NL West division title.

In that case, we pulled a Crime Dog out of our hats. And we were able to do that because our minor league system was flush with quality talent attractive to the San Diego Padres. And, once again, our major league scouts pinpointed the exact, right player we needed to fill this crucial need.

4

The Diary of a Major League Deal

To PARAPHRASE THE TRADITIONAL CHANT OF ROYALTY transition, the rotation is dead, long live the rotation. Hopefully, that will be the operative line following a pair of moves in the winter of 2004–05 that may have paved the way to another classic rotation—expected to be an even deeper one—for many Braves seasons to come.

The acquisition of All-Star closer Dan Kolb in a trade with Milwaukee permitted us to make the dramatic move of putting John Smoltz back into his preferred starting role. Just five days later, we acquired ace-caliber starter Tim Hudson in a trade with Oakland. Suddenly, the holes in our rotation left by the free agent departures of Russ Ortiz and Jaret Wright were not only filled, but we had aces No. 1 and 1A to go with Mike Hampton, John Thomson, and Horacio Ramirez, any one of whom would have been considered the staff ace on some teams.

As we entered the 2005 season, there was an excitement that we were armed with a starting staff that was, by all expectations, potentially another classic rotation for the ages. And one that might be even deeper than the Big Three that had blazed the way to that string of division titles in the '90s. Barring serious injury or unexpected developments, we were going to be all set. Alas, the injuries kept coming in waves.

But the key was not in just acquiring Tim Hudson, but signing him to a long-term extension. That would avoid "renting" him for one year as had been the case with several of our meaningful additions in recent years. The market value of Ortiz, Wright, Gary Sheffield, and J. D. Drew, after only one or two seasons with us, became too high for our policy of sensible payroll management. When we picked up Drew for the 2004 season, in fact, I had predicted to our staff that we likely would have him for only one season.

A year later, however, I told those same staff members that I felt we had a good chance of keeping Hudson for the long haul. Tim had only the 2005 season left on his Oakland contract (for $6.75 million) when we traded for him. Obviously, his deserved reputation as one of baseball's very best starters and team leader would push his market value considerably higher for his next contract. The objective for us was to entice him to choose a long-term extension with us rather than test the free agent market following the one season.

I saw two important factors on our side. Our projected payroll over the next five years had room enough, I felt, to commit a fair and attractive offer to Tim. Plus, the fact that he grew up two hours away in Phenix City, Alabama, as a Braves fan, and that his family and friends could more easily see him pitch would be a strong consideration for what our due diligence revealed was a genuine family man with rock-solid core values.

The initial step in making the trade for Tim came after I had read some articles right after the 2004 season speculating that Oakland GM Billy Beane might be willing to trade away one or more of the A's talented starters. I promptly called Beane and said, "Billy, if you decide to trade Tim Hudson, that's who we want. We'd be very interested in discussing a deal for Tim."

At the annual general managers meeting at the Ritz-Carlton Key Biscayne, Florida, we continued our pursuit. It was during the midmorning break on November 12, the last day of the meeting. We fanned out into the lobby off the meeting room to stretch our legs and Billy was standing against a wall. Billy knew his team's limited salary structure would not permit him to re-sign all three of his outstanding starters—Hudson, Mark Mulder, and Barry Zito. Supposedly, he would entertain a trade for one or more of them rather than losing them to free agency after the 2005 season with nothing in return.

I approached Billy to remind him of our continued interest in Tim Hudson.

"Yeah, I was going to talk to you before we got out of here," he said. "I think there's a deal to be made there."

Over the next couple of weeks, Billy and I kept discussing the possibility, mentioning several players that might be included in such a trade. He and his staff had been studying our major league and minor league rosters for potential A's. The name of Marcus Giles was floated in media speculation, but I quickly informed Billy that we could not and would not consider trading Giles. We knew we were losing Drew and did not feel our offense could afford to lose Marcus, too.

Beane, with his payroll concerns, wanted young prospects, especially pitching prospects. And once again, the quality of our farm system led Billy to determine we were one of the few teams with the kind of promising prospects he would consider in a trade for Tim Hudson. Several big-market teams wanted Hudson, but none had the prospects of quite the caliber we were offering to make the deal work for Oakland.

Billy Beane is among that genre of general managers I prefer to deal with—those who are straightforward. Terry Ryan of the Twins, Jim Hendry of the Cubs, Walt Jocketty of the Cards, John Hart of Texas, to name a few. I like guys who get right to it, value for value. When we open talks on a deal, we've all done our homework, we all know what we want, and we know what is a fair exchange. I don't enjoy dealing with some of the others who throw out a first proposal that is a senseless negotiating ploy. A waste of your time. Or you're trying to get a certain player from a team and they ask for five of your best prospects when they know two would be equitable. You shake your head, quickly end the conversation, and don't look for the next.

Because he was the poster boy for *Moneyball,* I kidded Billy that he and I doing a deal would be viewed as *When Worlds Collide.* As the baseball world perceives us, this was one end of the baseball universe meeting the other end. Billy was very prepared, very smart, just like we try to be in every trade discussion.

We agreed to continue our discussions at baseball's winter meetings December 10–12 in Anaheim. There, at the Anaheim Marriott, I assembled much of our baseball staff in my suite: Assistant GM Frank Wren, Director of Baseball Operations Tyrone Brooks, Scouting Director Roy Clark, Player Personnel Director Dayton Moore, Manager Bobby Cox, major league scouts Jim Fregosi and Chuck McMichael, and others. At times, there were up to fifteen staff members and sometimes as few as three or four as we brainstormed the Hudson trade and other possible deals. We laid it all out; making a deal for Tim will cost us this much in player talent—which is a lot—and discussed the fairly reasonable expectations of the financial impact that keeping Tim long term would have on us.

We looked at more statistics and analyses of stats about Tim Hudson than one can imagine. We had our team physician, Dr. Joe Chandler, thoroughly discuss and examine all aspects of Tim's physical status with Oakland's team doctor. We analyzed each player that came up as potential parts of various trade scenarios as Billy and I went back and forth. He and I talked briefly in the lobby one final time as we checked out of the hotel on December 12. Although the deal hadn't been made, I felt it was inevitable.

A few days later, we completed and announced the trade: Hudson for outstanding minor league left-handed pitcher Dan Meyer, reserve outfielder Charles Thomas, and right-handed relief pitcher Juan Cruz. We had just acquired the starting pitcher who most in baseball considered the best available. His record over the previous five seasons marked him as a preeminent starter.

Now came the real challenge to turn this headline trade into a possible historic milestone for the Braves by signing Tim Hudson to a long-term extension. Buckle up and come along behind closed doors for the ride . . .

LATE DECEMBER 2004. I ASKED FRANK WREN AND TYRONE BROOKS to begin the task of crafting various structures for a contract offer, taking into consideration a galaxy of variables of our projected payroll over each of the next several years and comparables throughout baseball that might indicate Tim's market value.

Time was at a premium because Tim and his agent, Paul Cohen, had established a deadline of March 1, more than a month before the start of the season, to negotiate a contract extension. After that, they wanted Tim to concentrate on spring training and the regular season without the distraction of contract negotiations.

In my first conversation with Paul Cohen after the trade, I said, "I understand having those kinds of deadlines. I think in-season contract negotiations are distracting to a player and ordinarily we don't negotiate with a player during the regular season. However, we have negotiated a number of contracts during spring training. I don't think a player has to worry about divided concentrations in spring training, because the agent and we do most of the work. The player is kept up to speed, but he can still concentrate on getting his legs in shape and his arm healthy and all that. So we have the same philosophy. I don't like to negotiate during the season and neither do you. We both want the player to concentrate on baseball. But, what we should do is extend the opportunity to reach an accord one more month, through the end of spring training."

They declined and kept March 1 as the end date.

This meant we had only January and February to complete all the projections to determine the bounds of our offer, craft a contract structure, get it insured, have it approved by my superiors, and sell it to Paul and Tim. To fail would have meant waiting until the end of the 2005

season, which would have only increased the likelihood of losing him
to free agency.

Early January 2005. Once again we decided we would want to include an evergreen clause in the structure, tying automatic option years
into the number of innings pitched over the course of a season. But
how many innings? Tyrone went to work on a statistical analysis of
how many innings every top pitcher had logged early in their career
and throughout their career. His chart:

Pitcher	Avg IP First 5 yrs	Avg IP Next 5 yrs	Avg IP Career	Avg IP/GS Career
Tim Hudson	207	—	207	6.8
Roger Clemens	214	222	214	7.0
Pedro Martinez	182	196	191	7.2
Randy Johnson	215	181	211	7.0
Greg Maddux	235	238	232	6.9
Mike Mussina	190	220	202	6.9
Curt Schilling	134	219	188	7.6
Tom Glavine	186	216	208	6.6
Bartolo Colon	191	225	200	6.5
Kevin Millwood	167	182	171	6.2
Brad Radke	217	201	209	6.6
Andy Pettitte	209	166	188	6.4

So now we knew how many innings the greats like Roger Clemens
and Randy Johnson and Greg Maddux pitched in their first five years,
the average yearly innings pitched by a No. 1 starter, and the career innings pitched by them. We provide ourselves with pertinent data and
then negotiate with this knowledge behind us.

And to think that some believe we traditionalists never look at or
analyze statistics.

From this data accumulation and analysis, we determined that somewhere in the 210 to 220 range would be a good and fair target to set the evergreen clause, so if Tim pitched that number of innings in the last season, we would add another guaranteed year onto the end of the contract at the agreed-upon annual salary.

With our evergreen threshold determined, it became necessary to obtain insurance coverage: With any contract of this length and salary level we always insure it, to protect ourselves against serious injury and loss of a player's services. So Frank worked on getting an insurance quote.

As I have done throughout my career as a GM when negotiating significant contract deals, I have relied principally on my assistant GM as my right-hand man throughout the process. In this instance, it was Frank, who has served in that role since 1999.

When I lost Dean Taylor to the Milwaukee Brewers as GM, I started looking for the right guy to fill that spot. Frank was highly recommended to me. I knew him a little, but not well. Dean and John Hart, my close friend and GM of the Texas Rangers, recommended Frank highly. I also called Dave Dombrowski, for whom Frank worked as an assistant GM with the Marlins, from 1991 to 1998. Dave gave a glowing report on Frank and his capabilities in that job.

He's a very bright guy, extremely computer-literate. "Gadget Man," I call him. He has the benefit of having played and coached professionally, worked as a minor league executive, did international scouting, and worked at the major league level. He has a rich background and a real knowledge of the game. Having a guy with his talents and background is a factor in choosing someone for that position because I spend a lot of time working with my assistant GM and rely on him considerably.

Thursday, January 20. Cohen fires the first shot in negotiations. They wanted five years times $12 million a year. Or, six years times $11 million a year.

He contended that proposal factored in a 15–20 percent "discount" that Tim was willing to give to play in Atlanta. "If we wait and go free agent in the fall," he said, "the price will be higher for any other city."

The asking price was high, I felt, but not so completely out of reach that it would be impossible to negotiate an acceptable deal.

I floated out to Paul our desire to include an evergreen clause, because one of the concerns we have nowadays with long-term contracts in general—and with pitchers specifically—is the health and well-being of a pitcher's arm and our ability to insure the contract over time.

Paul reminded us that during this same winter, there were some long-term contracts signed that he viewed as comparables. Outfielder Carlos Beltran, five years. Starting pitcher Pedro Martinez, four years.

At least we now knew what Tim and his agent were willing to consider. The only thing he and his player would have to provide us is the assurance that the player is physically able to do his job. The evergreen clause would do that. If he pitches X-number of innings the first year, or X-number of innings on average over two years, we add a year to the contract. It's automatic. No questions asked.

Isn't that fair? That's all we were asking. Just be healthy and we'll keep doling out the millions. But at this time, the numbers they were asking didn't fit into our long-term payroll of '06, '07, '08, and '09.

So it was plausible, not impossible, but very challenging. We vowed to keep looking at it and maybe we could come up with an idea, perhaps, how to off-load some money to fit in Hudson's money.

Tuesday, January 25. Frank, Tyrone, and I met in my office, kicking around the key parts of a contract response. I sat at my desk, Frank was off to my right, and Tyrone sat on the couch, his back to the stadium playing field below.

We talked about being creative and thinking outside the box to see if there was some way to do this contract to make it fit our payroll management requirements. We ran numbers. We looked at the payroll projections. We had been thinking all weekend about ways to get a contract with Tim Hudson that must accomplish several things. It had to balance the need to meet the market value that he and his agent felt was there. It had to satisfy that requirement, but also permit us to manage our payroll over the next four or five years to ensure we could still construct a team.

It would be a simple matter if all we were doing is negotiating on the basis of just one of those issues. We felt we could get a contract done for Tim Hudson, based on the talks I'd had with Paul Cohen.

The challenge in discussing variations of four-, five-, and six-year contract structures is that it's as if we were in a cage fighting not one, but two lions. It's almost like an animal trainer with two chairs and the one lion over here is the lion of negotiating the best contract. But with the other chair, we've got to fight off the budget lion, fitting this contract into our payroll. Thus, we can be assured that we can afford a shortstop and a second baseman and a center fielder—a team.

That's an interesting dynamic in terms of contract negotiations up against payroll management. Those are always the abiding considerations with every deal we make: What gives us the best chance to put the best team on the field? Is it keeping this player? Or is it saying a tough goodbye to a player, providing us with needed roster payroll flexibility?

The point is, it's not just simply negotiating a contract in an economic vacuum.

What we do, in part, is project over several years what we likely would have to pay all of our various players, plus factor in their scouting evaluations and statistics. I've been utilizing that analytical combination for twenty-five years, long before Moneyball was dreamed up. I've never made a deal in my baseball life where statistics weren't analyzed from top to bottom and sideways, and made part of the trade dossier.

Frank, Tyrone, and I updated our long-range, detailed, color-coded payroll projections chart, which we do at least once every three months. This is how most general managers have to operate now. With each additional player added, with each additional option that is exercisable or automatically vested, with each arbitration-eligible player, with each free agent, it has a different dynamic and impact on what our future payrolls are apt to be. We must manage that well.

Though always subject to unforeseen future variables, the chart provided us with a sense of how much overall money would be available over several years for a Hudson contract. It also indicated how the Hudson money would have to be apportioned each year to stay within our annual $80 million payroll budget.

After meeting for about forty-five minutes, we didn't come up with a final resolution, but Frank left me with some ideas that I could sleep on.

So as our workday ended, our plan was to study it at home, have another meeting the next morning to fine-tune our offer, and then call Cohen to present it to him. We wanted to keep the negotiations moving. It's important from a psychological standpoint that you continue to connect so there is not a drifting apart. Paul Cohen had called on this day "just to touch base" because the last time we had talked had been the previous Thursday. Part of the reason for that was we had been busy researching and doing our homework and trying to find the right salary number, right number of years, and a way to make this all fit. At this moment, we didn't have a shoehorn big enough to make it fit. But we were still working, not knowing how it would come out.

Wednesday, January 26. Internally we discuss an offer of four or five years, but decide we should lean to three or four years because of the insurance coverage limitation. We have gotten a price back on the insurance premium at $2.2 million, insuring the first three years of the contract.

We homed in on a counteroffer of four guaranteed years at an average of $11 million per year, plus a fifth-year evergreen option. The latter would vest with either an accumulation of star performance points during '07–'09 or an innings pitched threshold met on average during those same three years.

But fitting $11 million into our payrolls of '06 and '07 would be difficult. We would have to pay him something in the neighborhood of $8–$9 million in '06 and '07, then escalate to $13 and $14 the next two years to reach the total of $44 million over four years. Back-loading a contract like that helps solve a problem for the short run, but often creates new challenges down the road. But because we would have some large contracts expiring in those later years, this allocation worked best.

Friday, January 28. Wanting to keep my boss in the loop on a contract of this size and importance, Frank and I made the five-minute drive to the CNN Center, where Braves chairman and president Terry McGuirk's office is on the fourteenth floor. His office has a sweeping view of downtown Atlanta near Centennial Olympic Park where the infamous bombing occurred during the '96 Olympics. A big plasma TV adorns one wall and sofas and chairs are in a cluster arrangement around a coffee table. On an end table sits an encased, autographed ticket to the 2004 Chicago Cubs game in which Greg Maddux registered his 300th career victory.

The meeting was primarily a heads-up for Terry to let him know what we were thinking. This is normal for any big deals. We shared the proposal of four years plus the evergreen option year at $11 million per season. We felt that Tim's market value would be slightly higher than that following the 2005 season, though not as high as Paul Cohen was projecting. But Tim's desire to play closer to his roots and the comfort level we were confident he would develop in our clubhouse, as well as his declared willingness to give us a hometown discount, would lead him to accept a little less than he might get elsewhere to drop anchor in Atlanta.

We were comfortable with the terms of our offer for a player of Tim's accomplishments, character, and age. The challenge was managing a way to pay those dollars within our $80 million annual payroll.

Allow me to explain here that the $80 million budget wasn't going anywhere. It wasn't going to $85 million the next year, then $90 million and so on. At least as far as we knew. We had to operate on the assumption that it would remain at $80 million until such time that circumstances allowed it to escalate if revenues increased, or—heaven forbid—drop further if it's decided that it makes no sense to keep posting a red bottom line.

It was $80 million in '04 and '05 and we still lost money at that number. But $80 million is a comfortable number for constructing a championship-caliber team. No apologies for 80. The previous payroll totals of $100 million and $95 million had been inflated by a system that the agents and the union utilize to continually push salaries ever upward.

And while this was happening, our revenue in Atlanta was decreasing. Since our attendance surge that kept us above 3.2 million fans four straight seasons (1997–2000), we backed off to 2.8, 2.6, 2.4, and 2.3 in the next four years. That still ranks fairly high against the rest of the clubs, but not enough to offset an $80 million payroll.

But if you concentrate only on tickets sold as a measure of economic capabilities, it's misleading because there are some clubs that have greater TV and radio rights. Others have bigger marketing regions. Others operate in markets with a base of 8 to 10 million people to draw from or sell TV and radio spots to. We're not in the upper echelon of any of those factors in Atlanta. I have no complaints. Atlanta is a great city and a very solid major league market. But it's not New York, Boston, Chicago, or L.A.

We explained to Terry everything from the request Cohen had made to how we arrived at our counterproposal. We discussed the situation in its entirety, philosophized about baseball contracts, considered the implications of this contract on our ability to construct future teams, and the need to rely on the continued growth of our young minor league players.

Terry nodded. "I think your thought processes are right to protect us on the back end of the contract," he said. "Good luck." (Some months later, it was determined by corporate accounting that the payouts would be made in equal annual increments.)

Driving back to the stadium, Frank made a comment that at least we'd get a "second bite of the apple" after the season if this extension didn't get done. I had little interest in a second bite. They're so uncertain. I wanted to tether Tim to the Braves. Now.

Back at my office, we had set up a 3:00 P.M. speakerphone call with Paul Cohen. Based in Southern California, Cohen is a family guy with six kids. A personable and very detailed guy. This was the first time we had negotiated a contract for one of his clients. He had called a time or two to see if we were interested in one of his players but nothing ever developed.

I presented the four-times-$11 million offer and explained in great detail how we had come up with the terms and how such an extension would crowd our budget projections, but still permit us to maintain a championship-competitive roster behind Tim. I detailed how the evergreen clause would automatically add the fifth year if Tim pitched a minimum of 220 innings during one of the first four years.

Frank explained the insurance component.

We thought the phone call went well. From Paul's comments and reactions, we appeared to be talking on the same page. We got the sense that Paul seemed encouraged by our offer. None of his responses during that call indicated that he didn't like the contract package or wouldn't consider it. We wished him a good weekend and agreed that he would call with a response at two o'clock, our time, the following Monday.

Frank and I actually looked at each other after we hung up from that call and expressed that everything good happened on that phone call except that Paul didn't say yes to the deal right there. Yet in our minds it seemed close enough for that to happen.

But I also cautioned Frank that we didn't know this agent well enough to gauge his reaction for sure.

Monday, January 31. Cohen called at two o'clock on the button. It was as if we had never talked on Friday. It was not a good call.

Paul's counteroffer was $9 million higher—four years for $53 million.

Also, the evergreen clause was out the window. We were especially blindsided by that because Paul had expressed interest in the concept and even had asked additional questions about it.

The counter was shocking and surprising that we were as separated in this deal as we were. His number was so far removed from what we had proposed three days earlier and what he implied in our original conversation that our jaws dropped.

So we found ourselves with this very substantial difference in what they wanted and what we had offered.

Now, did the union get involved in that aggressive counter? With star-caliber players—and we know this to be a fact—their agents are in communication with the union. And agents have told us this directly, that the union has at times been unhappy with certain proposed deals or that the agent was "having trouble getting these terms through."

We know the union has that kind of persuasiveness on big contracts. Agents have told me so. I am not certain, however, that it occurred in this instance. But I wondered.

Although Tim's agent didn't tell me so, I feel confident that to one degree or another he shared our proposal with the union and probably didn't get a very positive reaction. All the world knew that after the '05 season, Tim would likely be the preeminent free agent out there. He'd be the poster child for high-priced free agents if he pitched well in '05 and hadn't signed an extension.

As knowledgeable baseball people read this, many will think we were absolute fools for not jumping at that chance to sign Tim Hudson, long term—at any price. Tim's age was not an issue. He was approaching his thirtieth birthday, was in great shape with no significant physical problems, and would be thirty-five or thirty-six at the end of the contract they were proposing.

After careful examination and analysis of our two positions, we felt that if you compared our offer and their counter and factor in taxes and Atlanta's cost of living vs. the other places he could go, it wouldn't have amounted to much difference in *spendable* dollars. However, having been through so many contract negotiations, I have learned never to be optimistic or pessimistic. Only realistic.

I had scheduled vacation time the following week at our second home on the southwest coast of Florida, and would then drive up to Orlando on February 15 to prepare for the start of spring training at Disney World's marvelous Cracker Jack Stadium. Paul and I agreed to talk further after I arrived in Orlando.

Though we were only one month from their March 1 negotiating cutoff, I felt we had to be patient and not be too anxious and avoid creating an impasse just yet. I wanted Tim to interact with Bobby Cox, his coaches, and our players for at least a few days of spring training to experience our appealing team environment before we made one last push to work out the extension.

At that point, I didn't feel optimistic that Cohen would be coming into camp to engage in further discussions. I feared in all likelihood our next chance to reopen talks on a contract extension would be conducted after the '05 season had concluded.

My hope was the long shot that Cohen would fly into Orlando and Tim Hudson would pull a Troy Percival on him and say, "Paul, I want to get this done."

Percival is the former Angels relief pitcher who tested the free agent market and went out to dinner one evening with executives of the Detroit Tigers. Troy was so taken with the Tigers' organization and offer, he picked up his cell phone right at the dinner table, called his agent, and said, "I want to be a Tiger. Get this done. In fact, get it done tonight."

His agent was at a basketball game with one of his kids, but had to hammer out the deal from right there. The agent, ironically, was Paul Cohen.

Wednesday, February 2. A new wrinkle arrived in my morning *Atlanta Journal-Constitution.* Chipper Jones, our star third baseman and highest-paid player, told a reporter he would be willing to defer part of his contract if that would help get Tim Hudson under a long-term contract. As I'll detail later, I called Chipper to explain how his well-intended offer would not help. A quick call to Paul Cohen put to rest the Chipper Factor in the Hudson negotiations.

I said, "Paul, Chipper said what he said in the paper, but you and I both know that is not a reasonable expectation for either one of us to think that the willingness of a third-party player is likely to solve our circumstances." He agreed with me.

We might have done something with Chipper to create a small footbridge across a creek. But at that point in time, we had to cross a gulf, not a creek.

All of the public speculation about an extension for Hudson was creating new levels of anticipation in Atlanta. Tim, who played collegiately at Auburn, had even the Georgia Bulldogs devotees among our fans excited about the prospect. As if Tim's spectacular 92-39 record with the Oakland A's wasn't impressive enough, one awestruck Bulldog fan recounted an Auburn-Georgia three-game series he had witnessed in Athens several years earlier. Tim struck out nine Bulldogs in six innings to win the opener, then played center field in the other two games, contributing six hits, including three doubles, to the Auburn attack.

Saturday, February 19. Two days after the pitchers and catchers reported, I had my first opportunity to engage Tim in an informal chat on the field about the ongoing contract extension talks. The March 1 deadline loomed just ten days away.

Tim said one of the factors in his mind was to develop confidence that the Braves would continue to be championship-caliber if he signed long term. He seemed to be fishing from me for some indication that I would continue as GM through the life of his extended contract.

I had talked to Tim several times at this point, but never about a possible contract extension until this day when we were standing next to the batting cage at Cracker Jack Stadium. "What's important to me," he said, "is the assurances I get that if I do a deal here, we're going to have a team that can win throughout the time I am here."

My answer to him was: "Tim, you know that our track record reflects that. It's what we do. We assure all of our players that we will continue to do all we can do to be a championship team. We've done it for fourteen straight years. What better evidence can there be? What greater assurance can you have than that?"

I reminded him that he had just come from a small organization not flush with cash, but was creative enough to get good players. And we've done that. Our payroll is in the middle now. Oakland's is near the bottom. But it doesn't matter. You do your job right, you can put a winning team on the field. "That's easy for me to defend and promise," I told him. "We've done it consistently."

His question did not relate specifically to me or Bobby, about whether we would be sticking around during the life of an extended contract for him. He was talking about the organizational goals and commitment in a general way.

I am aware, however, that players have commented that being in an organization and on a team led by me and/or Bobby is comforting to them, so our possible retirement looming on the horizon might be a concern. It's like in college recruiting, when a recruit is considering signing with a desirable, but aging coach. He may wonder if the coach is still going to be around for his senior season.

The significance of this brief chat was that I was communicating directly with Tim. He had a chance to hear my words, feel the depth of my belief, and look into my eyes to see if he thinks I'm telling it like it is. And I could look in his.

Without mentioning the name, I related to him the similar circumstance that Tommy Glavine was in when Tommy had to decide whether to stay with us or take a higher salary with the Mets. What I said to him, generally—and Tim is smart enough to figure this out— is that we had a player not too many years ago who, after having spent his entire career with us chose for reasons of economics, competitive ego, and likely persuasion of his agent and the union to take an offer to go elsewhere. And literally before the ink on that agreement had dried, he was calling around reaching out for a lifeline to come back. How could we help him come back? How can we throw him a life preserver to bring him back on board?

There was a way to put that bug in Tim's ear. I did it myself.

Some weeks later, Tim Hudson reflected on that meeting by the batting cage and the story about the player he assumed was Tom Glavine.

"For me, as an outsider looking in on that situation, I think it was obvious the reasons why that player may have regretted the decision to leave," said Tim. "Anytime you're in a comfort zone and you're happy where you're at, and you're in a winning organization and everything feels right, a lot of times you don't realize how great something is until you are elsewhere, or about to go elsewhere.

"I think maybe John was just trying to say how great it is here and how great my teammates would be. It's good to hear, but I don't think they had to try to sell this organization and team to me quite as much as they probably thought they had to.

"For me, the whole situation was this: Was I going to get a fair enough contract to stay? Obviously, I wanted to be here and was willing to give a discount to get that done. As far as the proximity to my family and friends and being part of the rich tradition of winning in Atlanta—everything was pointing this way. John telling me that story was nice to hear, but it wasn't a determining factor whether I was going to sign an extension here or not."

Wednesday, February 23. In a brainstorming session, Frank and I had a breakthrough realization.

We knew that Paul Cohen's last proposal for $53 million included a provision that Tim would spend $3.5 million with the Braves for tickets and boxes and other items through his charitable foundation over the course of his contract. What we quickly realized was that would be after-tax money. To generate $3.5 million, Tim, in his tax bracket, would have to earn nearly $6 million *before* taxes.

Subtract the $6 million from their $53 and—*voila!*—we're suddenly in the ballpark with our $44 million offer.

We decided that if we stretch our $11 million-per-year offer to $11.5 million, we might just sign Tim Hudson for an extended number of years. Frank further crunched the numbers, factoring in the tax angle, and discovered the difference in *spendable* dollars between a four-year, $46 million deal and Cohen's four-year, $53 million proposal with the $3.5 million charity arrangement would amount to somewhat more than $100,000 per season.

We prepared for a final, last-ditch meeting directly with Tim and Paul that had been set for the next day. There was renewed anticipation and precious little negotiating room.

Thursday, February 24. T-minus six days to the March 1 deadline.

The meeting was set for one o'clock in my office at the Disney stadium. Tim would be there in person and Paul would participate via speakerphone from California. We had set up an easel with a large flip chart on which Frank had put our revised offer and a detailed explanation of the tax angle.

When Tim came in and sat down across from my desk, he chuckled and said, "Did I tell you I have two big muscle-bound guys standing outside, just in case things get rough?"

It was a wonderful icebreaker.

With the speakerphone hookup with Paul confirmed, I began making our presentation, reviewing from notes on my desk the conversations we had had throughout the process. I mentioned our four-times-$11 million prior offer and explained again how appropriate and honorable, if you will, that offer was.

I continued by saying we had looked closely at their proposal, which was for $53 million with Tim buying back from the organization tickets and other things to put back $3.5 million over the life of the contract. We were appreciative of that, but explained that wouldn't work for us.

So Frank flipped over the chart outlining our new proposal: $46 million for a four-year extension, plus a club option for a fifth year. I explained why we felt that was a good move by us and a wonderful offer. Frank's diagram showed that our new offer and their offer, taking out the $3.5 charity arrangement, made a gross difference of $250,000 a year. The net, or after-tax difference—even factoring in a certain amount of tax deduction on the charity buybacks—was only $157,000 per year.

The look on Tim's face as he studied the chart told me we had taken a giant step toward his signature. He later conceded he knew, at that moment, he was destined to become a long-term Brave.

"It was exciting to me," he said. "Pretty much, my mind-set going into that meeting was that if they moved anywhere off of the 4/44, it was going to get done. The big question was if they held to the 4/44, was I willing to just get up and walk out of this meeting or take that offer? But once they moved off of the 44, I think then it was just a question of a couple of small things.

"In the days leading up to that meeting I put a lot of hours of thinking into it with my family and we really weren't quite sure what we were going to do. I would have felt foolish not taking the 4/44 and coming in to play just one year. It would have made it really tough for me. I mean, $11 million a year is a lot of money—probably more money than I would ever spend. There are only a handful of teams that can afford to give you top dollar. The question is would you be happy there? Is the happiness of your family worth an extra $3 million a year?

"But at the same time, you understand how hard you've worked in your career to get to this point and you're so close to free agency, you wonder what would happen."

Back to the meeting, we felt we were very close at this point. I pointed out the $11.5 million annual salary was the same amount of money we paid the great Greg Maddux, with four Cy Young Awards under his belt. And I agreed that we felt Tim is the kind of player who might be the next pitcher to do that for us.

Paul reminded me that it was an "old" contract. Yeah. Two years old. So that was the club talking and the agent talking. But when you're about to get a deal done, both sides start talking more. And we were talking up a storm.

Paul told us that Tim wanted to get this done. Paul came back with a counter that essentially accepted our $46 million package, but added not exactly a no-trade clause, but something very close to one. He wanted a salary escalator if we later traded Tim so that if he wound up on another team, that team would have to pay Tim something closer to what he would have gotten if he had waited until after the 2005 season and tested the open market. Paul was claiming that would be in the $14–$15 million range.

Paul had done his homework and knew we didn't give out no-trade clauses. "If we're not getting a no-trade," he said, "then we have to have the escalator."

I said I would have to think long and hard on that. Such a provision begins to erode the long-standing position that we've maintained against any form or fashion of no-trade clauses.

While we were able to significantly close the gap in terms of the money in the deal, this was an issue very important to us. We have to have control over our roster. We can't have our hands tied with any contract that we can't move if things don't go well. We have an obligation to pay players what they demand and what the market drives for them. And we do that. But we have to have unfettered freedom in operating this franchise. That's our right.

Paul also proposed that we have some sort of buyout rather than a blanket club option for a fifth year. He wanted a $2 million buyout if we chose not to exercise the fifth-year option.

We all agreed to think about these extra provisions overnight and we would talk to Paul again at one o'clock on Friday. I felt the session went well. Tim was in the office, directly involved, and I wanted that. There aren't many agents, quite honestly, that have the confidence to allow their player to do that. But there were still no high-fives in our office. You high-five when the deal is totally done.

So the rest of that day, I had to consider whether or not in this particular case to maintain the no-trade policy that we have jealously guarded and has allowed us the freedom and flexibility to dramatically revise our roster every year to whatever extent becomes necessary.

The so-called 10/5 players have the right to refuse a trade—meaning those who have ten years of major league service, the last five of which are with one team. Chipper Jones and John Smoltz are in that category. So there are some built-in roadblocks to managing your roster with some guys, but we just don't volunteer to add other roadblocks by putting in no-trade clauses. My operating philosophy—and it's also been our operating philosophy since I've been in Atlanta—is that no-trade clauses do you great harm, but no good. So we haven't included them in our contracts.

Now, we have acquired some players who already had no-trade clauses in their contracts and we are bound by those. But we don't put them into contracts that we initiate. It wasn't just that we didn't want to start a precedent. It was more that I believe it's the absolute wrong way to operate a franchise.

So that was the issue I had to wrestle with before we resumed talks with Paul Cohen the next day. We were so close. I wondered if this no-trade provision might be the deal-killer.

Friday, February 25. As I drove west on Interstate 4 toward the ballpark in the morning, I called Frank, who was also driving to the park. I asked him if he had any thoughts overnight about the no-trade clause. He agreed that we shouldn't do it because there were too many players in our clubhouse we had promised we wouldn't do a deal with a no-trade clause, or anything similar that would inhibit our ability to make a later trade. I knew it would be important to convey to Paul Cohen just how firmly we were against including that provision.

At one o'clock, Frank and I were in my office with Paul on the speakerphone.

It was not an antagonistic conversation. It was businesslike and pleasant. But I explained how adamant we were on trade restrictions. I noted that we hadn't given no-trade provisions to even Chipper Jones or Andruw Jones or John Smoltz or Tom Glavine or Greg Maddux. In fact, when A-Rod—Alex Rodriguez—had insisted a no-trade provision would have to be part of his contract, for all intents and purposes our discussions with him ended. That's when his agent, Scott Boras, said to us, "Well, if you won't do a no-trade there is no sense continuing these discussions."

I reiterated that to Paul Cohen. I also reminded him that we have never traded any of those star players that I mentioned. I made the point that when we sign star-caliber players, we intend to build around them as cornerstones of our team.

So the trade escalator was out, but we offered to meet him halfway on the fifth-year buyout. If we chose not to pick up the fifth-year option, we would pay Tim $1 million. And we would give him the right to decline our option on the fifth year so he could go elsewhere, but forfeit the $1 million buyout. If he feels like he can go out and get more at the end of the fourth year, rather than accept our $11.5 million, he would have the right to reject it, but in so doing would forfeit the $1 million buyout money.

If we, on the other hand, chose not to exercise the option, we would pay him the buyout provision: a fair and balanced compromise.

Paul had said he had the authority from Tim to make a deal on this call. Frank and I were doing hand signals to take a break. We agreed to talk again in fifteen minutes. Obviously, Cohen preferred to run all the final terms by Tim.

But as it turned out, Tim was in uniform on a back field at the Disney complex taping a public service commercial for the Boys & Girls Clubs, anxiously wondering what was going on with the contract talks. He was supposed to have his cell phone with him, but had unintentionally left it in his clubhouse locker. The phone rang and rang.

In a mild panic, Paul placed a call to the rented house where the Hudsons were staying during camp. "Hey, we're trying to conclude a contract here and Tim is nowhere to be found!" said Paul, flustered.

"Well, that's just Tim," Kim Hudson said of her husband. "What other guy in the world do you know who would have $46 million on the table and you can't get in touch with him about it?"

When we resumed our talks with Paul a few minutes later, he said with a laugh, "Well, you guys have sufficiently hidden Tim away from me."

"Yes," Frank joked, "we have cell phone jammers in the stadium to use when we need to."

We verbally agreed to the deal and complimented one another on how the negotiations had gone. Paul said he was particularly appreciative that our talks had stayed out of the media while we were negotiating. He said some clubs have told him they wouldn't say a thing and it hadn't always turned out that way.

We hung up and Frank and I reached across the desk and shook hands. It was one of those satisfying moments. We were happy with the fact that we were able to get Tim Hudson signed to a long-term contract with the Atlanta Braves. We were confident that he would be the leader of our pitching staff for five years or more.

It was important for me in the first conversation that day to lay out in the proper tone how adamant we were about the no-trade clause not being possible in this contract. It was important because of the historic component, the importance of being able to operate the franchise, the stance that we had consistently taken on that matter, and the integrity of my word to the players in that clubhouse who had come before and had heard these same words from me. So I set a firm tone that this was an important issue to us, and that this deal couldn't be done unless they understood and were willing to accept that.

After the call, Frank said, "I think he got your message."

We knew we had gone absolutely as far as we could have gone. Often, when you're in that situation, it doesn't turn out so well.

We had beaten the March 1 deadline by four days. But we couldn't publicly announce a deal until Tim could be given an extensive insurance physical and the insurance company signed off on the results. By coincidence, our player and staff annual physicals were scheduled the next morning at a nearby medical center. We could do the required MRIs on Tim's shoulder and elbow, fax the copies and physician notes to the insurance company, and hope for a green light on Monday or Tuesday.

We would have to tap-dance all weekend with the media, which ominously reported that the March 1 "drop-dead" date was imminent. Had we publicly confirmed an agreement had been reached, it would have become legally binding, with or without the insurance.

Tim later recalled that Friday evening was filled with relief.

"There was so much leading up to it, and when it's finally done it's like, 'Is this really done?' We didn't go out and crazy celebrate. We had a nice dinner with my two kids and my niece, who is going to be our nanny for a while.

"I called my parents and my brothers. They were all excited for us. I think my mom was really excited, not for the money but for the fact that we were going to be playing close to home for the next few years. They live in Auburn, Alabama, about a two-hour drive to Atlanta. They couldn't have been happier that we were going to be close to home and they were going to be able to see the grandkids and see me play whenever they wanted. So it was very exciting for all of us."

Saturday, February 26. At 8:00 A.M., I ran into Tim at Dr. Michael Link's office in Kissimmee where our team physicals were being conducted. I was going into the office for my physical and Tim was coming out. It was the first time I had occasion to talk to him after the negotiations had been successfully completed the previous afternoon.

I smiled and said, "You sleep well last night?"

"Yeah, I did. How about you? Did you sleep well?"

"I did."

My point is he was happy. And I was, too. And relieved. There was no need to verbalize that the deal was done, pending the results of his physical. He knew why I was asking. We were both happy campers. I wasn't asking so I could determine his sleep habits, but rather his contentment. It seemed to match ours.

Sunday, February 27. Paul Cohen called Frank in the afternoon to take care of some minor contract language housekeeping items. Some media speculation had begun to appear that the deal with Tim was close and Paul had read a number of stories online.

"I've read more quotes from Tim today on this than he's made since the very start," Paul said. Obviously, Tim was happy to get the deal done and couldn't keep a secret any longer. Quite understandable.

Monday, February 28. The results of Tim's physical were glowing. They were faxed to the Tampa hotel of a principal of the insuring entity, who was there doing business with the Yankees. It included the MRIs and a summary from our doctor on the overall physical exam and the radiological readings of the MRIs.

That afternoon, we got the green light from the insurance company. For a little more than $2 million, they agreed to insure half of Tim's contract for three years. But after three years, a new physical and MRI would be required and any injury sustained during the first three years would be excluded for the renewal period.

We immediately submitted the terms of the agreement to the labor relations department of Major League Baseball and Cohen submitted the terms to the players union. With that done, there was an official agreement of terms.

Then the official contract document was created where all of the twelve or fourteen pages of guaranteed language are included and ultimately that document is signed by all parties.

Some time ago, we developed our own language for those guarantees. Thankfully, the Commissioner's Office has taken over much of that process where most of that language is similar and universal for all clubs. There are only a few small changes that most clubs have to negotiate with the various agents who like particular wordings.

Brad Hainje, our publicity director, was notified to begin making plans for a formal press conference the next day.

Tuesday, March 1. The dreaded deadline day. One of the unique aspects of this deal is that it was done against the backdrop of this "drop-dead" date. That didn't allow us much time, since we made the deal to acquire Tim just two and half months earlier at the winter meetings in December. There is a lot of contemplation and consideration on the part of an organization—running numbers, projecting out how much of a contract you can carry on your books for the next four or five years and still put a team together. That takes time. We did the work we had to do to put ourselves in a comfortable position to either go for it or not go for it. And we put ourselves in a position where we thought we could carry his contract and still have a championship-caliber team. And we did it.

So there was a considerable feeling of pride as I sat behind a table in the front of the room alongside Tim and Bobby Cox at the press conference announcing our agreement with Tim in the auxiliary clubhouse at Cracker Jack Stadium. Before us were some two dozen local and national journalists and cameramen.

After the media session, Tim reflected on the moment.

"I've known a lot of guys who've gone elsewhere for greener pastures or more money, leaving organizations where they were happy and things were just great, only to regret it," he said. "All the money in the world isn't going to buy happiness for yourself and your family. How much money is enough? I understand what the market value would have been for me on the free agent market, but when you get to those dollars, you're talking about security for my grandkids' kids. I'm fortunate enough to play this game at this level, to provide well for my family. For an Alabama boy with a humble upbringing, it doesn't take a lot for me to be happy.

"I was willing to leave a lot of money on the table to sign a long-term deal. But I think John and this organization gave me something that was fair. When the time comes, I'd like to talk with them again about playing out my entire career in Atlanta. Ever since I could remember, all my family and all my Auburn friends thought it would be great if I could ever play for the Braves. I agreed, but I never thought I'd be playing for the Braves this early in my career. I thought I'd be some salty old seasoned vet ending my career there. It's great to come here in the prime of my career."

It was the biggest story in the baseball world that day. Was another classic pitching rotation incubating at Turner Field?

The Atlanta Braves didn't rent another superstar. We signed one to a long-term deal.

5

Dog Bites Man! Teacher Quits for Less Money!

Before I continue to wade into the principles and style that we have employed in managing the Atlanta Braves organization to fourteen consecutive seasons of championship-caliber success, let's turn back the calendar a bit in this short chapter.

I want to discuss some of the events and people that had a profound influence in shaping who I am and the management/leadership blueprint that I have used to help the Braves rattle off an unprecedented string of divisional pennants.

When I was in the sixth grade, I was unquestionably the leader of a group of friends and schoolmates at Public School 74, Oliver Cromwell in Baltimore. As a young Catholic growing up in a non-Catholic school, I was sent to catechism classes by my parents to be certain I was bathed in the world of Catholicism. My mother told me time and time again that the nun who taught the catechism classes—at St. Ann's on Greenmount Avenue in Baltimore—told her, "Johnny is a natural-born leader. He's going to be a real success someday."

In the ensuing years, as I went on to college and had a successful teaching career, was hired by the Baltimore Orioles, and began moving up the baseball ladder, my mother would constantly remind me of that story about what the nun saw and predicted.

I suppose what I am saying, in a roundabout way, is that others have suggested I apparently have displayed instinctive leadership qualities most of my life. But this isn't to suggest that only born leaders go on to lead. Some so-called born leaders never really take the yoke. And others develop leadership traits along the way as they embrace the kind of principles and policies that we will be discussing in much of this book.

My dad was a successful amateur and professional athlete. John Sr. played second base for three years in the minor leagues and was a great amateur basketball player. He was regarded as the Bob Cousy of Baltimore. He instilled confidence in me even though I was a more limited athlete, in terms of talent, in most sports. Baseball is where I succeeded most and achieved most. He would always nurture in me this great feeling of confidence.

Yet, here I was, 150 pounds, a little guy. But I didn't think that about myself. My self-confidence and competitive nature always exceeded my physical stature.

In fact, when I was presented with the Athlete of the Year award at Towson State in 1962, I was referred to by the faculty advisor, Dr. Martin, as a "banty rooster."

And that "banty-rooster-ness" is how I succeeded on athletic fields when I went up against bigger and stronger and probably more talented guys. I just had this intense competitive spirit, intense desire to succeed, to win, and to achieve that which my dad fostered in me.

That spirit and intensity migrated over into my personal, nonathletic life. I was a decent student and enjoyed success there. It all imbued itself in my leadership of people as I attained various leadership positions.

My dad, who died in 1994, lived his later years vicariously through me and my baseball job. As a former professional baseball player, he was extremely proud as I rose through the ranks of baseball administration. He died the year baseball died (the strike). Baseball resurrected.

At least dad got to enjoy some of our early success in Atlanta and was alive when we won the world championship in '85 in Kansas City and loved that. That was wonderful.

If I was blessed with a certain degree of natural leadership, there was one other facet of my life that has come naturally. Writing poems.

I've done it all my life. The first one I ever wrote, I was a freshman in college at Towson State in suburban Baltimore. In those old buildings without air-conditioning, on a spring day we'd open the windows. I was sitting in the back row, English Lit class. A just hatched baby bird started chirping. And out of me came this verse . . .

> A life is born in class one day,
>   by the outside world in early May;
> Poe and Longfellow we all know,
>   a life has come, a life must go.

The most poignant one I ever wrote, though, was about my dad, right after he passed away. Here is the first verse:

> A kind and gentle caring man,
>   has left our world too fast;
> Oh how I wish I could see his smile
>   and hear just one more laugh.

After I graduated from TSU in 1962, I took a job as an eighth-grade teacher and began working on my master's degree at Loyola College in Baltimore. I taught for four years at North Point Junior High School, teaching what was called CORE. That's short for Correlated Subject Matter, which was world geography, composition and grammar, literature, spelling, and current events.

No doubt my background as an educator is part of the reason I came to admire and identify with the late Commissioner Bart Giamatti many years later when I had the privilege to get to know him. I would have the pleasure—not often afforded general managers—of having dinner with him one night in West Palm Beach during the general managers meeting, which I co-chaired. We shared a limo ride to and from dinner at a fashionable restaurant over in Palm Beach and I had a delightful conversation with Bart largely about education and teaching. Bart, of course, had been president of Yale and a respected educator. I really enjoyed his intellect, integrity, and his passion for the game of baseball. He was truly a Renaissance man as baseball commissioner.

Bart really loved the game of baseball, and what a tragedy that we lost him so quickly in his term as commissioner. He was exactly what the game needed. He was a strong enough and smart enough and tough enough guy, I believe, to understand the issues and to negotiate on behalf of the baseball organizations and owners. Had his tenure lasted longer, I am certain that the economics of baseball would not have careened so far askew. Absolutely. No doubt in my mind. I'm only surmising that, based on my judgment of his intellect and his understanding of the game and his strength of leadership.

And no matter who would have followed him—you name the name—I don't believe it would have changed that. Bart was going to be a man, in my opinion, who could have done more in that office than all the others I had known. We'll never know. Sadly, he smoked too much and died too soon.

As an aggressive young teacher in 1966, I wrote a letter to Orioles owner Jerry Hoffberger, who forwarded it to Frank Cashen, who had just been hired as president of the Orioles. Frank was at one time a sportswriter in Baltimore and my family name was well known in sports circles in that area. I've told you about my father's athletic prowess. In addition, my grandfather Will Schuerholz is regarded to this day as one of the finest basketball coaches in Baltimore history. At one time, he coached a basketball team of all five of his sons—William, Gilbert, John (my dad), Wilson, and Donald. Uncle Gilbert also was a goalie on the U.S. Olympic soccer team. So as a former sportswriter, Frank Cashen was familiar with the Schuerholz family name as it related to athletics. He knew my grandfather and my father and my uncle and the sporting pedigree of the Schuerholz family.

The crux of my letter was that I had been involved in baseball all my life. Played baseball in college at Towson State, followed the sport closely, and was about to complete my master's degree in administration and supervision of secondary schools. I wrote this letter in a free period one day on an old Royal typewriter. I reasoned in the note that my advanced educational administration training, combined with my love for and understanding of baseball, would be a perfect combination for the Orioles. I didn't mention anything about my family. I just signed the letter and, as was his practice, Mr. Hoffberger forwarded it to Frank Cashen. Harry Dalton had been promoted to GM of the Orioles and Lou Gorman had just become director of player development. Lo and behold, Lou was looking for an assistant and they were well underway in this search process when I sent this letter, cold, not knowing they had an opening.

Frank Cashen, because I'm sure he recognized my family name, called me in for an interview.

We had a good meeting, then he walked me into Harry Dalton's office. Harry talked to me awhile and then took me to Lou Gorman's office. Lou and I talked briefly and he called me back in for another interview the following Saturday. About four weeks passed. I walked into my apartment carrying a trophy after having just won the Baltimore County recreation program's basketball championship as part of a faculty team at North Point Junior High. I was really feeling good and riding high.

There was a message to call Lou Gorman. I figured it was the old "Thanks for your interest, but . . ." I'll never forget. I was standing in the kitchen of this little apartment and dialed the phone. Lou answers.

"Hey, John. How're you doing?"

"Great, Lou. We just won a basketball championship."

"Good, good. Congratulations. John, we'd like to offer you the job as administrative assistant in player development."

My feet left the ground at that moment and I don't think they've touched since.

At that time I had been making $6,800 as a fourth-year school-teacher in Baltimore County. And I went to work, at age twenty-six, with my beloved hometown Baltimore Orioles for $4,700.

I'm no doubt the only teacher in the history of that profession who has voluntarily left teaching to take a job for *less* money. Most people leave teaching to make more money. I left to pursue my dream, to be a part of professional baseball.

I had always felt I was overlooked as a player. I made All-Maryland Scholastic Association second team in high school, all-conference at Towson, second-leading vote getter in the Mason-Dixon Conference my senior year. I was a player, so I thought. But I was still only about 150 pounds soaking wet. Though I felt the scouts overlooked me, my lifelong dream was answered another way.

I OPENED ENVELOPES AND I EMPTIED TRASH CANS, FILED LETTERS AND drove station wagons to the airport to pick up people and packages. I did as much grunt work as a person could do. My title was "administrative assistant," but, in truth, I was a glorified gofer. But what marvelous grassroots training that was.

Raises were minuscule, but I didn't care. I was where I wanted to be, doing what I loved, pursuing my dream. My workstation—I couldn't call it an office—was in the underground bowels of old Memorial Stadium, which was right across from my old high school. I could see Memorial Stadium from my high school classroom window. Baltimore City College High School. It looks like a castle on the hill. It was my early window to my dream world.

My work area had a linoleum floor and my "desk" was a portable typing table, the top of which was very small and it had hard, caster wheels. It had those little spring-lock wings on the side that snap up if you need more room. And every time I would write something on my "desk," it would scoot across the floor. But that's how I started, and I loved every minute of what I was doing. I was in absolute heaven. I was in baseball!

I was so nervous going to my first spring training for the Orioles' minor league system in Fernandina Beach, Florida—just outside Jacksonville—that I developed a case of what is called pityriasis rosea. Your skin dries and flakes off. And I had a textbook case. I went to a dermatologist in Baltimore and when he saw me his eyes lit up. He said, "Please, would you take off your shirt?" It covered my chest and was all down my arms—all from nerves. I was so excited about going to my first spring training. The doctor was so excited about seeing this textbook case, he took Polaroid photographs of my upper torso.

When the plane arrived in Jacksonville, some other guys on the staff, co-worker Jack Pastore and trainer Dick D'Oliva (who went on to become an NBA trainer), met me at the airport. Jack and I were friends, but also looking to move up to the next level. We were workmates, but in some sense, friendly competitors as well.

I reached out to shake their hands and as I did, the flakes of skin came flying out of my shirtsleeve. Like a snowstorm. They looked at me with the strangest looks. I will never forget that scene or my formative Oriole years.

TWO YEARS LATER, WHEN KANSAS CITY ACQUIRED AN EXPANSION TEAM in 1968, the Royals hired Lou Gorman away from the Orioles and he asked me to go with him as his assistant. That was a very interesting time in my life as well. I quickly came to love Kansas City, but was apprehensive when I first went there. I half expected to find cows roaming the streets and horses standing at hitching posts in front of the general store. Baltimore was where I was born and raised—never lived anywhere else. A real hometown boy. The fact that I would be working with Lou made the jump a bit easier.

Immediately, I was thrown into the fray of preparing for the expansion draft; creating the forms we would use to select players, accumulating and analyzing scouting reports, and doing considerable statistical research. The latter was one of my prime responsibilities.

What a great experience for me to be a part of laying the cornerstone for that franchise's foundation along with Lou, GM Cedric Tallis, scouting director Charlie Metro, and Herk Robinson, my fellow administrative assistant.

Working under Lou Gorman was one of the singular great breaks of my professional career and treasures of my personal life. He was *the* mentor of my baseball life for a lot of reasons.

A delightful human being, Lou taught me the most valuable lesson of all—the value of treating people respectfully, and celebrating with them their role in any success we might enjoy as an organization or department. He was the very best at that. He makes the switchboard operator feel like she's the most important person in the office just by the way he says hello. Lou always has a kind word for everyone. He's a special man and a special friend.

Herk Robinson and I were the two young assistants in the Royals office working for Lou. We worked closely together discussing ideas, sharing thoughts, making suggestions. We met constantly to plan for the Royals' future. On occasion during meetings, Lou would produce a malaprop or two and Herk and I would struggle to maintain our composure. Later, tears would run down our cheeks and we would bite our lips reflecting fondly on those meetings and Lou's comments. Lou's brain simply would outrace his tongue and really funny things would accidentally spill out.

Yogi Berra, of course, has long been widely acclaimed as baseball's prince of the malaprop. But I'm telling you, Lou could give Yogi a running start in the Malaprop Derby and blow him away by the quarter pole.

Here's just a sampling:

"McClure's arm is not damaged structurally or terminally."

"I'll stay at an airport near a motel."

"His eyes diluted."

"He left a bad taste in their mind."

"He was stopped by two underclothed plain detectives."

"I vaguely and vividly remember in my own mind."

"I'll keep my ears posted."

"You've got to be in a good frame of mood."

"Per capita, Frank White will make more errors than Freddie Patek."

"At the dinner, I was sitting with Reggie Jackson on the table."

Working with Lou was not only fun; we were also successful. We won a division championship in 1976, quicker than any expansion team at that point in major league history. I continued to grow and learn under Lou's guidance and direction and was rewarded with the ultimate promotion in 1981 when the Royals named me GM.

FOR MOST OF MY EARLY LIFE, I WAS ALREADY LEANING, IDEOLOGICALLY, somewhat to the right. I was more than conservative in my approach even as a young Royals staffer in Kansas City, a decidedly conservative region. However, I suppose those traits were overshadowed by another guy on one of those low administrative rungs with the Royals. A young guy named Rush Limbaugh.

Yep, same one.

Rush had been a disc jockey in the Kansas City area, spinning rock-and-roll songs and using the stage name Jeff Christie. He was hired by our Royals marketing and promotions department and was just another young guy in our office. I'd characterize him as a low-paid junior executive in that area. I liked Rush. He was obviously a bright guy, engaging in conversation and always talking around the coffeepot in the morning. And always talking around the water cooler in the afternoon. And always talking as we walked out the door in the evening.

He was always talking. Still is.

Very effusive, very bubbly, very upbeat, and he loved—absolutely *loved*—baseball.

You knew the players liked him because they would pull pranks on him. One of the responsibilities that Rush had was to supervise the ceremonial pregame first pitch. On one particular occasion, Rush escorted the honoree to the mound and realized to his dismay that he forgot to bring a baseball. So he turned toward our dugout and, in his very loud voice, hollered, "I need a baseball." As if in the midst of a major snowball fight, some sixty baseballs came flying out toward Rush, who burst into embarrassed laugher. He got his baseball.

Rush was always, always opining about the issues of the day. Local issues, local legislation, state legislation, national events, whatever. He was always talking, a very interesting guy and quite knowledgeable. He was well read and opinionated, as we've all come to know. But Rush was a guy who had substance behind his words.

We were office friends. We didn't share dinners and all that. But he did come out to our house one evening and personally installed the very first VCR to grace the Schuerholz household. Rush, having come out of the radio industry, had a working knowledge about hooking up electronic equipment and volunteered to do it for us.

So down on his hands and knees to install the VCR. *The* Rush Limbaugh, future mega-mover and shaker, was right down there in John and Karen's house in the classic plumber's pose. If only I had had a camcorder to capture that historic moment to play on our newly installed VCR.

Not long after that, the radio talk show business called him again and he launched his show in Sacramento, which has gone on to make him one of the biggest media icons in the world.

Fast-forward many years later. After I became general manager of the Braves, we were headquartered at the PGA Marriott in West Palm Beach for spring training. It so happened that Rush was having a book signing one afternoon in the lounge at that hotel. It was arranged by an Atlanta radio station, WGST, which at the time was carrying our broadcasts and Rush's talk show. Because I knew him and had followed his rise to talk show stardom, I wanted to see Rush and say hello. I hadn't had an occasion to talk to him for years.

So I bought his book and got in the line of about fifty dittoheads, careful to duck back and forth to keep him from seeing me until I worked my way up to the table where he was seated. He looked up and was surprised to see me. He stood up and we hugged and had a quick visit. His inscription inside the book: "Who would have believed we'd come this far? —Rush."

Then, just a few years ago after the Braves moved to the new Turner Field, Rush called and said, "John, I hate to do this, but I'm calling for a favor. I'm remarried and I have stepchildren who have been lifelong, avid Braves fans. I would love to bring them to a game in Atlanta. Can you get me some tickets?"

"Rush, I can get you tickets, of course," I said. "That's easily done. I'm happy to give you my six seats, second row right beside the dugout. But I know you couldn't watch the game because you'd be inundated with autograph seekers and whatever."

I suggested I find a better place for him to enjoy the game. So I arranged for him and his family to use one of our VIP suites. It was the suite normally used by our team president, Stan Kasten, who was not in town that evening. It was just a couple of doors away from the suite where I always watch the game. Karen and I walked over between innings to say hi, see how they were doing and make sure they had the Cokes and hot dogs and peanuts we had arranged. They were absolutely thrilled with everything.

His new stepchildren, Jeremy and Sarah Poole, had grown up in the Titusville, Florida, area faithfully watching our games on cable TV, but had never actually attended a game in Atlanta.

As a payback, Rush and his wife invited Karen and me to be their guests in Palm Beach for a few days. He said we could stay in one of the four guesthouses within his oceanfront compound if I ever needed to get away, that no one would even know we were there.

I told him I appreciated that, but it wasn't necessary. We never did take him up on that because I do enough traveling and spend a lot of time in Florida as it is. But it was a very nice gesture and I thought that was the end of it.

But, lo and behold, a week later in the mail, from Rush, came this package of four bottles of a very classy wine as a tangible thank-you to back up his verbal thank-yous for the use of the suite. This is the kind of guy he is.

The wine was Château La Fleur Petrus Pomerol, vintage 1961. A forty-year-old classic Bordeaux. Even a semiserious wine aficionado like me got suitably excited. Rush intended two bottles for me and two bottles for Stan Kasten, who is not much of a drinker. But because I was gushing about what a sensational and expensive wine this was, I suggested he open it for the special occasion of Stan and Helen's twenty-fifth wedding anniversary they'd be celebrating a few days later.

Unfortunately, I didn't explain to Stan that a wine this old should be opened and decanted and allowed to breathe for six to eight hours, not just fifteen or twenty minutes. So with his family gathered for an anniversary dinner, Stan pops the cork, allows it to breathe a few minutes, and then fills all the glasses around the table. He took a big sip and promptly spewed it out.

Stan is a funny guy anyway, but I really laughed when he said he took a sip and declared it was "the worst shit I've ever had." They poured it back in the bottle, which he brought back to my office with only his portion missing and the cork poking out of this beautiful Petrus Pomerol.

He tapped his finger on my desk while smirking and said, "I wasn't gonna waste it and I wasn't gonna throw it away because you said it was special. So you can have it."

That day, I did let the wine breathe and that night I invited Don Sutton, the Hall of Fame pitcher who is an analyst on our telecasts, to share that bottle of Petrus. I knew Don to be something of a wine connoisseur and would appreciate it. So we enjoyed that bottle of Petrus, finishing it off after the game.

I took great delight in later needling Stan by telling him the Petrus "was like nectar of the gods it was so good." His laughing response is not printed here to avoid charring the page.

Don said I probably didn't realize just how valuable that wine was and gave me the number and name of a rare wine specialist. I called the next day just out of curiosity. I introduced myself and told him the reason for my call. When I told him the wine was a '61 Petrus, there was a long pause. He asked if I were sure it was '61 and I read him everything on the label. There was another pause and I was floored by what the guy told me. He said the bottle of wine in my hand was valued at about $7,500.

That being the case, I guess the spatters on Stan's tablecloth were worth a couple hundred bucks.

MY HABIT OF STYLISH APPAREL, IT IS OFTEN SAID, IS ONE OF THE THINGS that characterizes me. It's not the essential thing that sets me apart, but when people are asked to describe me in a few words, one of those words is apt to be "clothes." And as Bobby Cox told a reporter, " 'Dapper' is usually in there, too."

Growing up in Baltimore, I had an uncle—Al Wyatt—who always took great pride in his appearance and had a very good sense of style. When I graduated from the sixth grade, he bought me a pair of cobalt blue slacks with saddle stitching down the side seams and a matching cobalt blue belt with a big gold buckle. While that's no longer my style, I mark that gift as the moment I really became interested in my personal appearance. Style and appearance became important to me then and remain so today.

I know I've rubbed off on the staff in Atlanta in the area of personal appearance and dress. Absolutely. It's a cyclical thing in our society about how we dress. I've always dressed up. That's always been my thing. When I was in college and had a major exam to take, I wore a dress shirt and tie to class that day. It just gave me the feeling that I would be placing the proper emphasis on it and be more capable of doing well. Of course, I also studied some.

I know we're in a casual environment in sports, but we're also in a business where first impressions are important. When I came to the Braves, it was a casual organization with a casual attitude. I instituted a dress code for the office staff and continued the one in place for the team. We're one of the few teams that travel in coats and optional ties. At the Braves, we feel it is important to portray professionalism.

In jest, I tell the staff I get casual by unbuttoning my top button and loosening my tie. Now, that's casual!

In my view, the way you dress is a reflection of not only who you are, but who you represent. We have an understanding in our organization that if you are representing our company, even in the new casual environment, you dress as a businessman or businesswoman and represent us properly. That's not too much to ask.

Most staffers respond to that. Over time, I have become somewhat comfortable with this casual trend. But I joke that I have invested so much in my clothes; and because I have some really nice outfits hanging in my closet with ties, I'm going to wear them.

There was a period when I typically wore suspenders. It was just a style that I enjoyed. That became my trademark, which has endured even though I haven't worn suspenders on a regular basis for some time now. That became the item constantly selected by people wanting to give me a gift for whatever occasion. I now have dozens of suspenders hanging in a closet at home.

One very special pair of suspenders I have was made and given to me by a hair stylist, Mara, who began cutting my hair soon after I joined the Braves. They were navy blue suspenders on which she hand-embroidered little red tomahawks. I wore them almost daily during the 1991 postseason, my first with the Braves, when we went from worst to almost world champions. After that, I weaned myself off them. I didn't want to feel like I was captive to these "lucky" suspenders. So I only wear them under extreme circumstances—like when a win is *really* needed.

Superstitious? Who, me?

I broke them out for the 2004 playoffs because I wanted to win another World Series. I was pulling out all the stops. We had a good team, won 96 games, and you can't be sure when the next chance to grab the brass ring might come along. So, 96 wins and a team that was well positioned and well constructed for postseason success, we thought. I needed to give it every chance for success, thus the suspenders were absolutely appropriate.

Unfortunately, Carlos Beltran and the Houston Astros somehow managed to fend off the mystical powers of those suspenders. But if our starter, John Thomson, hadn't pulled his oblique muscle on the fourth pitch of Game 3, I believe we would have won that game and the series. And we played pretty well all year against the Cardinals, whom we would have faced in the NLCS. So who knows what would have happened? But it didn't happen.

Maybe I should take the tomahawk suspenders into the wizard shop for repairs.

6

Building a Winning Organization

ON THE EVE OF THE WORLD SERIES EACH YEAR, MAJOR
League Baseball holds what it calls the Gala. This is just a lavish mixer
with free-flowing bars and heavy hors d'oeuvres where officials from
the baseball industry and the national baseball media gather to chron-
icle another fall classic. The Gala prior to the 1990 Series was staged
on a sternwheeler-restaurant anchored on the opposite bank of the
Ohio from Riverfront Stadium, where Marge Schott's Cincinnati Reds
would begin a shocking four-game sweep of the Oakland A's the next
evening.

Equally as shocking, the baseball world had just been informed that
I had departed my post as general manager of the Kansas City Royals,
one of the classiest and successful major league franchises of that era,
to become GM of the last-place Atlanta Braves, widely disparaged by
many at that time as the Brand X of baseball clubs. That unexpected
development had been formally announced three days earlier in a press
conference at the old Fulton County Stadium in Atlanta and the Gala
on this lovely October evening would be the first opportunity for most
of the league officials and club executives to interact with me in the
wake of this startling news.

Almost immediately upon arriving, I bumped into an old friend,

Orlando columnist Larry Guest, who assisted me in the writing of this book. Larry and I found a small table by a rail to share a libation and shrimp, and discuss my imposing new task. He was nice enough not to take my temperature or give me an ink-blot test.

One by one, and two by two, baseball's ranking administrators— my contemporaries and friends—filed by to offer their congratulations and wish me well in Atlanta. They shook hands, patted me on the back, made happy talk for a few moments, and then drifted back into the milling crowd.

Larry would relate to me much later their true sentiments, which he could plainly see over my shoulder as the well-wishers moved along out of my eyesight. Almost to a man, they would turn and gaze back in my direction with baffled, pained expressions. Their awkward body language was what you'd expect of someone who had just put on a good face while paying their respects to a deathbed patient.

What a shame. Schuerholz was such a talented guy, but now he's lost his marbles.

They can be excused for having such thoughts. During the prior few weeks as I wrestled with this dramatic career move, I, too, had often felt I must have gone daft. Certainly, a reasonably sane man wouldn't seriously consider leaving the revered Royals for a parallel move to flamboyant Ted Turner's perennial cellar-dwelling Braves. Although I could see the Braves' hidden potential and was aware of the rebuilt farm system under Bobby Cox while he served as the general manager, the public perception nevertheless was that I was more or less running away to join the circus. Monty Python's Circus in cleats.

The Braves had been dead last three years in a row, four of the previous five.

In truth, I knew what I was getting into. I knew in my heart what could be done with this Atlanta baseball team and the energy around the organization and the possible support of it and the fans' engagement of it. I had confidence in its key core personnel and the kind of organizational potential that went on to win 14 straight division titles, five National League championships, and one World Series, and grew attendance to above three million from the embarrassment of being the only major league team not to have drawn a million fans in that just ended 1990 season. I knew in my heart we could do something at least *approaching* that. Maybe it's my belief in the Pygmalion Theory, the self-fulfilling prophecy that if you believe so strongly in something and you have capabilities and a strong work ethic, you can achieve those things. I believed that very strongly then and I still do today.

It's just that during the Schuerholz-Braves courting process, there were repeated and nagging moments when I didn't believe it quite so strongly. Or even at all.

THE EARLY SEEDS OF MY KC-TO-ATLANTA MOVE WERE A HYBRID OF happenstance and a slight change in the Royals' hierarchy.

As Ewing M. Kauffman, the kindly owner of the Royals, grew older and had some health issues, he decided he wanted to protect the Kansas City community by assuring good, solid ownership. So he sought a co-owner and eventually partnered with a real estate developer from Memphis, Avron Fogelman. Avron became part-owner of the Royals in 1983. He was the new young gun in the owners' box.

Joe Burke, one of my mentors, was president of the Royals at the time. Joe was clearly Mr. Kauffman's guy. I was one of Joe's assistants, first as director of player personnel and then as general manager starting in 1981 when he moved up from GM to team president. Mr. K relied on and trusted Joe with anything—his franchise, his money, anything. And rightly so. Joe was a good, honorable, and loyal man. When Avron, a younger man, came into the mix, he wanted to have a different style of operations, direction, and leadership. He selected me as his point man to see this through. I was invited to branch out into other areas of operations to educate myself and involve myself more in matters of business as well as continue to operate the baseball side of the organization.

That plan simply didn't work as well as we had hoped. There was still a great loyalty factor toward Mr. Kauffman and Joe Burke, as there should have been. There was a lot of resistance—some more obvious, but most of it subtle and quiet resistance on the part of some key administrative staff. The transition wasn't going smoothly. I found myself being whipsawed between people who were my friends and colleagues and associates. They looked at me as the point man for this dramatic and unsettling change that was underway, where Avron Fogelman was about to take charge as the principal owner in place of the admired, respected, beloved Ewing Kauffman and Joe Burke. And they were most unsettled by that.

So these guys with whom I had walked the halls, became friends with, laughed and shared lunch with most every day, started looking at me differently. They were saying things to one another and it began to concern me. The place I loved so much was beginning to become more uncomfortable and negative than I ever thought it could be.

And here is the happenstance part: As this was happening, I was serving on a committee of Major League Baseball called the Player Personal Development Program. That was not in the traditional player development sense. This had to do with the afterlife of major league players. Once a player finished his career, we were concerned that they often lost their way. George W. Bush, the current president and owner of the Texas Rangers, was on that committee. And, as chance would have it, so was another president, Stan Kasten. Stan was president of a baseball club. The Atlanta Braves.

While this internal transition and turmoil was going on with the Royals, I was an active member of this committee that met periodically. One meeting was in New York when the Yankees were playing at home. Again by happenstance, I had a car available to me to take me to and from the airport and Stan Kasten did not. At that time, I didn't know Stan from a crate of apples. We had some time after that New York meeting to catch our respective flights. I offered Stan a ride and he suggested since we had time that we go to the Yankee game for a few innings. He was a Yankee fan growing up, but hadn't been to Yankee Stadium in years.

So we headed to the Stadium, and during the ride, Stan mentioned to me that he was going to make some big changes with the Braves. He had decided to bring Bobby Cox out of the GM office and return him to the field as manager. Actually, he had excused their manager, Russ Nixon, during the season and Bobby had taken on the dual role of GM and interim field manager for the remainder of that season. As we rode, Stan revealed his plan to permanently put Bobby back in the dugout and was beginning a search for another general manager. "I figured it would be a great opportunity," Stan later recalled, "to pick John's brain for possible candidates."

"Do you have any good candidates in mind?" he asked during the ride that day.

Had this been a Saturday morning cartoon, you would have seen the light bulb over my head right there in the back of the car.

I told Stan I would give it some thought—that I knew of some capable individuals and would get back to him about it. Well, the more I thought, the more I thought about myself as a candidate, in part because of what was going on in KC.

I'm convinced that Stan didn't toss this out as bait for me, because no one at that time had any idea that I might entertain leaving what most people in the game considered one of the best franchises in Major League Baseball. It was a characterization and reputation well-earned because of the way we had operated and succeeded. The Royals had earned a reputation for the consistency of operation. (That is the trait I have become most proud of in Atlanta: the consistency of our high-class, championship-caliber Braves organization.)

But nobody thought I'd leave Kansas City. Ever! Not even Stan, who would confirm years later that he wasn't fishing for me when we talked that day in New York. "I had no reason to think John would consider Atlanta for even a minute. We all assumed he was going to stay in Kansas City forever. He had been there twenty-three years," said Stan.

Terry McGuirk recalls calling Commissioner Fay Vincent to confide that the Braves were pursuing John Schuerholz to become GM. He said Fay laughed and declared that I would never leave Kansas City for Atlanta.

The irony of that is that during our daily lunches in Kansas City—involving Joe Burke, myself, VP for administration/business Herk Robinson, comptroller Dale Rohr, marketing director Dennis Cryder, PR director Dean Vogelaar—we'd constantly discuss all manner of baseball issues. We were like Joe's disciples gathered there in the Stadium Club at the ballpark, literally every day. One day, someone asked something like: What baseball team is struggling now but has the potential to be a really good franchise? We concluded Texas was one. And the other? Atlanta. I flashed back to that consensus opinion as I mulled over Stan Kasten's revelation.

Here was the president of the Atlanta Braves in the back seat of a limo telling me he was looking for a new GM. And all this turmoil was going on in KC, the ground shifting beneath my feet. What I had previously thought would be my permanent home in the Valhalla of baseball, Kansas City, was beginning to be unstable and bothersome for me.

So I became intrigued with the Atlanta situation. Stan and I had begun to talk often in the weeks after that New York encounter—about his candidate search, about issues with their playing field, and about other baseball developments. During one of those discussions, Stan felt I had "asked one too many questions" about his GM opening and *his* light bulb popped on. "John! Wait a minute! Is this something *you're* thinking about?"

"Well . . . maybe."

"You're shitting me!" Stan blurted in his typical shoot-from-the-hip style. "You kidding me?"

"No, I think I want to be considered a candidate."

He said, "You know, of course, you have to get permission from your team."

"Yes, I understand that."

So I went to Joe Burke and asked for permission and told him why and what was motivating me. He said he would reluctantly grant me permission to talk to the Braves. Then the fun really began.

PART OF MY INNER CONFLICT WAS THE KNOWLEDGE I HAD ALREADY backed out after accepting a job one time earlier in my career and I didn't want to feel I was establishing a pattern. The first time was when I became a New York Yankee for twenty-four hours.

In September 1975, the Yankees offered me the job of farm director. I had been the Royals' assistant director of player development under Lou Gorman for five years and felt I was overdue for a promotion. GM Joe Burke gave me permission to talk to the Yankees' Cedric Tallis, who had been hired by Gabe Paul to be his assistant GM. Cedric recommended me to Gabe to be their farm director when Pat Gillick left that position.

I was at a farm directors meeting in Chicago with Lou. While there, with Joe's permission, I talked to Cedric on the phone and negotiated a deal to become the Yankees' farm director. I flew back to Kansas City the next day, explained to Joe what I had done, and gave my notice.

"You've made the biggest mistake of your life," he said. "Can you give me twenty-four hours?"

I said sure. I loved Kansas City. I didn't want to leave. The thought of going to New York was exciting, but a little intimidating, too, for a young guy who had never spent much time in the Big Apple.

Twenty-four hours later, Joe called me in and said, "We'd like you to stay. We're promoting you to director of player development. We're promoting Lou to assistant to the GM." And they gave me a nice bump in salary.

I didn't give the Yankees a chance to sweeten their offer, and that was the hardest part about it. Cedric Tallis was a dear friend and I had loved working with him when he was the Royals' GM. A delightful man and really competent baseball guy. Just a good, good man. The hardest part of making that decision was telling him I would be going back on my word that I had given him a day earlier. I was taught not to do that. My word was important to me, as my father had always insisted it should be.

Cedric was irate. He said he was angry and disappointed. "I can't believe you would go against your word," he said, the words slicing through me like a rapier. I felt worm-high, but I had made the right decision.

He didn't talk to me for years, which hurt me deeply because I respected Cedric so much.

George Steinbrenner might have been aware of this whole incident, though maybe not. Perhaps Gabe Paul didn't feel it was necessary to tell him until after the ink was dry on my hiring. But I've never mentioned it to George in the ensuing years when my relationship with him began to grow.

I felt badly enough about Cedric's reaction that I sat down and wrote him a letter in longhand. I expressed my appreciation for his confidence in me, how difficult the decision had been to back out, and the fervent wish that I hadn't lost his respect and friendship.

I flashed back to that situation as I now wrestled with the Atlanta offer.

Here I was considering the job of general manager in one of the two cities we used to talk about at our Kansas City lunches that had the potential to become a grand franchise with good leadership and a good program. I thought I could bring that to Atlanta.

As a result of this move that was viewed by many as so unfathomable—Mission: Impossible, if you will—I received a number of calls. One that stands out in my mind was from Al Rosen, then GM of the Houston Astros. Al had become a real friend and confidant of mine. I respect him greatly, not only because of his standout playing career with the Cleveland Indians, but because of his demeanor as a general manager, the style with which he conducted himself, the manner he handled the responsibilities of his position, and the way he communicated to all of us as general managers.

He said, "My God, John, do you realize what you're doing?"

I said yes, it is a franchise that's not highly regarded, needs a lot of work, but has a lot of potential.

"And you left that grand Royals franchise in Kansas City for *this?*"

I said yes I did, but I have a lot of confidence we can get this thing going in the right direction. Real soon.

Little did I know.

In my conversations with Stan Kasten about possibly making the jump to Atlanta, we naturally talked about Braves owner Ted Turner. Stan praised Ted for his dynamic, enthusiastic support of the sports franchises, and Ted's willingness to let good, capable people lead and do their jobs. Stan referred to Ted as "the secret ingredient," reasoning that many owners will say, "Yeah, do it your way," but the first time you lose two games in a row they fire you. Stan insisted that Ted was an owner who would really let us do what we felt was best and would stand behind us.

"When I got there," Stan said, alluding to when he became president of the Braves in 1986, "I told Ted we had to stop with the free agents and start building from within. I explained to him in detail why and he said, 'Stan, just do it, please! I'm so tired of not winning. Whatever it takes.' And he meant it. That's a huge difference."

If we did our jobs right, Stan assured me, Ted would do nothing but support and praise and enjoy. And that was exactly what he did. He supported, praised, and enjoyed.

He was gregarious, engaging, a man's man, a bon vivant, a hunter, outdoorsman, vitality beyond measure, imagination and creativity to a greater degree than anyone I'd been around. He was visionary with the heart and soul of a competitor and a winner. Here was a man who sailed ships across violent oceans to win race after race after race. This guy knew about competing. He didn't necessarily know about our sport of baseball, but he was willing to let others who did know—Stan Kasten and myself, and Bobby Cox before me—do the things that needed to be done.

Before I joined the Braves, I hadn't had any direct interaction with Ted. I'd seen him. I'd hear him walking through World Series hospitality tents with that distinctive, *Gone With the Wind* voice of his. You could always tell Ted was present and the energy field was palpable. And his laugh was his special laugh. During my negotiations, I had no contact with or from Ted. He left it all up to Stan and Terry McGuirk to get that done. Hiring a new GM was their job and Ted chose to let them do it.

I appreciated Ted for his kindness to me and my family, but most of all for his leadership example. Ted displayed all the requisites for true leadership—strong self-belief, the power of positive thinking and self-imagery, pride, the will to win and achieve, unwavering courage, driven and—above all—competitive. His favorite leadership advice: "Lead, follow, or get out of the way."

One of the things that had comforted me greatly while contemplating this decision to become Braves GM was the knowledge that Stan had assured me Bobby Cox was going to remain as the manager. When I was GM of the Royals and Bobby was GM of the Braves, I sent scouts into Atlanta surreptitiously, trying to determine if Bobby really wanted to remain as GM or would rather be back in uniform in the dugout. I did that because he was always the No. 1 managerial prospect on my short list back in Kansas City.

I CAN REMEMBER THAT MANY IN THE ATLANTA MEDIA WERE SURPRISED and happy and positive about my announcement and arrival. That may have been their first and last day of positiveness. I kid, of course. A little.

As heart-wrenching and emotionally agonizing as it was to leave

Kansas City after twenty-three years, it was just that exciting, anticipatory, hopeful, and enthusiastic a feeling about coming to Atlanta.

And my understanding was that it wasn't just the baseball operations that I would be involved in, but the entire sphere of the Braves organization, knowing full well that the ultimate responsibility for those other areas rested with the team's president, Stan Kasten.

But no doubt I was going to be the front-line guy, the point person, the lightning rod of attention. I would be the *field general,* if you will, out there on the lines. As I told Stan, it was important for me to be able to interact with all of the department heads and to speak to everyone in each of the departments to communicate our new overall mission statement.

Among modern-day general managers, that is certainly atypical. In the old days, twenty or more years ago, the Haywood Sullivans, the Frank Cashens, the Lee MacPhails, the Al Rosens, there was a lot of crossover for GMs. Many had, in fact, direct responsibility for all facets of the organization. But by the '90s, baseball had become so sophisticated, so technically specific in each area, that it became impossible for a GM to manage it all. We're in that age of specialization.

Typically, the modern GM is in charge of just baseball operations, which takes into account the operation of the major league team, hiring of the manager and coaches and trainers, hiring the player development director, scouting director, assistant GM, and, of course, acquiring the *right* major league players to construct a winning team.

But when I came to Atlanta, even though it was in the modern age of general managing, what I asked Stan for—and he gave me—was sensible autonomy where I had the right to make decisions benefiting the organization, but also the opportunity and the authority to make observations and recommendations concerning other facets of the operation. I learned quickly, and communicated to Stan, that some areas of our business side were not only malfunctioning, but were very, very troubling and problematic for this organization's well-being.

I immediately talked to people who worked in those areas—

concessions, field preparation among others, and they knew I was a new listening post. Someone who would seek the input of the people actually doing the work. I established myself as a viable listener, as the safe haven of information and comments made about things that were bad and needed to be fixed if we intended to establish ourselves as a first-class operation. I learned quickly that people all up and down the organization—inside and outside of baseball operations in whatever department—were communicating directly with me or indirectly through my executive assistant, at the time June Cornillaud. June provided valuable and trusted assistance in this transformation process.

I would always share that information with Stan. Ultimately, he made the decisions from his leadership position that were proper and necessary in improving the operation of our entire organization. He changed some personnel at the high levels of the business side and we began to function in a more effective, cohesive, and successful manner.

As the baseball operation was being lifted to higher ground, the championship level, so, too, was the rest of the organization. The major league team is the product we are presenting to our community for their financial and emotional support. We can't do that if we just put a good team on the field and all of these other departments/areas are beset by problems and leadership issues. Stan, to his credit, would allow me to have input, or sometimes just validate for him what needed to be done.

And he would listen. He trusted me and trusted my instincts.

So we slowly and meticulously continued the transformation of this organization. The transformation of the baseball operation had begun years before under Bobby's leadership with the commitment by Stan and Bobby to rebuild through the farm system, through the draft, getting young players back into the pipeline. It was beneath the surface, but it was being done. All of a sudden, here's a club whose major league team had been very bad, but beneath the surface, unseen to most fans, was a pipeline of organizational talent that was pretty flush and was making its way to the Show.

In my first year, 1991, we didn't have an opportunity to utilize many of those young guys yet. But we knew they were there. That talent was in place and on its way up.

What we really needed to accomplish was to improve our major league club immediately, and we did that with the signing of some key free agents—Terry Pendleton, Rafael Belliard, and Sid Bream—and the trade for Otis Nixon in spring training. And the rest is history. Remarkable history.

And the entire organization, all of the other departments that interact with the businesses and the corporations and the people and the sponsors in the community were ultimately lifted up and improved and began to function as champions. A new spring in their step. A vibrant organizational pride became evident. Braves pride.

In that first year, in fact, we came within one run of a world championship, going from worst to first in our league and into the World Series. Actually, *three years* of worst to first. I repeat for emphasis: The Braves had finished last in each of the prior three seasons, and four out of the previous five. How proud we were of this remarkable, unbelievable turnaround.

Yet, if we score one run in the top of the 10th inning of Game 7 in Minnesota, when John Smoltz and Jack Morris hooked up in arguably one of the best pitching matchups and greatest games ever in the history of the World Series, we are the world champions. At least we were the outdoor champions of baseball. We did not lose a World Series game outdoors that year. We were 3–0 in Fulton County Stadium. The Twins couldn't beat us outdoors. Unfortunately, we also played four games indoors, at their place.

As I began my Atlanta adventure, it was clear that apathy had a stranglehold on much of the Braves organization. One of the first things I had to do was remove that bottleneck without necessarily removing all the people. And that was challenging. It would have been easier to take those who had been injected with the apathy drug and excuse them and bring in a whole new group of fresh people. I didn't want to do that. I didn't think that was right. That's not my style. There were too many lives that would have been affected. I wanted to provide them new leadership, new guidance, new attitude, new roadmap, new tools to succeed. And I believed I could do that. And believed they could, as well.

I did change out one staffer, bringing in groundskeeper Ed Mangan. I'll expand on Ed in the next chapter.

I tried to exude, as best I could, an aura of confidence. Thankfully, that confidence gradually became contagious.

I can remember walking down the halls in our offices at old Fulton County Stadium the very first week as general manager. As a staff member walked toward me and as I got close to him—and I'm a person who likes to look you in the eye and say, "Hi, how're doing?"—the staffer's head dropped to the floor and he wouldn't make eye contact with me. I can only imagine it was out of embarrassment, out of a lack of professional pride, a lack of personal self-esteem. And we're talking about a person in sales and marketing!

I was thrust into this kind of environment. I was this guy who was supposed to be a difference maker, wearing suspenders, walking briskly down the hall, looking people in the eye, trying to establish new levels of energy and new levels of expectations that this organization hadn't even dreamed of before. That was uncomfortable for a lot of folks. And I knew it would be. But I also had supreme confidence that it could be done, especially in baseball operations.

That particular hallway encounter struck me in a way that brought home all of the things I had heard about the current environment. It just verified and validated that those things were true and needed to be fixed. We needed to inject new energy, create new self-esteem and new ideas, a new roadmap with new goals—much higher goals than this organization had ever displayed. And we did.

My goal, which was stated the first time I addressed the staff, was not a nebulous goal to get better, to make strides, to improve, to get to

.500. It was, clearly and precisely, to become a championship organization. To win a world championship. It was direct, it was clear, and I thought it was attainable. And I was right.

That staffer I encountered in the hall became not a star member of our staff, but became productive, more positive and outgoing, and remained on the staff for several years after that.

BEING APART FROM MY FAMILY THOSE FIRST SEVERAL MONTHS IN Atlanta was bittersweet. I missed them terribly. But being there alone gave me a chance to completely immerse myself in the challenge. I got into the task vigorously and spent every hour of every day and night that I needed, to get that big momentum wheel turning in the right direction.

I had the opportunity that first week to speak to the entire staff. I spoke about working together to create the new Braves with new Braves pride.

"It's a new day. We start counting from today. We're going forward. We're going to be a championship-caliber organization. We're going to work that way. We're going to produce that way. We're going to think that way. We're going to succeed that way. We're going to feel that way about ourselves and each other."

I left them with one of my favorite sayings, "Winners make commitments. Losers make excuses." I reminded the people at that meeting there had been enough excuses offered to the Atlanta area and our great fans about why we haven't succeeded, why this team hasn't won, why the seats were dirty, why the ballpark food wasn't very good, why the ushers and parking attendants weren't more attentive or pleasant. Why, why, why . . .

I pledged we were no longer going to offer excuses for those things. Instead we were going to make commitments to fixing all of it. After all, winners make commitments.

In my first week on the job, Skip Caray, the Braves' venerable play-by-play announcer, invited me to lunch. Who better could I learn about the organization from but the guy who has been broadcasting them for decades? I saw it as a perfect opportunity to ask him about all that had gone on in the organization, on the team, in the clubhouse, how people think, how people act. To get Skip's perspective of the organization.

He took me to Bones, one of Atlanta's most popular eateries. I learned a lot about the Braves personnel and practices. The picture he painted was not a pretty one. At the end of it, Skip said, "After all these things I've told you I want you to know also there's a three o'clock flight back to KC. Or else I can drive you back to the stadium. Your choice."

I went back to the office.

We won our division that first season and went to the World Series that year, so Skip and I have had that lunch every winter since. Our agreement is that he buys unless we win the World Series, then I buy. The year we won the Series, the winter of 1995, I took him to Chops restaurant in Buckhead, credit card at the ready. We had this elaborate lunch and had a nice time. When I called for the check, the manager of the restaurant came over and said, "Oh, Mr. Schuerholz, thank you for what you've done in bringing us a World Series victory. The lunch is on me."

Skip was livid.

QUESTION: WHAT DO LIZA DOOLITTLE, PABLO CASALS, AND DON Quixote have to do with the Atlanta Braves winning pennants?

Answer: Everything.

Liza, Pablo, and Don Quixote—or at least the ideals and concepts they've represented in my various talks to staff and others—are the undeniable undergirding of the success that we have enjoyed in Atlanta. And those ideals and concepts are equally invaluable to any organization or company no matter whether the objective is to win baseball games, construct buildings, manufacture products, sell life insurance, eradicate termites, publish books, or whatever the endeavor.

I invoke these and other unexpected names to emphasize and to il-
luminate the various theories and precepts of the management blueprint that I have formulated, adopted, and implemented in guiding
myself and our staff and our players to succeed.

I break down the task of building a winning team—or company or
organization—as follows:

1. Create a new vision.
2. Establish organizational goals.
3. Develop a roadmap, or game plan, if you prefer, for success.
4. Inspire the staff.
5. Provide the leadership.

That's what we had to do when I became GM of the Braves prior
to the 1991 season. Here's how we did it:

FIRST I APPLIED THAT PYGMALION THEORY. IN *MY FAIR LADY*, PRO-
fessor Henry Higgins demonstrated the Pygmalion Theory with Liza
Doolittle, taking her from the street urchin she was and turning her
into someone who *looked* like an elegant lady of class and dignity. For
the longest time, if you remember the movie, she didn't speak well or
speak properly. It was because she didn't think of herself as a lady of
class and dignity. But once she was willing to accept herself as someone
who was actually deserving of that stature, then she began to take on
those characteristics in an honest and comfortable way.

That's what creating a new vision is about—establishing organizational goals and self-esteem. As I said, the first and foremost task fac-
ing me when I came to Atlanta was that I had to somehow get rid of
the losing mentality that the organization suffered from. We had to
first defeat and eradicate apathy.

And then the next thing, right on the heels of that, I had to be able
to convince people that they had the ability within themselves, individually and as a group or department, to be better and to achieve

more and to feel confident about that. To visualize a successful Braves organization—a championship. That's the Pygmalion Theory.

Winners make commitments, losers make excuses. That is the theme and principal theory I utilized throughout this transformation.

When we constantly talk about making commitments and not making excuses, feeling confident, doing what needs to be done and feeling absolutely certain that it can be done, only then can we do away with apathy, create a new vision, and then start establishing new goals—clear and precise goals.

We had to begin to believe in ourselves as an organization, as a team, and as individuals. We had to change the environment from one in which losing was not only expected and accepted, but had become comfortable. We had to create an environment in which new and higher goals were set, expectations raised, and, of course, the necessary work ethic and commitment were put in place. We had to raise our sights.

Part of defeating apathy was projecting positive physical body language. It was expressing trust in the people we had determined were going to remain and be a part of this new administrative/management philosophy and aggressive program. I needed them to have trust and confidence and actually show it and live it so that they truly would believe they could do these things.

As someone so accurately said, "It is better to aim at perfection and miss, than to aim at imperfection and hit it." We needed to raise our organizational sights.

Before I took the Atlanta job, I analyzed what the Braves were, analyzed their strengths, assets, and deficiencies. All before I took the job. I knew what was there. The vision I created for the Braves was done *after* analyzing all the things I had found to be good about the Braves, not so good about the Braves, and, quite frankly, downright disappointing or embarrassing about the Braves.

Knowing those things, analyzing them properly and accurately and intelligently, I then decided the specific fixes that would be needed for the Braves organization to get to where we wanted to go. And where we wanted to go, in establishing our organizational goals, was to win a world championship. We didn't accept any halfway targets. It wasn't, "Let's get better," or "Let's improve," or "Let's work harder." That's just too vague.

In my mind, I had to establish the priorities: What was the vision of this Braves organization that I expressed? As I said earlier, I saw an organization that exists in a town that I thought could be a dynamic, winning town that would support a winning team. And my vision was to create an organization that would have people in it who believed as I did. People who would work as hard as I would. I knew on the field we had a manager who was absolutely in lockstep with me and with the kind of team we wanted to create. Additionally, I wanted to create the same kind of administrative organization. That was my vision—to create a world championship organization, top to bottom.

One of the vehicles I have used to renew our yearly goals and motivate the uniformed staff is a heartfelt conversation with about thirty members of our baseball staff—manager, coaches, scouts, medical staff, and top administrative assistants—when we gather for the start of each spring training. This presentation sets the tone, creates a working theme for that spring training and season.

In recent years, these pre-spring staff meetings have been conducted in the auxiliary clubhouse at Cracker Jack Stadium, our excellent spring home at Disney World. This meeting to me is the most stimulating of the year. It signals the time of year that baseball is renewing itself as an industry and we as an organization are renewing ourselves, setting new goals and designing new roadmaps.

Judging from the comments after I make these presentations, it is motivational to our staff who listen to me discuss aspects of various staff and leadership responsibilities, and the assorted themes I try to create for these meetings. This meeting is also a reaffirmation of who we are as an organization and a celebration of our phenomenal continuity of success—this record-breaking run of success that we've put together.

I get wonderful feedback every year. Bullpen coach Bobby Dews, who is our literary man, an author of several novels; our team medical director, Dr. Joe Chandler; Jose Martinez, special assistant to the general manager and a key staff member in our baseball operations department; Bill Fischer, ex-major–league pitcher and pitching coach and our current minor league pitching coordinator; and Bobby Cox all approached me after the 2005 session, for example, and expressed they felt the talk hit the mark.

I try to create various themes for these meetings and make them as stimulating as I can. You can only say so many things about leadership and responsibilities of leadership. Year after year, I concentrate on what the players expect of them as staff members each season and their responsibilities of preparing these players physically and mentally to meet the challenges of another championship run.

During a stretch of four recent springs, we talked about change. First year: Change. Second year: Understanding Change. Third: Managing Change. Fourth: Managing Change Effectively and Thinking Outside the Box. I'll talk about managing change in more detail a little later.

As part of my 2004 pre-spring address, I read passages from the book *A Traveler's Gift,* written by a friend of mine, Andy Andrews. Andy is a Christian comic and motivational speaker and terrific bestselling author. I heartily recommend this book, just as I did to our staff—and even offered to purchase one for each of them and did for my daughter, Gina, and son, Jonathan. I read passages about self-improvement and other important elements of life.

I also shared one of my favorite stories, involving the famed cellist Pablo Casals, to underscore the never-ending task we all face of continuing to improve ourselves.

When Casals was ninety-five years old, a reporter went to him and said, "Mr. Casals, you are the greatest cellist who ever lived. You're ninety-five years old. Tell me, why do you practice your cello six hours a day?"

"Because," Pablo countered, "I believe that I'm making progress."

There can be no better example of Pablo's spirit than our ageless first baseman, Julio Franco. Playing well into his forties, Julio is constantly going the extra mile to hone his skills and condition his body. And you'd better believe that makes an impression on teammates half his age. Julio is our Pablo personified.

In our business or personal lives, we are all growing and progressing. Always! We need to be sure we give everyone else in our company, our organization, and our team the encouragement to do it as well.

We want our coaches, instructors, and staff to feel the same way. That's why we have early batting practice at 7:00 A.M. during spring training to give guys a chance to get extra swings. And even the stars, Chipper and Andruw and the others, are all there, setting the right example for younger players.

A truism I often recite to underscore that: "Only a mediocre man is always at his best." We are all works in progress. Always.

FOR 2005, THE THEME FOR OUR STAFF MEETING WAS THE RESPONSIBIL-ities of their leadership roles and the secondary theme was about attitude. The attitude that we have as individuals is our choice on a daily basis. Doesn't matter what happened in the past. Doesn't matter what successes we've enjoyed or failures we've endured. Doesn't matter what people write about us or say about us. Doesn't matter what other people do.

We have control over one thing—the *attitude* we take with us every day to our jobs. And I talked about how important attitude is. As an example, I pulled from the work of a famed Spanish author. Keep in mind these are rugged, salt-of-the-earth, tobacco-chewing baseball people listening to this.

"Last year when I talked about Pablo Casals and said, kiddingly, I was sure you all know Pablo. Half of you probably thought he was a tennis player."

This time I said I would talk about someone they were equally familiar with: Miguel de Cervantes. There were thirty question marks on the faces in the room.

I explained to them that Cervantes wrote the literary classic *Don Quixote* about this comical figure and what he did and the kind of attitude he possessed. As comical as he was, he was determined to be a knight in the world at that time and prepared himself to do that— making his own armor, creating his lance and helmet, and getting on his trusty steed to battle windmills in the back hills of Spain.

The book inspired the contemporary musical *Man of La Mancha,* in which the lead song, "The Impossible Dream," carried significant inspiration for us. I suggested that as they listened to the lyrics, they allow their minds to apply those words to what we face as the Atlanta Braves organization in 2005. I'm sure my colleagues were thankful, no doubt, when I announced that I would spare them the agony of my attempting to sing the song. Instead, I simply recited the words.

"The Impossible Dream" was not just about the 2005 season we were approaching, but rather any number of recent seasons. Over the past fifteen seasons rarely did people outside our organization think we were capable of winning a world championship. We were largely picked to finish third or fourth in 2004, for example, and we won 96 games and won our 13th straight division title by 10 games.

But this is about having the idea that you can succeed "fighting the unbeatable foe, striving with the last ounce of courage, running where the brave dare not go." On and on, I recited the words to that song and reiterated what a magnificent attitude that song reflects. I stressed how we should all embrace it and remember it as we dream what most think is an impossible dream for us, but we know is a very possible dream for us.

And the last story I shared with them was of the gazelle and the lion in Africa. Each morning the gazelle awakens knowing that she must run faster than the fastest lion to survive that day. And the lion awakens that morning knowing that he must run faster than the slowest gazelle so as not to die from starvation. Both of them realize that when the sun rises, they must be running for their lives.

So I suggested that as the sun rose on the 2005 season, this Braves team should be running with the determination of the lion, the survival of the gazelle, and the attitude of a champion to our goal of winning a world championship.

And I reminded them at the end, "This is our quest."

IN 1991 THE THEME I CHOSE FOR THE PRE-SPRING TALK IN MY FIRST year as Braves GM was this: "Out of adversity grows opportunity." It focused on taking the disappointment and frustration that the previous several seasons had produced and turning them into determination, motivating us to do what we could individually and collectively to get the Braves to the top. We also talked about the positive relationships—mine with Bobby, Bobby's with the staff, and the staff's with the players. All absolutely essential for success.

I challenged them to accept my premise that the talent was spread fairly evenly throughout Major League Baseball and that teams with the strongest attitudes and toughness separate themselves from the pack by making the commitment of winners.

I stressed the "team concept," noting that while baseball requires great individual skills, no team can win unless it creates and nurtures a strong team attitude. I told them that we as a staff could promote and strengthen the team concept by our actions, words, and attitudes. You can't simply say, "These guys are pros. They know what to do to get ready." They must be challenged and they want to feel part of a team effort of becoming winners through hard work and smart work.

I charged that each of them, individually, could be contributing architects of this new structure. "Someone in this room could very well be the catalyst with the player or players that key our efforts and success this year and in the future," I implored. "Winning is hard; losing is easy. Winning won't come easy, but if we truly want it, it will happen. We can win, so we *will* win!"

Then I did something unprecedented, before or since, in my baseball career. A few days later, I gave essentially the same talk in the clubhouse to the players when the full team had assembled in West Palm Beach for my first spring training with them.

It was in much the same fashion and much the same message about having pride in the Atlanta Braves. To underscore my own pride in the organization, I put on a Braves warmup jacket and wore it as I stood before the group in the clubhouse. I told the players then what I believed we would accomplish, how I felt about the team we had constructed and what my view of what the past had been and how we were going to commit ourselves to doing what was necessary to win and how we felt we had accomplished some of that over the winter with the signing of some new players. (Fast-forward a couple of weeks and we made the deal to add fleet outfielder Otis Nixon from the Expos early in spring training, which really rounded out the team. We had already added Terry Pendleton, Rafael Belliard, and Sid Bream.)

I just shared my personal feelings about the pride I expected all of us to have in the Braves. I wanted everyone to have a sense of that pride and be proud to wear that uniform and not feel they had to apologize or be the butt of anyone's jokes about it anymore, because those days were gone. Those days were over, I insisted. Forever!

"We're going to be the proud Atlanta Braves and we are going to prove to people that we are winners," I told them. "And we are committed to that. And that's going to be the way we approach everything this year."

The speech, as far as I could tell, was received very well by Bobby and his staff and the players. Especially the players who had been there battling their butts off and struggling to win—Tommy Glavine and Steve Avery and Kent Mercker and John Smoltz and David Justice and Ron Gant and others. Those were people who were really busting a gut to get out of that last-place rut they were in. As for the new players we had signed and brought in, I had assured them we were committed to winning and that things were going to be different in Atlanta.

"Trust me on this," I told them that day in the clubhouse. "We are putting a winning team together. We've got a good nucleus and we're going to build on it. And we're going to have a winning team here and it's going to come quick."

That's what I said and I could tell from their faces it was exactly what they wanted and needed to hear and what they believed.

Bobby said to me right after that talk—I'll never forget it—"Great job. That was outstanding."

BUT MY GENERAL VIEW IS THAT THE CLUBHOUSE IS NOT THE GENERAL manager's place, especially if you have trust and confidence in the manager and the coaching staff, which obviously I do. In fact, that's the one and only talk I've ever made in the Braves' clubhouse. Thankfully, there's been no need for me to be a constant clubhouse spokesman.

In Kansas City I had to deliver a sad message when I informed the players of the diagnosis of manager Dick Howser's brain tumor. And then again to advise them of his death. But in terms of directing my comments to players in a motivational way or in a leadership fashion, that day in West Palm stands alone.

The primary playing talent asset we had with the Braves when I came to Atlanta was a young, emerging pitching staff that was going to be really good. All you had to do was look at the statistics—there's that word again—measuring how those young pitchers performed the year(s) before and listen to scouting reports about how they would make a good pitch to get a groundball that should have been a double play or an out. Too often, though, an infielder would boot the ball or throw it away. Instead of giving the opposing team three outs in an inning, they were giving four and five.

The pitching quality was there. So my plan, from the very beginning, was to (a) improve the playing surface, which was horrible, and (b) improve the infield defense, which we did by adding Pendleton at third, Belliard at short, and Bream at first, and (c) get a center fielder who could play the heck out of center field, which we did early in spring training when we acquired Otis Nixon in a deal ironically hammered out with Expos GM Dave Dombrowski and his young assistant GM, Frank Wren. Eight years later, in 1999, Frank Wren became my assistant GM and still serves in that role.

Later on in that spring training, I was over on one of our back practice fields, standing next to the batting cage, and Terry Pendleton quietly came up beside me and whispered in my ear, "John, we're gonna have a lot of fun around here this year. This team's going to be real good."

We were launching our long, remarkable streak of division titles. And Terry won the National League MVP award.

ONCE YOU GET PEOPLE TO START FEELING CONFIDENT ABOUT THEM-selves, you can establish goals that had seemed unreachable. Setting goals is very important. If we are to succeed in life, we must set definite and specific goals to strive for. We must focus our mind's eye on the specific purpose. They have to be clear and precise goals and I believe it is best to write them down.

Write down goals for every phase of your life, and especially for your business. Write down daily, weekly, monthly, short-term goals and goals for the next year and review them constantly.

Naturally, you will find it necessary from time to time to modify, change, alter, and improve your goals as you raise your consciousness. But at least you will have a roadmap with your destination clearly marked.

Always remember your goals must be logical or your mind won't accept them. Practice goal setting constantly. You'll be amazed how the positive changes will occur.

I guess I learned on my own the concept of writing down goals. That worked for me as a young baseball administrator and before that in my days as a teacher. I would have personal goals I would write down. I wanted to examine where I wanted to be as a teacher. Did I

My grandfather William Schuerholz at one time coached all five of his sons on the same team: William, Gilbert, my dad, John Sr., Wilson, and Donald.

SCHUERHOLZ FAMILY

HERE YOU ARE! REAL CHIPS OFF THE OLD BLOCK

William Schuerholz, Old-Time Player And Coach Of Champions, Has Five Sons In Basket Ball

The Baltimore City College High School baseball team in 1958, the year I was voted to the All Maryland Scholastic Association second team.

My son, Jonathan, and I visit with Hall of Famer Reggie Jackson at Royals Stadium in 1986.

Here I am with George Brett, Willie Wilson, and Don Quisenberry after all four of us had signed "lifetime" contracts with Kansas City.

My son Jonathan and I with Royals manager John Wathan in 1988.

With Gene Autry, the owner of the California Angels from the team's inception to his death in 1998, at Major League Baseball's winter meetings in Palm Springs. Sadly, Gene never got to see his team win the Series.

Royals manager Dick Howser and I met President Reagan during the White House visit of the 1985 World Champion Kansas City Royals.

It's been my privilege to work with two of the greatest managers in the game during the last fifty years, Dick Howser and Bobby Cox.

With third baseman Chipper Jones, whom I con-sider the face of our franchise, a leader by exam-ple and produc-tion since he came up to the majors in 1995.

Fred McGriff, the "Crime Dog," made as great an impact on our team's success as any player we've ever acquired in a trade.

In addition to being a potent offensive threat, Andruw Jones is the best center-fielder of this era, whose defensive skills often defy description.

Maddux, Smoltz, and Glavine: Three Cy Young Award winners, and the heart and soul of one of the most successful and consistent pitching rotations of all time.

Greg Maddux is as prepared,
competitive, and determined
as they come.

Tom Glavine's mental toughness
and never-surrender attitude gave
us all confidence every time he took
the mound.

Our most remarkable athlete and the
ultimate competitor, John Smoltz has
continued to grow as a team leader.

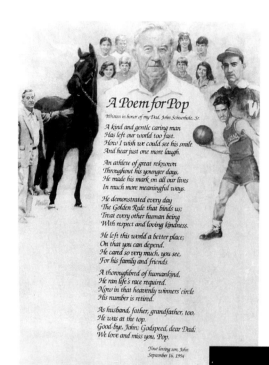

A Poem for Pop

Written in honor of my Dad, John Schuerholz, Sr.

A kind and gentle caring man
Has left our world too fast.
How I wish we could see his smile
And hear just one more laugh.

An athlete of great reknown
Throughout his younger days,
He made his mark on all our lives
In much more meaningful ways.

He demonstrated every day
The Golden Rule that binds us;
Treat every other human being
With respect and loving kindness.

He left this world a better place;
On that you can depend.
He cared so very much, you see,
For his family and friends.

A thoroughbred of humankind,
He ran life's race required.
Now in that heavenly winners' circle
His number is retired.

As husband, father, grandfather, too,
He was at the top.
Good-bye, John; Godspeed, dear Dad;
We love and miss you, Pop.

Your loving son, John
September 16, 1994

The poem I wrote honoring my father after his death in 1994. My friend from Kansas City John Martin did the artwork.

Dodgers manager and baseball icon Tommy Lasorda at Turner Field.

I joined Mickey Mantle at the Hall of Famer's charity golf tournament in Lake Oconee, Georgia.

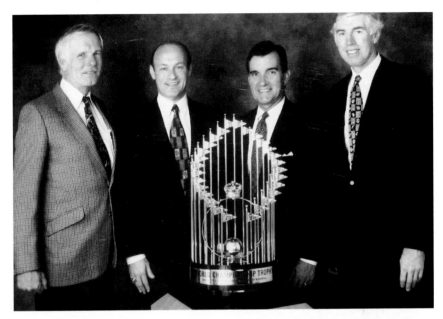

Then Braves owner Ted Turner believes in allowing good, capable people to lead and do their jobs: Turner and I with team executives Stan Kasten and Terry McGuirk behind one result of that philosophy, the 1995 World Series championship trophy.

I was welcomed by President Clinton when the 1995 World Champion Braves visited the White House.

Carrying the Olympic torch in 1996 when the Games came to Atlanta was a huge personal thrill.

Braves president Stan Kasten and I hosted Colin Powell when the former secretary of state visited Turner Field.

The Schuerholz family—my wife, Karen, and children, Jonathan and Gina—celebrated Thanksgiving in Kauai, Hawaii, in 2004.

want to remain a classroom teacher or become a supervisor or administrator or principal? What kind of graduate work should I do to meet my obligations for advanced degrees? Where should it be? I decided it would be in administration and supervision of secondary schools. What timetable do I want to give myself beyond the requirement of the state of Maryland to get this accomplished?

Those are things that I wrote down. For me, doing that just evolved. I don't recall anyone telling me to do that. It was through self-involvement in this process that I learned it was effective and that it worked.

I did that as a rising young staffer for the Orioles and Royals. I did it when I rose to become general manager of the Royals. And I did that when I came to Atlanta.

I wrote down what I wanted to accomplish and what I wanted to do and how I wanted to go about it, and still do. Some were ideas I had about the team. Some were ideas I had about organizational guidelines and some were personal and family goals.

As a leader, it's also extremely important how you verbalize your goals, your plans, your commitment, and your passion. This, to me, is a critical leadership tool.

If you're sitting behind your desk with your visor pulled down over your eyes and looking down at this pile of stuff on your desk and you won't look up and don't feel energized, you don't feel you can do much more than just shuffle papers around. But if I say to you often enough that I feel you are going to be a valuable part of this team, it's my job—or someone who is your immediate supervisor's job—to convince you that we've got to get you energized. We have to get you believing in yourself. If we feel that you have the innate ability to do this job and do it better than it has been done before, then we're going to have to work to get that out of you and clearly and effectively communicate that to you.

That was accomplished in Atlanta by showing confidence in the staff that was in place. By expressing how much we needed them, by giving them meaningful tasks to do, clearly explaining the new goals and guidelines for their areas. Each was told this is what we need you to do to present your organization as a world championship public relations department. As a world championship baseball operations department. As a world championship minor league department. As a world championship scouting department. As a world championship sales and marketing department.

And you know what? Before too long, ol' Liza began speaking eloquently and carrying herself with pride and dignity.

But with this new self-belief system starting to take root, we had to change the attitude of the entire organization. We needed to establish clear and appropriate goals and provide guidance on how to achieve them. Goals that were attainable.

Several years ago, the London Transit Authority had a more mundane problem. It seems that their buses were sailing past the people who were standing at the bus stop waiting to be picked up and carried to their destinations. Naturally, the Transit Authority began receiving thousands of calls from angry people who were late for work.

Finally, the London Transit Authority issued a public statement about the problem. They said this: "It is impossible for us to maintain our disciplined schedule if we must continually stop to pick up passengers." Do you get the feeling they had somehow lost sight of their purpose or their goal?

Our goal in the Braves organization was simple and repeatedly defined: Create a world championship team and organization.

In the words of Thomas Carlyle, "A man without goals is like a ship without a rudder."

NOW THAT YOU'VE ESTABLISHED YOUR GOALS, HOW DO YOU GET THERE?

In our situation, it gets technically specific. The roadmap is: What are the goals of your department? For instance, scouting department, what are your goals? You want to start blending more young guys into a veteran staff that has grown old together? You want to begin to balance that out a little bit better so you will continue to do your job well now, but preparing to get the job done over a long period of time? You want to change the scouting reports and how the information of a player is transmitted? You want to change how we get information about a player's makeup? Do we want to create a test instrument that allows us to find out more specifically about a guy's makeup? And how do we go about that? What kind of testing device do we want to use? Who do we know to talk to about that kind of issue? Are our territories covered properly? Do we need to change the territorial coverage? How are we doing in international scouting? Do we need to strengthen our international scouting component? What's our production been in that area? Let's analyze our drafts for the last ten years. Where are we strong? Where are we weak?

On and on and on, just in that one area.

And in player development, it was about reviewing our entire program. How are we training our guys? Do we have the right methods? Are we using the right approach? Do we have the right programs? Are we doing enough to physically condition our guys? Do we need to run more? What is the nature of the fundamentals we're using? Are they appropriate? Do they need to be changed? Who are the staff members we're giving that responsibility to? Are they worthy? Do they need to be improved? Where are our minor league teams aligned, geographically? Do we like the facilities we're in? Do we like the towns we're in? How can we improve? We want to put the best overall minor league affiliate package together to make our organization attractive to somebody we're trying to sign. Who are the people who work in the office on this administrative staff that are principally responsible for those functions? Do we want to improve or change them? Do we need a new perspective? Do we need a fresher view of those responsibilities and those challenges? Who do we have in those leadership positions?

Those are the questions I asked myself and our staff. And I'm still asking.

Remember, we are always making progress!

7

Leadership: Good People, Good Listening, Enthusiasm

The first and most important element of the leadership policy that has allowed me to enjoy whatever level of success I have had is valuing people and understanding the importance of creating the strongest possible team. It is selecting the right people, educating them well in their jobs, and motivating them to do their very best while asking them to make the commitment to winning.

If you select the right people and develop them through education and motivation and challenge, then success will inevitably follow. You will have created a cadre on whom you can rely as you explain your vision, outline the mission, establish the goals and objectives, and explain their responsibility in this mission.

That is leadership. If you embrace this philosophy, it becomes the essential element of good leadership, provided you do one more thing:

Listen to your people. Be an active, engaged, and interested listener.

You assure yourself and your business of succeeding if you create and listen to the strongest team possible.

You do that by:

1. Selecting the right people.
2. Investing in them, improving them, and leading them with enthusiasm.
3. And by listening—*truly listening*—to them.

I'VE ALWAYS CONSIDERED MYSELF A RAPT LISTENER, A PERSON WHO wants to learn. That is partly due to the fact that I became completely deaf in my right ear when I contracted measles at the age of five.

In 1945, parents didn't run children to the doctor at the first sign of a fever as we do today. When temperatures rose, they simply applied ice packs, administered aspirin, and tried to make the kids comfortable. That is what my parents did for me. However, my fever kept rising and it finally got so high that it destroyed the nerve in my ear, disintegrating it. There is no surgery or mechanism or device that can restore hearing to that ear.

My early days in grade school were difficult due to a combination of my hearing problem and the practice of seating children alphabetically. As an S, I was usually seated near the back of the room. Eventually, my parents intervened and had me moved closer to the teacher. I began to instinctively compensate by learning to read lips and listen intently. To this day, I can still read lips and I still listen carefully.

I never considered having a deaf ear a disability. In fact, in some ways it allowed me to be the center of attention. As teens in Baltimore, my friends and I would hang out on the street corner by the drugstore and shoot the breeze or sing and harmonize songs of the '50s. One day one of the guys brought a trumpet. Just for laughs, he blew it directly into my deaf ear like the "Call to the Post" at Pimlico. I could feel the percussion but could hear nothing. They found this bizarre and entertaining.

In college, I played soccer and baseball so I was always assigned a seat at one of the athletic tables in the dining hall. My teammates loved practical jokes and I was an easy mark. They would pretend to be telling a joke but would utter no sound. Then they would laugh at the pretend joke. Not wanting them to think I didn't get it, I would laugh, too. Then they *really* laughed!

My wife says I have a bionic ear and finds it a little odd that I can't hear her in a direct conversation. But let someone in another room say something about me or about something I'm not supposed to hear, and it comes through clear as a bell.

Of course, you don't have to have a hearing deficiency to become a good listener. I've always told my children that active, engaged listening is one of the great, underappreciated tools for success.

Being an active, engaged listener has helped me understand that you learn more by listening and being attentive and keeping your eyes and ears and brain open to what people are saying. It has helped me in every endeavor, whether academically, professionally, or personally.

Today, I sit here with these championship rings and consecutive division pennants strung across the facade just below my office at Turner Field and the strong belief that success will continue. The reason I am confident each year is that I am surrounded by good people and I do my best to listen to them. I view my role as general manager—in terms of making decisions—as the final filter. In virtually every case where we acquire a player, sign a free agent, or construct the team, I ask everyone involved in the analysis and judgment process to give me their opinion, give me their analysis, give me their judgment and ideas. Then I ask them, "Why? What makes you say that?" Then I listen *very* intently.

There might be a disparity of opinion on any issue or player. My job is to listen, evaluate, and, ultimately, make the final decision. I have to decide who is the best judge of pitchers, who judges hitters better, who has the best instincts regarding Latin infielders, and so on. I listen to all that input, then engage in the analysis, evaluation, and judgment process and, finally, the decision-making process.

That listening skill, that attentiveness that I learned in my early years, has served me well.

*　　*　　*

UNLIKE SOME OF TODAY'S SPORTS AND BUSINESS EXECUTIVES, I VIEW communication as a two-way street. I emphasize to our people the importance of communicating by reminding them of a favorite saying of mine:

Your conversation is your personal advertisement; for every time you open your mouth you allow others to look into your mind.

That's the element of communication that distinguishes you as a person of knowledge and strength, as a person of clear vision, and as a person of leadership. But in order to communicate effectively and to demonstrate those leadership qualities, you first have to be willing to listen. You have to be an active, effective listener in order to gain knowledge. There are only so many sensory elements that provide our input—what we see, what we read, what we hear.

This transfer of information must go up the chain of command as well as down. You can't have an effectively operating company or enterprise if you don't have your ears open and your mind open to the people who are working the line, or out in the field, who are giving honest, valuable feedback. In baseball, it might go from the scout to the scouting director to the player development director to the director of player personnel to the assistant GM to the GM. It might have several layers to travel. It might be something as subtle as gathering information about an amateur, draft-eligible player's schedule and communicating it in an effective way to a central command center where any changes can be noted. So if cross-checkers or double-checkers are coming in to scout a prospect and render a second opinion, they won't show up at an empty ball field. It may be a change in a form, or a change in a computer format, now that we've computerized virtually everything we do. It might be as subtle as that. Enough of those small pebbles left in the road, if not cleaned up and swept away, will create a far rockier road in the operation of your organization.

I know our people in the field communicating in an upward fashion feel little or no frustration because an open line of communication always exists. I'm sure they have a greater sense of involvement. I'm sure of that because we develop and foster good two-way communication in the Braves organization.

EARLIER, I MENTIONED WORKING WITH RUSH LIMBAUGH WHEN WE were both aspiring young executives with the Kansas City Royals. Rush recently made some observations that were both flattering and also assuring that I must have been an effective listener even in the early part of my career—even with only one good ear.

Rush correctly observed that the Royals were very corporate in the front office, which was divided into two sides—the baseball side and the business side.

"If you wanted to go anywhere in the Royals organization you had to be on the baseball side," Rush reflected. "I was in marketing and sales and that was on the business side. And everybody guarded their turf. Everybody wants to work for a baseball team, so the baseball-side people were very guarded and we business-side people typified that by looking across the hall and wishing we were on that side.

"Schuerholz was one of the few people on the baseball side who was actually nice and open to me. I'd walk into the press room during dinner before games and I could sit at his table and it wasn't a problem. I couldn't do that with too many of the other executives. And I could talk to him about my circumstances and situation and do it with trust.

"When I got a couple of promotions, he was one of the few people who came up to me and congratulated me, saying it was well deserved. I've never forgotten that. I wasn't very high in the chain of command, but he never treated me that way. When I first went there, John was the guy in charge of scouting and negotiating player contracts and it was clear he was going places. So it was flattering to me that he was willing to take time for me when I needed it or wanted it."

Not long after I had become GM of the Royals and near the end of Rush's five-year tenure with the organization, he was put in charge of producing the home games. That means running the scoreboard and putting all the elements of the commercials on the scoreboard and coordinating the organ music and that sort of thing. He wanted to incorporate for the first time recorded music in the ballpark, and not just organ music.

"This was like telling the Pope we were going to change a religious dictate," Rush recalled. "The Royals were a very staid and very conservative organization. On opening day, we were in the scoreboard booth getting some of this stuff ready. John came down to listen to it and see what I was doing. I thought he had a little concern on his face, but he always stood behind me on these little innovative ideas I wanted to try. So I always felt he was someone who would *listen* to new ideas and was on my side."

Those are kind and reassuring words that maybe I was already trying to go about making positive changes the right way, even way back when.

WHEN BROACHING THE SUBJECT OF HIRING GOOD PEOPLE, TWO INDIviduals leap right to the top of my mental short list. One I hired; the other I enthusiastically inherited.

In Kansas City, I hired the remarkable Buck O'Neil.

I'm honored and proud to call Buck a friend. Of all the people I know on this earth, when I see him across a room—before he gives me his big bear hug—his smile is so bright and genuine, he lights up the room. His eyes sparkle when he sees me, and it makes me feel so good.

Buck is a legendary star of the old Negro Leagues and became an invaluable staffer in Major League Baseball. When you see a guy like him who is the man and gentleman that he is, the baseball historian he is, the remarkable person he is, and to know he is your friend, that is a special honor. And, in turn, you feel he cherishes being your friend.

He'd typically give me that bear hug and say, in that wonderful deep bass voice, "Hey, boss!"

He's as special a human being and as remarkable a man as I've ever known. Even into his seventies he was still shooting his age in golf.

I had a chance to catch up with Buck on a recent visit to Turner

Field as we were honoring members from the Negro Leagues. After talk of family and mutual friends, I asked him about his golf game and whether he was still, at ninety-some years old, shooting his age. Without hesitation, his eyes gleaming, Buck said, "I sure am, boss, but that's not a good score now."

He's got vibrancy, energy, character, spirit.

In the mid-'80s, I hired Buck as a Royals scout. He had worked for the Chicago Cubs for a long time. I hired him for two reasons: First, I thought he had a lot of ability as a scout. Second, we had some young black players—Willie Wilson, U. L. Washington—whom I thought Buck could help. So I invited him not only to scout our opposition at the ballpark, but anytime he wished to visit our clubhouse, attend batting practice, and talk with the players. I encouraged him to be around the batting cage, not just for the black players, but for everybody—the manager, myself, the entire team. We all benefited from having Buck share his baseball knowledge and spirit.

If you were a young major league player, and knew about his fascinating background, or you realized what he'd accomplished, what he'd endured and his remarkable countenance about that; if you knew of the great glory of the days he played and managed in the Negro Leagues, you were sure to be lifted by Buck's positive energy and positive attitude and positive influence and his levelheaded counsel. His approach to everything in life was so very positive and so energized that you were better just by being in his presence. We all were.

Buck talked to everybody in our clubhouse. He was like a magnet. If I suggested he talk to a player about attitude or behavior, Buck would go on a mission to seek and help that player out.

Frank White and George Brett—who didn't need that kind of help—spent as much time with Buck as anyone. Here were two excellent, high-class All-Stars, who were still attracted to, listening to, and learning from what Buck had to say. He was just a wonderful influence.

I can remember before a day game we were standing in the tunnel leading out to the dugout in Royals Stadium. Buck and I were just talking about baseball and all of a sudden he puts his hand on my arm and said, "Hold it, boss. Stop. Listen."

I listened and you could faintly hear the crack of the bat in batting practice.

"Listen, boss," Buck said. "It's Bo Jackson hitting. We have to go out and watch, boss."

I asked how he knew it was Bo Jackson.

"Boss, I've heard that sound three times in my life," he said. "Josh Gibson, Babe Ruth, and Bo Jackson. Let's go see Bo hit."

We walked out and, sure enough, Bo was hitting.

Buck was the guy who was the real push behind the effort to have the Negro Leagues Baseball Museum developed and located in Kansas City. I had the great honor and good fortune to make several visits there and have been supportive of their efforts. In 2002, 2003, and 2005, I was selected as the National League Executive of the Year by the Negro Leagues Baseball Museum and was honored at their banquet with the Rube Foster Award. Busts of Rube Foster, the awards I received for that honor, rest in a prominent position on my office credenza at Turner Field. Buck was thrilled that I won and was happy to be there with me. I consider it a very high honor, indeed.

I WAS FORTUNATE TO INHERIT BOBBY COX AS THE BRAVES MANAGER when I came to Atlanta. As I mentioned earlier, when Stan Kasten offered me the GM job in Atlanta and explained that Bobby was moving out of the front office and back into the dugout, he said it was his intention to have Bobby continue as manager. Stan asked how I felt about it. Was I okay with that? Not only was I okay with it, I was delighted. I've always had great respect for Bobby.

When I first arrived in Atlanta, Stan said, "C'mon, let's go see Bobby. He's in the hospital and just had an operation on both knees."

Off we go to Piedmont Hospital. We walk into Bobby's room to a jolting sight. There were cinches and pulleys and ropes. Both of his legs were harnessed up into the air in casts from his ankles to his hips. They had done what is called an osteotomy on both knees, where they remove pieces of bone from his knees. The gruesome procedure seemed almost like medieval torture. Maybe worse.

That was the prescribed treatment in those days before knee replacements became routine. I don't think they do osteotomies anymore.

In that first face-to-face meeting with Bobby, he was sort of groggy and pain-riddled and his cast-confined legs stuck up in the air like a couple of traffic cones. Stan and I were up in that hospital room with him trying to make small talk. In his typical, lighthearted style, Stan was laughing about the uniqueness of this odd circumstance of his new GM and manager holding their first meeting in this strange setting.

Bobby was happy that I took the job. We've always had a healthy respect for each other. And there was never the least bit of friction over the fact that he was going back into the dugout and I was replacing him as GM. Of the two roles, Stan and Terry had clearly determined that Bobby was better suited as a field manager and, indeed, Bobby was eager to return to the field. He also wanted to stay in Atlanta. That is one of the main reasons he'd left the Toronto Blue Jays a few years earlier when he returned to Atlanta as the GM.

I've always believed that I've had the great privilege in the role as general manager of working with two of the best managers in the game in the last fifty years, Dick Howser and Bobby Cox. They were similar in their approach to their responsibilities and to their jobs as managers. And they were similar in how they interacted with players, how they led their teams, the kind of environment they created for their teams and in their clubhouses, and the way they approached games. Not a lot of fanfare, just a lot of good, solid, deep baseball knowledge and instincts. Both men had a calm demeanor on the surface, but a fierce, competitive fire crackling inside. Dick and Bobby matched up in the 1985 American League Championship Series, Dick's Royals against Bobby's Toronto Blue Jays.

In Kansas City, I was faced with the task of replacing our field manager after Dick died from a brain tumor. I wasn't as effective in that change process as I feel I would be now. That was very emotional and personal, not cold and calculated. It was human, and not a change I managed very well. I thought I had the right guy, Billy Gardner, to replace him, but the team didn't respond to Billy. I learned from this experience that your first instincts are not always the best. I learned when you think you have the obvious solution, it may not be so. I learned that more time and more thought and more consideration and more in-depth investigation of all the issues have to take place—especially in such an emotionally charged environment.

Dick and I worked together well and we were good friends. It was a tough situation because I hurt personally and, at the same time, had this challenge and responsibility as a relatively young general manager to continue the Royals' success.

That's a situation I think I might have handled better. But I know I have grown from that experience. We all can learn from a mistake or inappropriate action if we go back and honestly peel the layers away, examining what we did wrong. Then if we push ourselves to make the necessary changes I think we can become better. We can grow. We can improve in everything we do, always. Remember Pablo Casals?

Dick was the manager of the 1986 American League All-Star team, having won the World Series the previous fall. It was on that trip to the 1986 All-Star Game, in Mr. Kauffman's private plane, that we first began to notice Dick failing. He complained of headaches. He was unable to remain on the field during the All-Star Game workout and he momentarily forgot Frank White's name—who was the Royals' All-Star starting second baseman and one of his best players. During the flight home, Dick called me Joe.

It was frightening to us all how quickly this began to happen to Dick. His lifelong friend Trevor Grubbs—who became a friend of mine when Dick became our manager in Kansas City—and I began to worry greatly about what we were witnessing with our good friend.

When we returned after the All-Star Game, we arranged for the appropriate medical people to examine him. That's when the stage four brain tumor was found.

Dick put up a brave fight, but it was a horrible ordeal. He began taking chemotherapy, which was very debilitating. One of our coaches, Mike Ferraro, had to take over the team for the remainder of the '86 season on an interim basis. We were hopeful that the next spring training would be part of Dick's path to recovery. We wanted him to have something to look forward to, something to live for; that was to put that manager's uniform back on.

We gave him that opportunity but it was hard for all of us because we quickly knew that he wasn't going to be able to do the job. But he wanted to and we respected him and wanted to give him that opportunity. And we did.

Dick opened that '87 spring training as our manager, but couldn't do it. He had to leave for treatment. To fight for his life.

Some would say we did some things as an organization for Dick during his battle with cancer out of compassion and out of love and respect for him that wouldn't ordinarily be done in corporate settings. We might not have managed change properly or effectively as it relates to managing an organization in the traditional sense, but I think we did what was right from a human emotional standpoint, as best we could.

I have no regrets about that. That was not a mistake. The mistake was in not effectively working the process of who the appropriate replacement would be.

Dick was a lot like Bobby Cox in terms of how the players admired and respected him. A tough, quiet, disciplined gentleman. It was hard not to respect and admire him.

I wrote a poem about Dick, which I recited at his memorial service in Kansas City. The first verse:

Connie Mack and Casey Stengel and Walter Alston wait,
  To greet their newest brother outside the Pearly Gate;

Connie was the first to speak as their new member passed,
  "You've taught us all something more about this word called 'class.'"

LITTLE DID I KNOW AT THAT TRYING TIME THAT I WOULD LATER HAVE
the opportunity to work alongside yet another manager who is so dis-
tinctly a cut above the crowd. The years I've spent in Atlanta have been
made more enjoyable by having Bobby Cox as our manager and a partner in this great endeavor. He's as good a leader-manager as I've ever
been around.

The environment he creates around our team is the best anywhere
in baseball as far as allowing players to succeed more consistently. That
is an environment that is even-keeled. The challenging, turbulent seas
of baseball always appear to be calm under his guidance. While the seas
themselves may be rough with turmoil all about, he has his steady hand
firmly on the wheel steering this team's ship through those troubled
waters. He makes it *seem* smooth. He makes it *feel* not so intimidating,
not so dangerous, not so tumultuous. A calm and steady hand.

A great example of that steady hand took place in the first half of
the 2004 season when we had to retool the roster after losing Javy
Lopez and Gary Sheffield and Vinny Castilla and got hit with a rash of
injuries. We were written off by so many sportswriting pundits. Even
before the injuries made the situation even more daunting, we talked
internally about how it was going to take a long while for this new roster to blend. We felt we had put together a very good team, talent-wise,
but knew it would take a good month or two into the season before
this bunch would come together as a team and show their true ability.
And that's exactly what happened.

We believed they were talented and we thought success was going
to happen, but I also knew that under Bobby's leadership and with his
steady hand, it would happen for sure. After significantly retooling
again for the 2005 season, I was confident this same *melding* would
happen again. I felt Raul Mondesi and Brian Jordan and Tim Hudson
and Dan Kolb and the other new guys we brought in would respond

well to Bobby, and I was right. In the face of injuries to our starting pitching rotation as well as to Chipper Jones, and disappointing seasons from some key players, we substantially reconstructed our roster with seventeen rookies from our minor league system. With his managerial magic, Bobby molded these players into an exciting, energetic team and led them to our 14th consecutive division title.

He can manage twenty-five guys more effectively than any manager I've ever observed. There is also a toughness about Bobby Cox that the players and everyone else around know is there, but rarely has to show itself.

Bobby will explain to a player in a private way how he doesn't appreciate the way the player is going about his work, or how he is representing his profession or our team.

That he always does this in private is one of his great strengths. He's not looking for theatrics. He's not looking for points—*Look at me, media, how I deal with people, how I scold people, how I embarrass people, how I criticize our players. Look at me, how honest I am about that criticism.*

That's not being honest. Bobby is *very* honest, but he handles those issues in a professional, sensitive, and private way. Players really respect that.

There are very few players that Bobby doesn't feel like managing and doesn't want around. Without naming names, he felt that way about a few players. They weren't willing to put the team first and their ego second. Their attitude and interactions created friction in the clubhouse and they didn't add to the strength of our team. If ever any of these circumstances existed, he and I would have a short talk and that player would soon be gone.

There have been some guys who performed very well after they left here. But they just didn't fit the mold of what we wanted our team to be.

We think we acquire good players and Bobby and I have always been on the same page, philosophically, about the kind of players we like. He and I think a lot alike in that regard, and did even before we were together. So when we have a hole to fill on our roster—significant, moderate, or otherwise—we usually bring players in that fit into Bobby's team mold. And we really don't have to talk about it. It's more or less an unspoken understanding that he and I have developed about the type of player we want on this team. Obviously, I bounce ideas off him and talk to him about players he may know or has seen.

To me, the most important relationship that exists in baseball is the one between the manager and general manager. There have been very few times that we have disagreed on player decisions, but also some times where we both have deferred to the other's opinion. The vast majority of time, we're on the same page.

We do our due diligence before we are ready to propose or make a trade. I'll say, "Bobby, here's a guy we're ready to acquire and here's what we know about him. Do you have any feelings, one way or another?" Ninety-nine percent of the time, Bobby is willing to take the players that have passed our litmus test. Obviously, our consistent track record in determining who earns our seal of approval has gained Bobby's confidence.

When he won his 2,000th game as a manager late in the 2004 season, we honored him with a trip anywhere in the world. He and his wife, Pam, chose to go to Europe that off-season. He had never been to Europe and Pam wanted to go. Terry McGuirk, our chairman and president, and I had kicked around ideas about an appropriate expression to Bobby on that momentous occasion. I talked to our traveling secretary, Bill Acree, who knows Bobby really well. They work together every day. I got ideas from Bill and we ultimately felt a trip would be the right thing to do. So I went to Bobby's office the next day to tell him.

His reaction was so typical of him. He's so low-key and understated. He was thankful and appreciative, but said something like, "Awww, John, that's so great. You guys don't have to do anything like that."

True. We didn't *have* to. But we *wanted* to.

When I was still at KC and Bobby had become GM in Atlanta, we made three trades, the most significant of which sent solid starting pitcher Charlie Leibrandt to Atlanta for infielder Gerald Perry. In an interview not long ago, Bobby looked back on that time when we were both GMs. "John was always up front," he said. "He was a guy you would actually call 'honest.' In those days, everybody wasn't above-board. But John was always one of the good guys out there."

Bobby did a fine job as GM rebuilding the Braves' minor league system. He is a very astute judge of talent. I've always felt that way about him. While the team was finishing last in its division three years in a row, his plan, with Stan's support, was to rebuild and refill the minor league pipeline while they were taking their lumps at the major league level. And through Bobby's involvement along with his scouting director, Paul Snyder, they did that. I knew Bobby to be not only a solid judge of talent, but also as one of the best managers—and felt that is probably where he should be. I just felt baseball deserved to have a manager of that Hall of Fame caliber down in the dugout. That's where he really shines.

Bobby was fine with moving back to the dugout. He loves Atlanta, has made his home here, and wanted to stay. So that was the best of all worlds for him.

But he left the GM office with the knowledge in his heart that the work he had done to replenish a farm system was well done. He was able to look at his efforts and slough off the criticism about how bad the big-league team was performing.

Bobby has a very professional, respectful view of baseball and baseball players. He has a lot of admiration for guys who possess the talent to play major league baseball. He knows how difficult it is to succeed as a major league player. He knows how hard these guys have had to work and he realizes the pressure they're under. He understands how difficult it is to play a game and win. He knows how difficult it is to deal with the daily baseball onfield confrontations—hitter against pitcher, pitcher against hitter, base runner against catcher, outfielder against gap-hit fly ball—and to succeed. Bobby truly understands and appreciates how difficult it is to play this game and to play it well.

That natural and honest understanding he has, and that natural and honest appreciation he has for the players, is felt by them. In turn, they display that same measure of respect and admiration and appreciation for him and for the way he manages the team.

The guy is a Hall of Fame manager. That says it all.

PART OF WHAT MAKES A GUY LIKE BOBBY COX A GOOD MANAGER IS that he, in turn, surrounds himself with good people by selecting good coaches. Just as Bobby has a keen eye for player talent, he also has exhibited the ability to pick and choose his own quality staff. He has tapped coaches who are not only blessed with specific coaching talents for their roles, but also possess the desired character and personality to meld together as a productive coaching unit and support the kind of player instruction, discipline, and deportment that we demand.

One of his staff promotions that occurred just before I came to Atlanta was minor league pitching coach Leo Mazzone, an engaging, innovative fellow Maryland product. He is best known to our TV fans as "Rocking Leo" for his nervous habit of rocking back and forth on his dugout perch while watching his pitchers work. Leo takes a lot of ribbing for his rocking, which he's done all his life and is usually unaware that he is doing it. "My mother said that even as a baby," Leo recalls, "I rocked back and forth in my high chair, banging my head."

In a game against Philadelphia back when one of our top scouts, Jim Fregosi, was manager of the Phillies, Leo glanced across at the other dugout to see the entire Philadelphia team rocking in mock unison. Jim grinned from around the dugout wall and flashed a playful gesture to Leo.

More importantly, Leo has come to be known as one of the best pitching coaches in baseball. In fact, in a 2003 *Sports Illustrated* survey of major league players, Leo was named *the* best pitching coach by a phenomenal vote margin of 3-to-1 over the second-place choice.

Bobby and Leo, in concert with some of our other key personnel, have created and nurtured an Atlanta Braves legacy of pitching excellence that has developed a momentum of its own.

We have the best pitching environment in Major League Baseball, for three main reasons. First, we have the best pitchers' manager I've ever seen in the game. Bobby manages pitchers more effectively than anyone. It's not so much about how he uses them in games and when he brings in a reliever. That's the traditional measuring stick for handling pitchers. But in addition to that, Bobby will never abuse a pitcher. That is to say it is more important to him to protect a pitcher's arm or to protect a pitcher who is having some nagging physical problems, to the extent that a pitcher's arm and well-being over the course of the whole season are as important to him as any particular game.

"I learned one thing right from the first time I signed a contract in 1959," Bobby says. "If you don't have some pitching, you don't have any kind of chance to win a ballgame. So I've always set my sights on pitchers, and try to take care of pitchers and figure out a way to make them last longer. They're the biggest asset a team can have."

During spring training, all the pitchers throw in the bullpen the first thing every morning and Bobby sits on a bench right behind them. He carefully watches their delivery, their release point, the movement of the ball, and—most important—how consistently they hit the catcher's target with each type of pitch they throw. And he does that every morning, all spring. He doesn't leave that bench until the last pitcher has thrown. He studies pitching.

Bobby said right from the start of his career he became intrigued about the care and handling of pitchers. While playing for the Yankees, he delighted in picking the brain of legendary pitching coach Jim Turner. For us, Bobby gives much of the credit for keeping our pitchers healthy and productive to Leo.

"Leo has been a part of that as much as I have," Bobby says. "You can blow out pitchers real fast if you don't watch it. At least I have a relationship with them such that they trust that I'm doing the best I can to take care of them."

That relationship didn't come instantly. As a young minor league manager, Bobby went out to the mound to remove a guy named Eddie Ricks one night in Toledo. When Bobby reached out for the ball, Ricks angrily whirled and threw the ball over the center field fence. As has remained his style throughout his career, Bobby didn't embarrass or admonish Ricks right there before the fans; but once they were in the clubhouse after the game and out of public view, he gave Ricks a stinging earful.

Bobby understood and admired Ricks's competitive spirit, but over the years his pitchers have learned not to embarrass him or themselves, not that he would let them get away with it very long after the game. Although they have become few and far between, he still has an occasional disagreement with a frustrated pitcher after they are removed from the game. Most recently, he engaged in some screaming matches in the dugout with controversial John Rocker after Bobby lifted him. It was one of the signs we saw that made us believe Rocker had some issues.

Often, Leo has to bear the brunt of a pitcher's frustrations when the lifted pitcher reaches the dugout and Bobby is still on the field with the new pitcher. "There have been a few times," says Leo, "when Bobby makes it back to the dugout and finds me and the lifted pitcher going at it so that he had to tell both of us to shut up. But after a cooling-down period, we usually have a lot of fun with it."

Bobby recalled that he and John Smoltz, the ultimate competitor, got into it a little when Smoltzie first came up to the majors and Bobby took him out of a game.

"I told him he would appreciate someday what I was doing," Bobby recounted. "He was behind, like, 7–4 in the fifth inning, and there was no reason to keep him going. Now he was going to have to pitch at least a couple more innings, just so he might get a win—for all the wrong reasons. My best interest is for them."

He will just not let a guy continue who says he doesn't feel right or can't go another inning. Bobby will not abuse a pitcher.

Ever.

Ever.

Under any circumstance, for any reason.

So pitchers last longer, they pitch deeper into the season and to the end of the season more effectively because of the way Bobby manages them and cares for their mental and physical well-being. (That assessment is made on a track record stretching over many years. I can only view the uncommon string of mostly freak injuries we suffered during the 2005 season, when three-fifths of our starting rotation spent extensive time on the disabled list, as merely an aberration, not a glitch in Bobby's methods or our time-tested pitching program.)

Second is Leo's throwing program. Leo has a tried-and-true throwing program that is different from the traditional tactics. He believes that pitchers should throw more often between starts, with less energy, and that's the physical part of the plan.

"Touch and feel" is another facet that Leo feels is vitally important. A pitcher throwing from the mound more acquires more of that feel. Leo wants them to have their hands on the baseball more often and "feel" the delivery point and have "touch" on their pitches without overexertion. Leo's method began to evolve after he extensively picked the brain of the great Johnny Sain in spring training in 1979 when Leo first joined the Braves as minor league pitching coach. Basically, the program calls for our starters to throw two days between starts, rather than just one, to get the pitchers on the mound as often as possible.

"The key is that the coach has to regulate the effort," Leo explains. "For example, if I told you to run seven miles in a week, would you rather run one mile every day, or run seven miles and take several days off and then you can't move? We feel the same with a pitcher's arm."

Leo isn't a big fan of two modern baseball developments: the five-man rotation (instead of four) and the obsession with pitch counts. He feels pitchers stay sharper in a four-man rotation, but baseball thinks they stay healthier in a five. Keeping a pitch count, he suggests, tends to psyche pitchers into thinking they are tired when their pitch count gets up around 90. To combat that, Leo has been known to occasionally "forget" to click the counter he uses to keep up with the pitch count during a game. As the late innings approach, a pitcher who is going well and has actually thrown, say, 95 pitches, might not feel as spent if Leo's clicker swears he's only thrown 85. (Naturally, Leo is not at all happy that the scoreboards in many ballparks now display a running count of pitches thrown.)

Leo believes all pitchers should command the low-and-away fastball. Whether a right-hander or a left-hander. And he also has a lot of competitive pitching theories about challenging hitters and feeling confident in your approach. He does an excellent job.

Leo is a taskmaster. He is demanding and at one time a pit bull and at another time a belly laugher. He has extremely high expectations for pitchers and is in their ear on almost every pitch they throw in the bullpen. Now, that varies with the experience of the guy. But he is very, very intense. You only have to look at the records of our pitching staffs over these past 14 years, where we finished in team earned run average to appreciate his contribution.

I haven't always understood Leo's approach, but I keep looking at the statistics. Consider this: We've finished first or second in team ERA twelve of thirteen seasons, 1992 to 2004. That's pitching excellence!

Our pitching staff was hammered by injuries in 2005, but we were nevertheless able to win our 14th consecutive division title. We finished the year with a team ERA of 3.98—good enough for sixth place in the National League.

At season's end Leo decided to leave the Braves and join his longtime friend Sammy Perlozzo, manager of the Baltimore Orioles, as his pitching coach. After 26 years with the Braves organization, 15 of which were spent as our major league pitching coach, Leo felt the opportunity in Baltimore was one he had to take.

So it's the outstanding combination of Bobby's managing of the pitchers, Leo's coaching of the pitchers, mentally and physically, and, finally, the support of our medical staff. That gets broken down into three components. One, Dr. Joe Chandler, who heads up our medical team, has great diagnostic ability with respect to the nature of injuries, the depth of injuries, and the prognosis for cure and recovery. Joe has been a nonpracticing orthopedic surgeon since he ruptured a tendon at the base of his right index finger during a hip replacement operation. He was straining to separate the tendons on a man's hip and they were so strong that he tore that finger tendon, and he permanently lost use of that index finger. It is extended at an odd angle and thus leaves him unable to operate. At my suggestion, he went to surgeons for concert pianists and concert violinists in New York, but they were unable to restore mobility in Joe's finger. He is still a sensational doctor, a real treasure for this organization. I can't sufficiently express how fortunate we are to have him doing his work for us.

Second are our two trainers, Jeff Porter and Jim Lovell—and before them, Dave Pursley, who retired in 2003—who have done and continue to do a remarkable job of keeping our players on the field by their attention to small, nagging problems, by their care of a pitcher who has an injury, and their tireless work with our pitchers to keep their arms healthy and in shape.

And the third component of that medical team is our strength and conditioning coach, Frank Fultz, who has developed pitcher-specific strength and conditioning programs. And those are not all the same. Some are tailored unique to a particular pitcher—the way he likes to work, the way he likes to strengthen his legs, the way he likes to strengthen his back, and, most importantly, how he likes to condition his legs and arm. Whatever the preference, Frank creates these pitcher-specific and individual-specific programs.

So the combination of all that—good, committed, dedicated, talented people, highly motivated—produces what I believe to be the best pitching environment in Major League Baseball.

Then, on top of all that, comes one other very important factor. It is the caliber of the mentality of the pitchers we have wearing our uniform. These guys are talented professionals, and accept their professional responsibility of being part of this grand pitching legacy that has been established here. And they work hard to enhance that legacy. They are willing to commit to it, willing to work at it. It doesn't always come easy, but every pitcher on our Atlanta staff understands that he is part of the Braves' pitching tradition and also part of perpetuating this historic pitching legacy that has been created here. And they take great pride in that. Ultimately, it is the pitchers themselves, and the kind of competitors and the kind of people they are, in conjunction with top-notch staff, that make all this work.

BEFORE I LEAVE THE SUBJECT OF HIRING GOOD PEOPLE, I WANT TO correct one common misconception. Terry Pendleton is commonly credited with being the first free agent I brought on board after coming to Atlanta. Terry was the first free agent *player*.

Actually, my first free agent signing in Atlanta was my assistant GM, Dean Taylor, who had earlier served me in that same role in Kansas City. When I accepted the job and even before I left Kansas City, I called Dean, who was then working in the Commissioner's Office.

I said, "Dean, you won't believe what I'm about to tell you. Are you sitting down?"

"No, but I can be."

"Well, sit down," I said. "I have decided to leave the Kansas City Royals and take a job with another organization." I could hear him gasp.

He said, "You're kidding me! I don't believe that. I know how much you love Kansas City and that organization."

"No, I'm not kidding you. Are you sure you're sitting down?"

"Yes I am."

I said, "You'll never guess who I'm now working for."

"Well, tell me."

"The Atlanta Braves."

There was silence. A pregnant pause.

He was shocked. He knew what the baseball world thought of the Braves at that time.

"You're not serious," he scoffed.

"I am serious," I said, adding: "More shocking and serious than all of that is that I want you to come join me."

"I'll do it."

And he did. Dean came with me as my right-hand man.

Ed Mangan, our excellent groundskeeper, was our second "free agent," then Terry Pendleton.

I hired a new groundskeeper because one of the first things Al Rosen and countless others reminded me was that we had the very worst playing field in the history of professional baseball. A veritable field of screams.

The fellow we had here as groundskeeper was a young guy, Brandon Koehnke, who comes from a groundskeeping family. It wasn't as if I was blaming him. I just knew Ed Mangan, who worked for Boardwalk & Baseball, where the Royals conducted spring training for several years. I knew him to be exceptional. George Toma, the recognized Michelangelo of groundskeepers, would come down to prepare our main field in the spring and Ed became an ally and student of George's. George would praise Ed as the best young groundskeeper he had seen. They now work together in the off-season every year, preparing the Super Bowl and Pro Bowl fields.

I had known Ed and knew his work. When I came here and received the feedback about the playing field at Fulton County Stadium, I wanted Ed to help me fix that piece of the puzzle.

In fairness to Brad, who has gone on to have success as Cleveland's groundskeeper, there were tractor pulls and Motocrosses and football games and marching band contests on the playing field at our ballpark. The poor guy didn't have a chance.

It was important to me to get that playing field in as excellent a condition as we could. Ed did that. He did a remarkable job. He worked his magic then and still does today. Of course it did help that I howled about the tractor pulls and Motocrosses, which began to disappear from the stadium events calendar.

AMONG HIS OTHER ASSETS, ED MANGAN HAS THAT ONE QUALITY THAT I consider so very vital to personal or organizational success.

Enthusiasm.

In the words of Ralph Waldo Emerson, "Nothing great was ever achieved without enthusiasm."

I often utilize two yarns combining baseball lore and some real-life observations when the need arises to illustrate baseball enthusiasm.

First is the home-to-first rundown. This was at the Rookie League level, brand-new professional baseball players, most of them right out of high school. I was in Bluefield, West Virginia, evaluating our aspiring young Orioles. The situation called for a bunt. The hitter knew it. The catcher knew it. The pitcher knew it. People in the stands knew it. The guy selling popcorn knew it. It's a bunt situation.

The young batter drops a perfect bunt, right down the first base line. Anticipating the bunt, the pitcher is off the mound quickly and fields the bunt about halfway between home plate and first base. And the runner stops. The pitcher, in his youthful inexperience, does not turn to throw to first but rather throws to the catcher at home plate. Now the runner is caught in a rundown on the first base line between the pitcher and the catcher, unsure what to do and dancing back and forth. In an effort to avoid the tag, the runner races back to home plate and dives into home plate as the catcher caught the ball from the pitcher. The umpire calls him out.

When I came back to Baltimore, I asked my boss, Lou Gorman, what would have happened if the umpire, swept up by the zaniness of the situation, called him safe? Is that minus one run?

The other example I use was the home-to-dugout rundown. Funny story. Again, this was in another Rookie League game years later, this time in Corning, New York, after I had joined the Royals. Tying run at second base. Line drive base hit to center field. Our center fielder gets a good jump on the ball, catches it, and fires a perfect laser, one hop, to our catcher. The ball and the runner arrive at exactly the same time. In a cloud of dust, the runner goes sliding across the plate as the catcher makes the tag. He thinks. However, the runner thinks he beat the tag and proceeds to the dugout where he takes his seat among his teammates. The umpire makes no sign. The catcher's manager yells: "Go touch him! He didn't touch home plate!"

Now this catcher, who doesn't know many of his own teammates yet, turns to the other dugout and sees twenty-five guys he doesn't know at all. Doesn't know which guy was the runner. So he runs over and starts making his way up the dugout, tagging each player as he goes. The runner, seeing the catcher getting closer to him, suddenly bolts out of the dugout and starts racing toward home plate. Seeing this, the catcher turns and throws the ball to the pitcher, who by now is standing at home plate.

The runner, who doesn't want to get tagged out, stops in the area of the on-deck circle. The pitcher comes running toward him, so he turns and runs back away from the pitcher, who throws the ball back to the catcher, who has emerged from the dugout. They get him in a rundown between home plate and the dugout and finally tag him out.

Keystone Kops, baseball version. Youthful enthusiasm.

I complimented our guys on the rundown play.

It's an enthusiasm story. Nothing great is ever accomplished without enthusiasm, on the baseball field or off.

IF THERE WERE SUCH A THING AS A BASEBALL DICTIONARY AND YOU wanted to illustrate the word "enthusiasm," that would be easy. You just paste in a picture of George Brett, the remarkable star of the Royals during most of my time in Kansas City. If you want more, throw in a shot of Brooks Robinson, the legendary Oriole.

Here are the two guys who have stood out in my mind as people who love the game of baseball, loved being on the baseball field, loved not only playing the game, but practicing the game. I am pleased that George and Brooks remain good friends of mine.

George had a joyful countenance about him. Always. He looked like the young guy who found his most heartfelt and sought-after gift under the Christmas tree that morning, and he looked that way most every day he stepped on the field.

We drafted George in the second round at Kansas City when I was the assistant scouting director. Obviously, he should have been ours or *somebody's* first-round pick.

And Brooks, the human vacuum cleaner—the consummate pro and gentleman.

Here are two Hall of Fame third basemen who exemplified—to the zenith—enthusiasm for what they did.

Not long after I joined the Orioles in 1966 as an office assistant, we had a game scheduled on a rainy day in Baltimore. The game was likely to be rained out. It was one of those midsummer downpours. I was doing my chores, running errands in and out of the clubhouse. I was walking through this labyrinth of hallways in the bowels of old Memorial Stadium. As I neared the dugout, I heard this "thump, thump, thump." I kept following the sound, which led me into the dugout tunnel and out into the empty, soaked dugout.

Rain was pelting down outside on the field and streaming into the dugout. At the far end of the dugout is a guy throwing baseballs up against the concrete wall and backhanding the caroms in a very narrow space between the dugout bench and the steps leading up onto the field. Short-hopping balls was Brooks Robinson.

Brooks Robinson—the human vacuum cleaner enthusiastically honing his skills. (Remember Pablo?)

This was after Brooks had put on that tremendous performance a year earlier against the Dodgers in the 1966 World Series, where he was throwing guys out from the third base coaching box. Here was a guy who was already established as the preeminent defensive third base-man. Ever. Here he was working on his skills, enjoying it, wanting to be out there, wanting to play a game, wanting to be in uniform, want-ing to go make a tough play and win a game.

To this day, if you sat down and talked with Brooks Robinson, you'd know he is one of the nicest, most enthusiastic people you'll ever meet in your life.

I welcomed George Brett to the Royals when he arrived in Billings, Montana, as a seventeen-year-old from El Segundo, California. He was a shortstop who stood at the plate, à la Carl Yastrzemski, with his bat held high in the air, barrel pointed skyward.

That was George Brett, who made himself into a Hall of Famer. He was one of those proverbial guys who could step out of bed in the mid-dle of the winter and hit a line drive on the first pitch he saw, no mat-ter who was pitching.

Etched into my mental George Brett highlights film is that classic blow against Rich "Goose" Gossage in that showdown with the Yan-kees when we finally beat them in a playoff in 1980. He hit a 103-mph fastball up into the third deck in Yankee Stadium. It was just a thrill to watch a guy like that grow and become the kind of incomparable player he became.

He was a leader, but not a vocal guy. Brooksie was not a vocal guy either. But by their enthusiasm, their work ethic, by their everyday de-meanor, by their desire to win, by their coming through in the most tense situations when the game is on the line with a play or a hit or a home run, they were leaders. They embodied on-the-field baseball leadership every day in a professional fashion. Day after day, week after week, month after month, year after year, they did that their entire careers.

The bizarre incident that will forever be a major part of George's legacy occurred on my watch as general manager of the Royals: the fa-mous Pine Tar Incident against the Yankees.

July 24, 1983, Yankee Stadium. George hit a two-run, two-out homer, again off Gossage, the hard-throwing closer, to push us ahead, 5–4, in the top of the ninth inning. But while George was being congratulated by all of his teammates, Yankee manager Billy Martin jogged out to demand that home plate ump Tim McClelland inspect George's bat for having pine tar too far up the handle.

Pine tar is one of several substances the players are allowed to use to obtain a better grip on the bat. There were regulations in place that spoke to the authorized amount of pine tar a player could use on his bat—no farther than eighteen inches from the knob—though it was loosely enforced. In the natural course of things, some of the pine tar will stick to a player's hands or batting gloves, and when he touches other areas of the bat, traces of the pine tar will appear in those areas.

Billy Martin was lying in the weeds all the while waiting for this particular development to occur. He probably sensed that if any Royal was going to hit a home run to win a game it would be George Brett. And when he did, Billy planned to go out, pick up the bat, and have the umpire measure how far up the bat handle the pine tar had migrated.

Well, it all happened just like that. George hit the home run and circled the bases. Our team was euphoric. Here comes Martin out of the dugout. A meeting of all umpires ensued at home plate. The pine tar on George's bat was measured, using the seventeen-inch front edge of home plate as a guide. (Afterward, McClelland announced there was "heavy pine tar" nineteen to twenty inches from the end, "lighter tar" another three to four inches.)

McClelland then took the bat and pointed to our dugout—there are a thousand pictures of this—and gave the "out" sign.

I can remember like it was yesterday, seeing the veins in George's neck exploding, his eyes bulging out of his head, his long blond locks flowing behind him, arms flapping as he charged out of the dugout— and there must be two thousand pictures of that—pushing our manager Dick Howser, coach Rocky Colavito, and others out of the way so he could get to McClelland. I don't think his foot touched the top step of the dugout as he bounded to home plate in two strides, into the face of Tim McClelland, as angry as I've ever seen George Brett protest anything.

By declaring George out, that ended the game with an apparent 4–3 Yankee victory. Dick Howser lodged an official protest. Watching on television back in Kansas City, our assistant director of scouting and player development, Dean Taylor, immediately began researching Rule 1.10(b): "The bat handle, for not more than 18 inches from the end, may be covered or treated with any material of substance to improve the grip. Any such material or substance, which extends past the 18-inch limitation, shall cause the bat to be removed from the game." Dean and I talked about it at length and it was our interpretation of the rule and its genesis that the clear intent of the rule was not to disallow actions created by a pine-tar-violate bat, but rather disallowing the use of such bat *before* the play took place. It was *never* the intent of the drafters of the rule to undo action that had taken place to penalize a player or team.

In crafting our written protest, we also cited Rule 6.06(b), which gives umpires the authority to call a batter out (and eject him) for using a bat that had been altered or tampered with. It specifically lists such alterations and tampering, and pine tar was not mentioned anywhere in the rule. Our protest argued that, based on the language in both rules, the umpires had no authority to call George out.

By the judgment of American League President Lee MacPhail, we were right and he overruled the umpire, noting in his decision that he did so because of McClelland's misinterpretation of the rules and not because of an error in judgment. At that time, it was the first known overturn of an umpire's call that had ever occurred. As a result, there was a clarifying footnote added to Rule 1.10, which specifically states that the batter shall not be called out or ejected for using a bat with pine tar or other allowable substances extending beyond the eighteen-inch limitation.

The Yankees, naturally, were livid. George Steinbrenner was quoted as saying: "I wouldn't want to be Lee MacPhail living in New York!"

We had to reschedule the makeup of that game, resuming from the point of the home run with one out remaining in the top of the ninth. Because we had no remaining games scheduled in New York that season, we had to go back three weeks later on a Monday off day to play out that remaining inning in the eerie setting of a virtually empty Yankee Stadium.

Billy Martin was so perturbed at the ruling, when he came to home plate just before the resumption began, he whipped out some sort of legal paper challenging that no umpire could say they watched George Brett touch every base after he hit the home run.

The umpires brushed it aside. But to demonstrate what a sham the whole thing was in Martin's mind, when the Yankees took the field for the bottom of the ninth, he made a mockery of it by putting pitcher Ron Guidry in center field and left-handed-fielding outfielder Don Mattingly at second base.

The resumption lasted just twelve minutes as our Dan Quisenberry shut down the Yankees in order in the bottom of the ninth, giving us an official 5–4 decision.

It was an interesting experience in my career that got worldwide attention. At the conclusion of that game, we went directly to Baltimore for a series against the Orioles starting the next day. I was on the *Today* show with Bryant Gumbel from a local TV station in Baltimore and also appeared on ABC's *Nightline* with Ted Koppel via satellite hookup from the Cross Keys Inn, where the Royals stayed while in Baltimore. This "sticky" Pine Tar Incident was not only a unique sports item, but a worthy and captivating general news story.

George was such a major part of the good image of the Royals. He was all about winning and positive representation of the club. To this day, he is still part of that staff and does a great job for them. Officially, his title is vice president/baseball operations, but his primary job is to keep being George Brett, which is a most valuable asset for the Royals.

We still talk occasionally. If he's coming to town, he'll call. We bump into each other periodically, most recently at the twentieth anniversary of our 1985 Royals world championship team, and we exchange greetings and catch up.

George was as talented and determined a player as I have ever been directly involved with in baseball. And his talent was a direct result of his effort, of his commitment. A major part of that was born out of his joy and his desire to have fun at being a baseball player—his great enthusiasm.

8

Coping with Baseball Economics and Agents

I DOUBT THERE IS A GENERAL MANAGER OF *ANYTHING* WHO has to deal with change more than a baseball general manager. From free agency to arbitration and, in my case in Atlanta, from a $100 million-plus player payroll down to an $80 million payroll, we have had to manage change effectively.

This has become such a significant issue in baseball that I began making presentations on managing change to businesses in and around Atlanta. In it I discuss the issues of understanding change, getting comfortable with change, not rejecting it out of hand, but learning about it, working with it, and embracing it.

Perhaps the best way of coping with change is to be as fortunate as I have been to have key personnel in your organization with the Chipper Jones Attitude.

Larry Wayne "Chipper" Jones, Jr., as you likely know, is our star third baseman and highest-paid player on the Braves. Since 1995, when he moved up to our major league roster, Chipper literally has been the face of our franchise, for a number of very important reasons.

First, he quickly established himself as an All-Star-caliber player and became an almost perennial third base fixture on the All-Star roster. He was the player who got the big hit for us, hit a late-inning home run, or made the sparkling defensive play to save a game. He has great, youthful enthusiasm that rubbed off in a very positive way not only on our team, but throughout our community. He became the face of our team because of his stellar performances, exceptional skills, and his leadership by example and production, not only to the local and national media, but also in the eyes of our fans.

To this day when you see youngsters wearing Braves hats and Braves T-shirts being interviewed and asked who their favorite player is, inevitably their answer is Chipper Jones. He *still* is the face of our franchise. And deservedly so.

Chipper demonstrated very early on that he not only had exceptional skills, but uncommon baseball instincts. Bobby Dews, our veteran bullpen coach, managed our Rookie League team in Bradenton, Florida, back in the summer of 1990 when Chipper was a teenager just weeks out of high school.

In the ninth inning of a game in which his team trailed, Chipper was on first with one out. Respecting Chipper's speed, the opposing first baseman held him close to the bag and was in perfect position when the batter hit a sharp, one-hop grounder just inside the bag—a made-to-order double play ball to end the game. Instantly anticipating that the first baseman would step on first—thus taking off the force play—and throw to second, Chipper faked three quick steps and, just as the first baseman fired to second and yelled, "Tag!" Chipper casually returned safely to first.

Bobby Dews was startled by the impressive move. "You don't see this kind of instinct in the Rookie League," Bobby recounted. "In my entire baseball career, I'd only seen the play twice before. Once by Mickey Mantle and once by Pete Rose."

Not only has he been an All-Star-caliber player, but one of the most productive switch-hitters in the history of the game. He has often played through pain when bothered by injuries. He has the respect of his teammates, plays hard, and has been a tremendous contributor to our record-setting string of division championships. Chipper has been the cornerstone. He cares about winning. He is a fierce competitor.

Next, he always has a strong interest in the well-being of this team, as demonstrated a number of times in conversations I have had with him. When it becomes apparent that we're making deals or when we have an obvious need on the team, Chipper will come to me privately in the clubhouse, in the dugout, or out on the field and ask me what we are doing about this, or how we are handling that. He has a real abiding interest in seeing our team and our organization succeed.

He certainly demonstrated that in capital letters a few years ago when we were trying to strengthen our team's defense. We had to make a change to improve our defense and Chipper assisted us greatly in the process by his willingness to relinquish his third base job. Because of his injuries, he wasn't the same caliber of third baseman he had been in the past. We had a chance to sign free agent Vinny Castilla, who was an exceptional defensive third baseman, as well as a dangerous hitter. In order to do that, we had to move Chipper from third base. But before I could go to him, Chipper actually came to me and said, "Vinny is a better third baseman. Go get him and I'll move to the outfield."

Here is a guy who had been a perennial All-Star third baseman who took the attitude, "The Braves winning is more important than my playing third base, so I'll give that up for the good of the team and go to left field."

In his very first play in left field that next spring training, Chipper threw out a runner at home plate.

He went on to play well in the outfield for two-plus seasons and continued to hit well. Unfortunately, during the 2004 season, Chipper then suffered some leg injuries that severely affected his ability to play the outfield. He let it be known that he felt he needed to come back to third base, not for his own personal preference, but simply because of his legs. We also felt he would be more productive there. And when he moved back to third base during the last half of that season, his game actually elevated and he was a key in helping us win our division again. After the All-Star break, Chipper drove in 62 runs and hit .337 in August as we surged into the division lead en route to our 13th straight division title.

He has had so many big at-bats, game-winning hits, carrying the team on his shoulders for a game, or a week, or a month. He's done so much of that for so long, it would be tough for me to single out just one instance of excellence on the field. Off the field, a couple instantly come to mind.

In the spring of 2005, we were trying to stretch our budget and reorganize our payout schedules to find a way to sign a long-term contract with pitcher Tim Hudson, to make that very significant acquisition even more meaningful by keeping him with the team for several seasons. Chipper, without any prompting or without any inquiry from us, volunteered to discuss a restructuring of his contract where we would have more spendable cash to accommodate Tim Hudson on our payroll.

In an interview with Braves beat writer David O'Brien, Chipper intimated he would be willing to defer some of his salary over the remainder of his contract if that would help get Tim Hudson signed to a long-term extension. "I've made my money," Chipper was quoted. "I want to win and I want to continue to keep this team competitive as long as I play here. If I have to make sacrifices here and there so that we can bring guys in or keep guys, I'm open to it."

I called Chipper and told him I saw his comments in the paper that morning. I said that I knew those comments were born of his abiding concern for this team, as everything he did always is. Chipper has always tried to do what is best for this team and this organization.

But I also let him know those comments might not be as helpful to the Hudson situation as he thought they might be. I further explained that it can be harmful to the process. If an agent thinks there is more money out there because our star player with the biggest contract is willing to restructure his deal, that could stall any progress in negotiations.

It's quite unlikely that a player is going to give any of his money back. He might defer a small portion to a later year, but that only creates a new budget dilemma for that later year.

The point, though, is that Chipper was willing to do something. He went public with his good intentions and I spoke to him about how much we appreciated his concerns but also how problematic a comment like that could be, despite his best of intentions.

Chipper understood.

The reality, as I stated at the time, is I don't know of another instance where adjusting an existing contract of a third-party player was the answer to a substantial negotiating difference.

After talking with Chipper, I called his agent, B. B. Abbott, an attorney who was a high school classmate of Chipper's in Florida. B.B. picked up the phone and, before I could speak, said, "John, I know why you're calling." I told him I just wanted him to know that I had talked with Chipper about what I read in the paper.

"I understand your concern and we understand it very well," he said.

Two weeks later, I had another conversation with B. B. Abbott just before the start of camp. I knew he was going to visit with some of our minor league players that he represents and told him, "When you're in camp, let's just sit down and try to pin down what we're talking about specifically with regard to this general offer of contract reconstruction. But understand that this would be totally unrelated to the Hudson negotiations."

When we talked at Disney, B.B. told me: "Chipper has complete respect and confidence in you and Bobby and wants to finish his career as a Brave, not anywhere else." Chipper is signed through 2006, plus two option years that vest with 450 plate appearances or All-Star selection (thus assuring he stays healthy and productive).

His offer to help with the Hudson deal was just another example of a team player who always has demonstrated his concern for the organization, always cared about this team, and is willing to put his actions behind his words. Indeed, in the winter of 2005 he did restructure his contract, allowing us greater payroll flexibility and helping to assure he'll be a Brave for the rest of his career.

LIKE CHIPPER, JOHN SMOLTZ IS ANOTHER PLAYER BLESSED WITH THAT wonderful leadership/winner attitude.

For the last several years there was considerable attention and debate on the issue of whether John should remain as a closer or go back to being a starter, much of which was fueled by comments John made about his desire to return to the starting rotation. I decided the best way to deal with this was for him and I to talk it through, face-to-face, alone. So I arranged a lunch with him the first week of December 2004, at McCormick & Schmick's restaurant at the CNN Center. We slid into a private booth with a curtain that could be drawn to avoid interruptions.

John offered this opener: "I believe I could be far more valuable to the Atlanta Braves if I am back in the starting rotation. As I sat in the bullpen these last several years watching our team not often getting to the position where the closer was needed and essential to our winning in postseason play, the frustration began to build in me and I had ever-growing confidence that being a starter is what I would be able to do best and contribute most to this team."

I said, "John, we would love to have you as a closer and we'd love to have you as a starter. In fact, if we could find a way to clone John Smoltz that would solve all of our issues."

He laughed and I added that he was excellent in both roles and that I knew if he were in the starting role again he would handle it in excellent fashion. I told him Bobby and I have great confidence in that.

"I am at peace with this entire issue," he said. "I know in my heart what I could be best at for this team. I know how I would contribute best to the Braves in 2005. But if you choose to keep me as a closer,

I'm okay with that. I'm not demanding to start. I'm not kicking up a fuss over starting. My point is I just want you to know in my heart how strongly I feel about how much more valuable I would be to the organization."

"John," I said, "you couldn't be much more valuable than to be the Rolaids Closer of the Year."

John was adamant. "I think I can. I really think I can."

Bobby Cox and I had discussed the matter. But after that lunch I was convinced that John was right. Moving him back into the starting rotation was the right thing to do. But we could only do that if we could obtain a quality closer to take his place in the bullpen.

A week later, we made the deal with Milwaukee to acquire Dan Kolb, who had been an All-Star closer and had 60 saves for the Brewers during the previous two seasons. That allowed us to confidently move John back into the starting rotation.

I also knew in my heart it was the right thing to do. I was so convinced it was the right thing to do that in our discussions with the Brewers for this All-Star closer, we were willing to give up one of the highly regarded fine young arms in our system, Jose Capellan. That got the deal done.

So we were able, with a high level of confidence at that time, to realign our pitching staff with John as the bell cow of our starting staff.

During this luncheon, we were so intent in our discussion—Smoltz's eyes burning into me with great intensity and mine back at him—we were unaware that a famous person was drawing a lot of attention to the table just outside our booth. When the waitress pulled back the curtain to serve our meals, John and I recognized what we were sure was the familiar face of former Soviet premier Mikhail Gorbachev sitting just a few feet away. Later, it was confirmed to us that Gorbachev indeed was in town that day to address an awards dinner for Green Cross, an international environment organization that he founded. But in truth, Gorbachev's presence, while surprising and interesting, didn't alter the seriousness or focus of our conversation.

To move John out of the closer's role in which he had been so effective and to gamble that he could once again be an effective starter at age thirty-eight—especially after several arm operations—set off the peanut gallery. Most every "expert" opined that we were flat-out nuts. Considerable debate ensued, the second-guessers having a field day at our expense. I would bet that even Gorbachev had an opinion on the matter, although he probably would have preferred John be a "lefty."

Even before the 2005 All-Star break, John let the air out of the debate and rendered the Critics Choir deathly silent. Despite some rotten luck in the early season when our sputtering offense provided two or fewer runs in seven of John's first 10 starts and Kolb blew two saves in consecutive Smoltz starts, John was 9-5 with a strong 2.81 ERA. He had pitched well enough as a recycled starter to have 12 or 13 wins by that point.

Fueled by his strong will and his intense competitive spirit, John had returned as the ace of our starting pitching staff. And although the demands of the regular rotation began to take a physical toll, his season-ending stats were still quite remarkable: 14-7, with a 3.06 ERA. With a sore shoulder, he recorded our lone playoff victory over Houston on pure grit.

But like Chipper, John's willingness to do whatever we thought best for the team—that true, selfless *winning* attitude—is a godsend to any GM faced with managing change effectively.

Here's another revealing glimpse at what a stand-up team leader John Smoltz is for us. Each spring, we host a presentation by a rep from the Baseball Assistance Team (BAT), an organization managed out of the Commissioner's Office that maintains a charitable fund to assist ex-players who have fallen on hard times. At one end of our clubhouse at Disney's Wide World of Sports prior to the 2005 season, a BAT representative made the annual appeal to our players for payroll-deduction commitments to the program. He had placed a sign-up form in each player's locker. His talk was sad and profound as he detailed some of the daunting stories of several players' circumstances. At the end of the presentation, there was this extended silence. The room stood still. Nothing was happening.

But then John Smoltz got up and walked to his locker at the other side of the clubhouse, picked up the form and returned to the table in front of the BAT rep. He filled out the paperwork, listed a sum to be taken out of each paycheck, signed it, and handed it over. Catcher Johnny Estrada, our player rep, then grabbed his form and followed suit. There was a rustle in the clubhouse as many of the other players also followed, pulling the form out of their lockers and signing up to be included.

To me, this was an example of John not only taking a leadership role, but also understanding the full power and impact of his leadership. He knew by initiating that action, others would follow. And they did.

IN BASEBALL, CHANGES HAVE COME IN A MULTITUDE OF WAYS: THE explosion of media coverage, enhanced fan comfort and facilities, computerization of the industry, dealing with performance-enhancing substances, and many other areas. But the most pronounced and dramatic change in baseball has been the evolution of our dysfunctional salary system and its impact on baseball economics.

It's a flawed system that feeds off the successful, accomplished egos of businessmen who have put together magnificent, successful business ventures. I'm referring to owners who have amassed fortunes and find themselves in a system that compels them—or attracts and motivates them—to spend wildly. Some have big airplanes, big boats, big successful businesses, and sometimes big egos, and they want to have a big, winning team—no matter the cost!

It happened with the Marlins, who admittedly overspent for a championship in Miami in 1997 with a stratospheric payroll. More recently, the Texas Rangers signed the biggest player contract in baseball history when they bought Alex Rodriguez for $252 million. It is a classic mistake of emotional decision making which has happened to many teams and owners. We are all vulnerable in this crazy system.

And quite often, they wake up one day and exclaim, "Whoa! What did I just do?" Wayne Huizenga no doubt said that to himself. He determined that his Marlins were not a sound business operation and began dumping high-salaried players like crazy once he had won a World Series.

From recent accounts, the Rangers also pulled back the reins to where their talented baseball staff, using good, solid baseball decisions, have begun to operate on the basis of spending what makes sense. Not millions more.

Wow! What a unique economic concept! Spend only what you earn!

People who write about, or talk about, this "unique" economic concept typically focus only on some notion that these owners simply have an obligation to put a winner on the field at any and all costs. They have an obligation, so the mantra goes, to do whatever it takes to put a winning team on the field. Forget about how many millions of dollars these owners lose. That's not important. Most often, these are the opinions of individuals who've never managed anything.

Operating economics may not be important to the talkers and writers, but it is very important to the people earning, spending, and losing the money.

Wayne Huizenga and other owners weren't alone in being drawn into that skewed thinking. Many other bright and extremely successful businessmen were attracted by baseball's appeal and then trapped in its bizarre economics and have suffered severe Monday morning economic hangovers.

The Atlanta Braves experienced a similar situation, gradually pushing our payroll past $100 million. We ultimately decided that double-digit red-number losses each year for the operation of this baseball team, no matter how good we were, didn't make sense. It was economic stupidity. We've chosen *not* to participate in baseball's economic stupidity any longer.

So we reduced our payroll by more than $20 million.

As a prelude to our dramatic cutback to the $80 million payroll level in 2004, it wasn't like there were simply whispers of concern about the money we were losing. There were actual meetings at the corporate level to discuss the issue. Like any good company, ours knew about the loss level and the bottom line. The feeling was: *Let's bring this thing into a more sensible range of cost management.*

This wasn't something that ownership and team management were at odds over. We all agreed it was wrong to continue paying players money we didn't have. It was a unanimous opinion that we were not acting in a very brilliant business fashion by continuing to lose upward of $10–$20 million more than we made simply to fund player salaries. The decision was made to cut our payroll to $80 million. A year earlier, then-president Stan Kasten advised that it was going to happen. Unfortunately, our attendance was dropping from previous remarkable highs of over three million down to 2.3 million, so our revenue still didn't match our costs.

Stan's heads-up was sort of a severe weather advisory. Except this was a severe financial advisory, blowing our way.

He had knowledge of how adamant our company was going to be in making these reasonable and intelligent changes. He was telling me, get ready. After all those financial adjustments were made and we still won the division in 2004, Stan told me he was convinced it was the best off-season I ever had as a GM. He admitted that he, too, didn't think there was any way we could lose all these quality players and still put a championship team on the field. "And you did that," Stan said over lunch one day early in 2005. "I'm convinced. I'm never going to bet against you. If you did that last year, you'll probably do it again this year ['05]."

Stan left the company in 2003 and Terry McGuirk assumed the Braves' chairmanship and presidency. Terry has been an executive with the company for a long time. When Time Warner sold off the NBA Hawks and NHL Thrashers, teams for which Stan was also president, the company and Stan felt there was no reason for Stan to stay in a job where so much of his responsibilities were gone. So Terry had his responsibilities altered to include the presidency and chairmanship of the Braves.

Stan has gone on to explore other sports and business opportunities.

The key challenge for the baseball general manager is understanding how to do this job in an environment where giant contracts, the players union, agents, salary arbitration, and media intrusion have become increasingly more powerful, and sometimes *oppressive,* factors.

From 1985 to 2005 the economic change has been dramatic. In '85, when we won the World Series in Kansas City, we didn't have a single player making more than $1 million. Our highest-paid player was George Brett, whose salary was precisely that.

Now, only the raw rookies make less than $1 million. The *average* major league salary in 2005 was $2.64 million.

Dealing with player agents was dramatically different in my early GM years because neither one of us had out-of-balance clout. There were player agents doing the bidding on behalf of these players, who themselves were not experienced or prepared to do it. That was understandable.

But because of the unique nature of baseball business, owners who were flush with cash could dramatically raise the bar on salaries, which affected all of us. We don't negotiate player contracts in a vacuum. There is always a measure of comparability, whether signing a free agent or one of your own players. That system of comparability can either force you to pay a player a salary you can't afford or, worse, have to trade or release that player.

The conversations with agents in those earlier days were, for the most part, civil and reasonable with regard to the financial parameters we were working within. But as the salaries began to escalate dramatically, agents became more aggressive and some even arrogant.

There was no stopping a system that combined free agency and arbitration, the double-edged sword, the runaway train of financial gain for players. Charlie Finley, the irascible and iconoclastic former Oakland A's owner, said providing both free agency and arbitration was "the stupidest thing baseball would ever do."

What I know from practical experience, from negotiating contracts, it is a system that completely works to the benefit of the player and the agent. I am amused that some of them are regarded as "super-agents" who are viewed as special and accomplished. Agents know—and those I talked to more often in the early days would acknowledge—the way you become a successful agent in this system is simply to learn how to say the word "no" and continue saying it.

When the bidding clubs with more money started getting more aggressive and signing the players they wanted at any price, all agents had to do was somehow convince an interested club that one of the big spenders was after their client and the offers kept increasing. The impact on other player contracts became obvious. We work in a competitive environment, in a business where competition drives us all. Believe me, the agents and the union know this and use it well.

Most new owners come into the game with saddlebags full of money that they earned from other businesses. They applied hard work and intellect in their enterprises where good business paradigms existed. Enterprises where people who invested their capital actually could make a profit. They came into baseball, easy targets for the agents to play off the egos of these successful businessmen who brought their same business aggressiveness and competitiveness to baseball. Early on, many owners didn't consider or concern themselves with the long-term impact of signing outrageous contracts. Now, most do, but not all.

It all began with a 1975 arbitration case tried in Kansas City, presided over by independent arbitrator Peter Seitz. He ruled, based on language that had been in Major League Baseball's uniform player contract for decades, that players became free agents after playing for their clubs for just two seasons. The blame goes to whoever wrote the contract language clause, which provided that "the Club shall have the right by written notice to the Player . . . to renew this contract for the period of one year on the same terms . . ."

After the Supreme Court rejected its claim for free agency under the antitrust laws in *Flood v. Kuhn,* the players union filed a grievance on behalf of pitchers Andy Messersmith of the Los Angeles Dodgers and Dave McNally of the Montreal Expos, both of whom had played one season under their clubs' renewal and declined to sign a contract for the 1975 season. Union chief Marvin Miller argued that since the players' clubs only had the right to renew their 1974 contracts for the period of one year, both players, who were not signatory to a 1975 contract, became free agents upon the conclusion of the 1975 season. Seitz agreed and as a result of his ruling, Major League Baseball was forced to negotiate with the union to establish some period of time at the end of each contract that the clubs could reserve the player contracts.

Don Fehr and his brother Steve Fehr, then Kansas City lawyers, assisted the union in the case. Miller was so impressed with Don Fehr, he was later hired as general counsel for the union and eventually Don succeeded Miller as head of the union, a position he still holds today.

Until then, baseball's reserve clause effectively bound a player to a club in perpetuity. But it was the carelessly worded clause in the uniform player contract that created the one-year loophole that the union seized upon. The wording had not taken into account the possibility that a player would play through the club-imposed extra season without signing a new contract. Thirty years later we're still trying to plug the dike that oversight created.

That arbitration case started free agency as we now know it. Salary arbitration, the other side of the players' double-barreled shotgun, had already been utilized by baseball to resolve individual salary disputes with more senior players. But now the Seitz ruling provided the union and agents with the lethal combination of arbitration and free agency. In free agency, a limited group of experienced players with substantial major league service time can command very high salaries. In salary arbitration, younger players with less major league service time can use these free agent salaries to support demands for their own large salary increases. This combination set up this whole troubling financial environment in which we find ourselves. It was a seminal milepost in baseball history.

Managing change effectively is challenging enough. Factor in aggressive organizational or ownership agendas, naturally competitive spirits, and a dysfunctional economic system and it often becomes nearly impossible.

AFTER THAT MONUMENTAL RULING, THE SYSTEM THAT EVOLVED BEGAN to widen the competitive gulf between the large- and small-market teams. I, of course, was in one of the latter in Kansas City. The frustration of being at that disadvantage boiled over in an interview that I did in 1983 with a writer in Jacksonville. I expressed my feelings about how, at the very least, challenging, and at worst, impossible it was to do battle with the Yankees and their payroll. It wasn't just about making good baseball decisions, good judgments, and getting the best talent, I fumed, it was about how much money you had in your saddlebags to spend. We didn't have a fair chance. It was an uneven playing field.

I likened it to a shootout on the main street of an old Western town. Here were the smaller-market teams getting ready to face off against the Yankees, as the characterization of the big spenders. They, of course, were the biggest and still are. Imagine if you could, I said, the small-market teams likened to a little freckle-faced kid with a big straw hat pulling out his popgun. At the far end, dressed in black with a big hat and two giant six-shooters, were the Yankees, more than ready to duel.

George Steinbrenner sent me a letter, with that article attached, saying if I felt the system was unfair and I wanted to complain about it, he understood. However, he thought it was equally unfair that I would single out the Yankees and characterize his operation as the sole reason for baseball's economic disparity issues.

I responded by saying, "You know what, George, you're right. In my zeal to make my point, I singled you out and that might not have been appropriate." My point in the interview was there is this great disparity. In my response to George—in a firm but respectful fashion—I said it wasn't meant to single him out. It was meant to make a point. It was made to draw as stark a comparison as I could to express this sham of competitive equity. The very uneven playing field. The one that existed then and still does today.

"My efforts to characterize the problems we all face in our business, especially those of us in smaller markets, should have been more broad-based and not as personal," I wrote. "You have my word that when the frustrations of a small-market general manager bubble over in the future, they will deal in generalities . . . and not with personalities."

He seemed to appreciate that. He appreciated that I was willing to respond in that fashion. And we've enjoyed a respectful relationship ever since.

In fact, I have been honored by a number of complimentary letters from him during the ensuing years of our championship runs.

I had another chance to rebut George seven years after that first exchange. In late 1990, after Ewing Kauffman had sold his company, Marion Laboratories, to a large conglomerate, he was prepared to use part of these proceeds in the pursuit of a couple of significant free agents. George responded with a public claim that this new aggressive attitude by the Royals debunked the old large market/small market competitive disparity. I wrote to George, strongly pointing out his fractured logic, noting that he knew the funds had come from the sale of Mr. K's company, not baseball earnings.

"More importantly," I wrote, "the great game of baseball has been enhanced and has benefited tremendously from the involvement and presence of Mr. Kauffman. . . . While I admitted my [1983] comments were inappropriate, they don't hold a candle to the inappropriateness of your comments about Mr. Kauffman. I made my apology. Now it's your turn."

THE FACTS ARE, THOSE FREE AGENT SIGNINGS IN 1983 BY THE ROYALS were funded by self-made money outside baseball that artificially pumped up the modest financial capabilities of that small-market team.

But over the years, the system has grown to the point where the average baseball player's salary is well over $2 million per year, and continues to be driven upward by deals approved or initiated by these very successful owners. They bring with them a desire to win—including winning in negotiations, which means getting the player they want at any cost. The agents know that, so they just keep driving the numbers up. They keep using the agents' magic word: "No."

However, I'm not blaming any individual owners, team presidents, or GMs because purely and simply it's the *system* that causes that to happen. Several organizations continue to spend more money than their baseball teams' economics would allow, or what their baseball operations rightly afford them to spend simply because of our responsibility and pressure to compete. Too many owners believe they can apply that same competitive drive from their outside business ventures, that same negotiating ego, that same winner's pride and business sensibility to baseball. How wrong they are.

Joining this competitive free spending to drive baseball salaries upward was the other terrible twin—salary arbitration. It's part of the double-barreled shotgun of salary escalation.

Players can compare themselves not only to others in their class of service, but one class ahead. Let's say a player becomes a free agent and gets $10 million a year. Now another player, who is in his fifth year in the majors and thus not a free agent yet, but has had production similar to that of the $10 million player, can stand before the arbitrator and rightly compare himself to that player.

What has made this especially challenging for us in Atlanta and many other franchises to compete for top-quality players in this fractured system is that we don't operate with a blank checkbook any longer. Nor, thankfully, do we have an owner eager to say, "Look what All-Star I was able to sign!"

That's not a criticism of Time Warner, which owns the Braves, or any other sensibly run franchise. To the contrary, I agree with and embrace our operating philosophy.

In the early '90s during spring training, when Ted Turner still owned the team, we were negotiating a multiyear, guaranteed contract with Jeff Blauser, our starting shortstop. The media were aware of these negotiations and in an interview I said something like, "Yeah, we'd like to sign Jeff Blauser. We have a lot of interest in him. He's an important guy for us. But the fact of the matter is we've got to operate this club sensibly and we do have a budget that we have to work with."

The next evening in my room at the PGA Marriott in West Palm Beach, I received a call from Ted.

"Hey, John! This is Ted. How you doing, John?"

"Great, Ted. How are you?"

"Hey, great job! Way to go. Keep doing a good job. (Pause) John, what's this shit I read about a *budget?* You wanna sign Jeff Blauser, sign him!"

That was the owner of the club! He was getting on me about posturing about a budget, which I felt was the right thing to do, letting the agents and the world know through the media that we have a budget and are going to operate within that budget.

I told Stan Kasten, president of the Braves at the time, about that call and we laughed like crazy. That's just classic Ted. A great owner and boss—shooting from the hip.

Since the ownership of our team was transferred from Ted to Time Warner in 1996, my line of communication to the owners is no longer as direct. Now my direct reporting is to Braves chairman and president Terry McGuirk. Any matters regarding our team that need to be communicated to ownership is done by Terry. We talk often, if not daily, and communicate effectively.

That's how we've continued to communicate in Atlanta after we reduced our 2004 payroll by more than $20 million and still won 96 games, our 13th consecutive division championship, and won our division by 10 games. This in spite of being written off by every pundit in the world.

Well, this is finally the end of the Braves' run. Such was the cry of the media.

Just as before, the core of how we operate, make decisions, evaluate, and construct our roster is the traditional baseball model. We rely on aggressive, intuitive scouting, sound scouting judgment, and knowledge of a player's ability, as well as knowledge of a player's makeup and character. We've always relied on those core traditional baseball values and did so again in the construction of our roster in the winter of 2003 and again in the winter of 2004.

We headed into the 2005 season operating again with an $80 million payroll. Over the past few years, we lost players of the caliber of Greg Maddux, Tom Glavine, Gary Sheffield, Javy Lopez, Kevin Millwood, Jared Wright, and Russ Ortiz. These are quality people that we had to excuse from our organization, or who chose to leave as free agents, because we could not begin to accommodate the kind of salaries they could now command in baseball's crazed economic market.

It's a system where there is no correlation between player salaries and the club's ability to generate income. It's only how much a team or an owner is willing to spend to construct that particular team. It's usually a feast for the players and the agents. An absolute feast. They know it. They can't deny it. It's an easy system for them to get rich.

MY MANAGEMENT STYLE HAS ALWAYS BEEN ONE THAT CONFIDENTLY delegates responsibility and authority to people who work with me. Eventually it evolved into my practice of talking directly to agents on a very limited basis. Frank Wren, my assistant, has the day-to-day contact with agents and does most of the contract negotiations for players on our roster based on the parameters we've established as an organization.

However, on the multiyear, multimillion-dollar obligations we make for the company, I still get directly involved.

In my earlier days as a baseball GM, I dealt with agents on every contract for every level of player. The high school or college draftees, raw major league rookies, and the potential free agents. I negotiated and did arbitration cases, all of it. But as the preparations to negotiate contracts became more challenging and time-consuming due to their escalating value and financial impact, I found it more effective to have someone else dedicate the hours, days, and weeks required to research and prepare to negotiate with the agents.

That person for a long time was Dean Taylor, my assistant at Kansas City and, until 1999, in Atlanta. Dean is now assistant GM for the Cincinnati Reds and at one time was the general manager of the Milwaukee Brewers. Since 1999, Frank has taken on that responsibility for me in Atlanta.

Now we have a full cadre of staff who get involved in information gathering, statistical analysis, and so forth so that we know that our proposed number is valid, well researched, and appropriate for a particular player and our overall team payroll.

Even before the negotiations begin in the case of a free agent signing or an acquisition by trade, we thoroughly engage in determining a player's character, ability, and how well he matches the needs of our team and many other factors before we get to the point where we decide this is the player we want to offer a contract.

As noted earlier, before this age of specialization, I had professional relationships with agents that were open and somewhat friendly. I had congenial relationships with many of them while I was in Kansas City and in my early days in Atlanta. As I've grown older, I've become more cynical and more bothered by this whole economic madness that has engulfed baseball, and the influence this system allows agents to have on our game.

There are usually a few markets each year where the teams make more money than any of the other teams, or where new owners have come in with fresh money in their pockets and are prepared to spend it, sometimes wildly. The so-called super-agents line up to take advantage of this situation. And they often have.

I don't have any desire any longer to deal with agents any more than necessary. I've determined that my having a slightly less-than-chilly relationship with them might be counterproductive. But I understand that Frank—and Dean before him—must interact with agents. They cannot be complete adversaries. They have to have some level of collegial and congenial relationships with agents because they are on the front lines, having to deal with them almost daily. Some believe you should foster a more affable relationship with agents to give you the best chance of signing their players.

Agents are just doing their job. I understand that. And they are merely taking advantage of the flawed system that is in place. A bad system. A dysfunctional system that inures to the benefit of players and their agents.

Agents play the system. Some have played the system so extensively they've gotten cocky and pompous simply because they represent these talented professional athletes.

My old boss, Stan Kasten, a lawyer by training, frequently makes a popular, one-hour presentation to law schools on the subject of sports agents. He begins the lecture by asking for a show of hands by those law students who think they might want to become sports agents. He says a number of hands go up. Then he spends the next hour telling them horror stories about unethical agent behavior and puts up a quadrant chart with "HONESTY" across the top and "COMPE-TENCE" down the right-hand side. In the lower left quadrant, he scatters a number of dots representing agents who are least honest and least competent. "Naturally, we hate those, right?" he'll say as the students nod. "We all hate people who are both dishonest and incompetent." Same for the adjacent quadrants with dots for those agents who are either honest, but incompetent, or competent but dishonest.

The remaining quadrant is for agents who are both honest and competent. "Yes, there are agents in this box. In fact, there are more that go here than the other boxes," Stan will announce, furiously dotting the remaining box. Then he further surprises them by arguing that we should disdain this group even more, because they are the most successful in siphoning money out of baseball or football or whatever the sport. He explains that everyone involved in baseball makes a positive contribution to the sport, whether it's the player, the sportswriter, the usher, the parking attendant, or the person who cleans the bathrooms. Only the agent takes money out and runs up the costs for everyone else while adding nothing to the sport.

Stan concludes the lecture by asking for another show of hands of agent wannabes. Rarely do any hands go up.

I go back to my early days as a general manager. I had a friendly relationship with some agents. Ron Shapiro in Baltimore, for one. I even consulted with Ron regarding a personal business matter.

Another agent with whom I shared a friendly relationship is Alan Hendricks, from Houston. But not Alan's brother, Randy, believe me.

The three of us were sitting in my hotel room in West Palm Beach negotiating Ryan Klesko's contract. By then, I had negotiated contracts for nine years in Kansas City and several more in Atlanta, and had developed, through other lawyers and various people representing us, certain contract language that we routinely used. It covers things like guaranteed payments, when the contract becomes un-guaranteed, how it transfers from guaranteed to un-guaranteed, the kinds of acts that a player can't do, the list of prohibited physical activities, his civil comportment, his moral character, and so on.

I told Randy and Alan, "If we're gong to pay this kind of money, we're going to have our guaranteed language in the contract."

Randy instantly became huffy and obnoxious. "That's what happens," he sneered, "when people try to act like lawyers who aren't."

I thought that was uncalled-for, unprofessional, pompous—classic Randy.

The veins on my neck popped out and I tersely excused the two agents from my room.

I'll paraphrase it.

"Get the hell out. This meeting is over."

That's the G-rated version.

I remember that moment like it was yesterday. I got so mad that if a fight had broken out it wouldn't have been surprising.

Ultimately, we got the Klesko deal done—a multiyear deal for about $5 million a year—but I don't deal with Randy anymore. I still talk to Alan. We've made a lot of deals and talk occasionally. He'll call most every year and go over the list of players he represents, either sixth-year free agents or major league free agents. We'll go through them quickly and I'll make a comment about one guy or make a smart-ass comment about another guy and he'll laugh and I'll laugh. We still maintain a professional relationship.

From time to time, in our early years, Alan and I would enjoy an evening drink at the Adam's Mark Hotel across from Royals Stadium in Kansas City and assorted other watering holes around the country. We don't do that anymore just because of the way GM-agent relationships have evolved for me.

I like Alan. There's a humorous story that underscores agent-think and what our player contract system is like. At Kansas City we had a right-handed pitcher named Keith Creel, a good guy from Texas, who was represented by Alan. Keith was a marginal kind of player who had just staggered through an awful year for us. As we were negotiating, I began reciting all of these statistics that reflected very badly on his client and making the case that he should be paid much less than what they were asking.

One of the great comments ever made to me by an agent—which

really pinpoints how this system works on their behalf no matter what the circumstances—came tumbling out of Alan's mouth: "Spare me the fucking stats."

Now, what should contracts and raises be based on if not performance stats? But when they don't work or benefit the player and his agent, their view is, *"Spare me the fucking stats."*

To this day, when I talk to Alan, we laugh about that. It was one of the great, revealing comments of all time by an agent.

When agents are in that situation, they only want to talk about how many years their player has played, how many innings he's pitched. Not how many times opposing teams lit him up like a Christmas tree, or how many times he walked the bases full, or that his earned run average looks like the national deficit. None of that. All that becomes irrelevant.

Let's not kid ourselves. Agents are the adversary. They are not our friends. I understand the need for people who deal with agents on a daily basis to have some level of civility, so they can do their jobs. But, again, we must never lose sight of the fact that agents are not our friends. Their job is to take as much money from our organization as they possibly can for every player they represent.

THE LAST TIME I NEGOTIATED A CONTRACT WITHOUT AN AGENT BEING involved was when Andruw Jones signed his current contract. Andruw, who is represented by Scott Boras, came to me in the last year of his previous contract and said he wanted to continue as a Brave. He knew Boras would take him out as a free agent. Andruw knew that was Scott's plan, as it is with virtually all of his big clients. Andruw did not want that.

We originally signed Andruw out of Curaçao as a young sixteen-year-old. We have been his baseball family since he put on a professional baseball uniform. He has a feeling of comfort with and loyalty to this organization.

When he came to me late in that 2001 season, he said, "John, I want to negotiate a long-term contract. I want to stay a Brave."

I told him that was great and expressed that I was glad to know he was making decisions on his own, but that he had an agent and it was and is my operating policy not to circumvent an agent. I said he needed to call Scott to say he intended to do this.

Andruw's response?

"That doesn't bother me," said Andruw. "He works for me. I don't work for him."

Stop the presses!

This was shocking. Refreshing.

A few weeks passed and on November 2, I was playing golf at the Golf Club of Georgia with Nick Trigony, the former president of Cox Broadcasting, and another friend, Mike Franke. I remember that I had just striped a pure drive on the narrow dogleg 11th hole. I don't usually have my cell phone on during golf, but Andruw and I had talked back and forth in the preceding few days and I didn't want to miss him if he tried to reach me. The phone vibrated and it was Andruw, calling from Curaçao. He said, "I want to get this done. I want to meet with you. Can I bring my dad in?"

"Absolutely. Bring him in. I'd be delighted."

I had already come to know his father, Henry Jones, when he came to watch Andruw play in his minor league days. A wonderful guy.

Henry served as our guide several years ago when my wife, Karen, and I were invited by our Curaçao scout, Giovanni Viczaise, and some local political leaders to visit the island, which is in the Caribbean just north of Venezuela.

It was late December and we stayed at a beautiful resort on the beach and spent a wonderful week traveling through the countryside, snorkeling, and visiting some historic buildings. We were taken by the beauty of the place, the gorgeous water, the soft breezes, the tranquillity of it. And the stark contrast of the highly developed capital city of

Willemstad and the raw, undeveloped, almost farmland-like country-side of Curaçao.

I had met Henry on several occasions, of course, but it was on this trip I came to know and truly admire him. Henry is a sensational man, a gentleman who is interested in his son's well-being. He's a great force in Andruw's personal and baseball development.

Henry himself played competitive baseball until he was fifty. He was an athlete and, in fact, when we were about to sign Andruw to a contract, we did the usual thing of sending a scout in there to see him throw and hit. Our scout wanted to clock him in the 60-yard dash and Henry wanted to participate in the race.

"For him to get out there and run against me was a huge thing to me," says Andruw, picking up the story. "I idolize Henry. He wanted to be in the race because he always had pushed me, motivated me. Who jumped higher. Who did this better, who did that better. We used to go to the beaches and go snorkeling and see who could go deeper. He always challenged me in anything."

Remember, Henry was nearly fifty that day, Andruw sixteen.

Andruw won the race. But not by much.

THE CONTRACT MEETING WAS SET FOR MONDAY, NOVEMBER 12, IN MY office at Turner Field. Henry and Andruw sat on the couch and we began to talk. Just the three of us.

From my personal notes on that meeting: "After exchanging some general ideas about contracts, we began talking about Andruw's desire to remain with the Braves and his strong feelings about not needing to be the highest-paid player ever on the Braves and not wanting a 'Jeter-type contract.'" Derek Jeter had just signed a ten-year Yankees contract for $189 million—baseball's all-time highest at the time.

I was prepared to negotiate and knew what we felt we could do. I explained that we would be willing to discuss a six-year extension at somewhere around $12 million per year. I explained why we thought those were the right terms. I gave him the comparables and talked about other players' salaries and about the parameters of our organization and what we could do. We had an honest, straightforward discussion of the issues.

Henry and Andruw asked for a chance to talk privately. I invited them to stay right there and I walked out of the office. A very short time later—maybe ten minutes—the door opened and Andruw asked my executive assistant, Melissa Stone, to have me come back in.

Andruw's father asked if we would be willing to do a $75 million deal for six years. Their counterproposal. I said we'd do that, but would have to structure it this way: a six-year contract through 2007, starting at $9.5 million the first year and progressing to $13.5 million in '07, plus a $3 million signing bonus. Which was slightly higher than we felt we wanted to go, but still something we could do that wouldn't cripple our overall projections. Besides, at that time, Andruw, just twenty-four years old, was being viewed as an enduring star for at least the next decade and was fresh off of a season in which he had 34 home runs and led the team with 104 runs batted in for the second year in a row. And no one knew where this crazy economic system was headed.

We shook hands. Deal done.

Again, from my notes: "Andruw said he would call and advise his agent of his decision. He and his father expressed their great appreciation and thankfulness for the Braves." Something that, sadly, doesn't happen very often in this day and age.

The following day, November 13, I spoke with Andruw in the clubhouse prior to a media gathering to announce the hiring of Terry Pendleton as our hitting coach. Andruw assured me once again that his signing was exactly what he wanted to do and he didn't care what anyone else felt or said about it. And he further said, "I want to sign the contract today."

Much later, Andruw confirmed my suspicions that he had caught flak from his agent and union officials for negotiating the contract on his own. "Yeah, they were calling me and saying I should not have done that, and all that stuff," he reflected. "The union, saying it was not right and I should have had my agent there. Right after that my agent called. He was not mad, but he was saying I should have just told him what I wanted and he would have gone in there to do it for me. But it was something that I wanted to do and just did it."

I think his instincts were accurate.

I contend that if Andruw had given his agent those very same desired terms, it wouldn't have gotten done. Boras would somehow have created a negotiating impasse between Andruw and the Braves and shrugged his shoulders to Andruw that they would simply have to go the free agent route to maximize their leverage.

We expedited preparation of the contract and he signed it in my office. He said—and I wrote this down—"I couldn't imagine playing for anyone else. The Braves gave me my chance to play professional baseball. I want to stay with the Braves."

Not once in this process did I have a conversation with Scott Boras. We did talk afterward. When Frank Wren and I initially met with Scott on July 23 of that year about re-signing Andruw, it was clear from that exchange that it was going to be difficult if not impossible to get Andruw signed with Scott.

My assumption is that Scott shared all of that with Andruw, because on July 25, Andruw approached me in the clubhouse after a game, asking questions about that meeting with Scott. In that conversation he expressed a desire to get a new contract done because of his upcoming wedding. He wanted to make plans for that and build a house in Atlanta. And he wanted to do it especially if we could get the contract done soon.

In that conversation, it was clear to us that he hadn't been made aware of the spring training talk we had with Boras about the kind of contract we would be willing to do for Andruw. Which was somewhere south of Chipper Jones's contract. I told him we'd talk at the end of the year.

I discuss the signing of Andruw Jones in great detail because I think it is historically significant. It was one of the very few times in modern-day baseball—who knows, maybe the last time ever—that a star-caliber player directly negotiated his own contract. He received a lucrative, fair deal to remain with his team and organization, to play in the town where he wanted to stay and without all the angst and posturing of either free agency, arbitration, or hard-line negotiations.

I can't remember the last time I dealt with a player without an agent. Even guys in the minor leagues have agents now. Most of the high draft choices have agents while they are still in college, some even in high school. They won't admit it, of course.

The old joke is when you go in to negotiate with a high school senior or college junior and you see the shoes sticking out from under the living room drapes, it's the "family advisor." Well, that's a lot of BS. It's an agent. And everybody knows it. And the NCAA, with respect to high school baseball players, has been willing to turn its back on that, and refuses to acknowledge that a player who is negotiating his contract and is being "counseled" by this "family advisor" in reality has an agent. They get away with it and lose no eligibility.

WE WEREN'T AS SUCCESSFUL WHEN WE TRIED TO SIGN ANOTHER BORAS star player the next year. The Braves jumped into the A-Rod Derby when superstar shortstop Alex Rodriguez left Seattle to test the free agent market. We wanted Alex and developed what we felt was about as generous an offer as we could possibly fit into our payroll parameters.

With Alex and Scott seated on the couch in my office, I looked Alex square in the eyes, said we wanted him on our team and offered a ten-year deal for $12 million a year. To be exact, the total contract package, with signing bonus and what-have-you, was worth $126 million.

Scott laughed at it and said we simply didn't "get it." He said that's why he needed to speak directly with owners. "They get it," he sniffed.

Well, we "got it" all right. Scott's request/demand for a no-trade provision and additional unique perks, combined with the exorbitant financial terms, were simply unacceptable.

As it turned out, our $126 million turned out to be exactly one-half of what he eventually signed for with the Texas Rangers. The Rangers had obviously been convinced that they had to offer much more. Ultimately, the Rangers signed Alex to a $252 million contract.

It was later determined by investigative baseball writers that our offer of $126 million, remarkably, was the next-highest offer. Another case where an agent bypassed knowledgeable baseball people and got to an owner. And he *really* "got it."

John Hart, the GM of the Rangers at that time, is a close friend. But John and I couldn't, and wouldn't, talk about our offers. That's collusion. You are not allowed to talk to another club during negotiations. It's not only against baseball's laws, it's against the labor laws of the United States. Management representatives in a competitive economic environment cannot talk to another company—or, in sports, another team— about what they've contemplated, what they've offered, what they've talked about. Can't do it.

But agents talk among themselves and with the union, sharing negotiating information all the time. That's allowed! What a system!

9

Crisis Management:
Rocker, Furcal, et al.

Earlier, I likened the responsibilities of a major league GM to a conductor of an orchestra as well as being the final filter in the decision-making process. Primarily, that characterization is regarding information and recommendations made by our baseball operations staff with respect to player acquisition.

Another characterization I would offer is this: Field General of Crisis Management.

During the winter prior to the start of each year we create a blueprint for our upcoming season. We establish our clear goals, map out our course to reach those goals, and communicate to our baseball staff the level of commitment we all must have to be successful.

Despite this thorough planning process and our overriding confidence in it, we must also be prepared for the possibility of potholes, roadblocks, obstacles, and even major crises confronting our mission. As the GM during these unexpected, challenging developments, I must serve as the "crisis management leader."

First, by displaying strength and confidence in our ability to confront these circumstances in a calm and confident fashion—void of displayed panic no matter how damaging the situation. Next, by communicating to our involved staff in a clear, precise, and confident manner how we will confront the issue and work to repair it.

Once this is accomplished, we tackle the situation head-on, constantly reminding our staff of the supreme level of confidence we have in our collective ability to resolve it in a most positive fashion.

In 1980, before I became GM in Kansas City, catcher Darrell Porter became involved with drugs and was sent, as part of his attempted recovery, to a rehabilitation facility in Arizona. As a result of my involvement in this process, I became a central figure in a well-intended idea that unfortunately worked in a way opposite to what we had expected.

Joe Burke was our GM when Darrell was sent to the Arizona facility. In the meeting we had to discuss this challenging situation, he said, "I think it would be a good idea for you to go to this facility during family week." Family week usually takes place at the end of a person's rehabilitation program and is designed to enlist others in support of the recovering addict.

Joe believed this would give me a better understanding of the problem and understanding of what friends, loved ones, and companies should know about this problem. Then, if Darrell has a need to discuss the issues, he would know that there is someone on the staff who understands his issues and challenges that he could confide in.

So I participated in this rehab program for one week. It was one of the most emotionally gut-wrenching, unbelievable experiences I've ever encountered. I sat in the classes, attended the lectures, went to the dining hall. I joined with members of Darrell's family in these very intense, personal, and raw moments when they all were talking from the gut and depths of their souls about their emotions. It was extremely unsettling.

It was as if I were watching a surgical procedure where they're opening up a body and digging into the soul, opening up the brain and digging into the psyche. I'm there watching it, listening to it, feeling it. It was very emotional for me. In one part of my brain, it was intellectually stimulating, while in the other part of my brain it was personally very uncomfortable.

The week ended and I participated in the graduation as a family member of someone who had attended the program. Darrell was there for four weeks and I was there only for the final week. I had become friendly with a lot of people in the class and some of the therapists and counselors. They presented me with a symbolic medallion that signifies you understand your weaknesses as a human being, understand the obligation you have to be strong, and the need you have to rely on God's help and guidance in your journey of recovery.

The medallion is a universal symbol, half of a coin with a flat edge, signifying that we humans are just one piece of the whole and we should always understand that we need balance.

They also invited me to speak. It was a humbling experience. I thanked Darrell and his family for allowing me to be a part of this with them. I expressed my appreciation to the staff for the good work they were doing, and how impressed and honored I was to be able to see their dedicated professionalism firsthand, and offered my support and best wishes to every graduate.

During the week I was there, I played catch with Darrell almost every day. He used his catcher's mitt and I was still a young enough guy with decent athleticism and arm. In my view, that was probably the greatest value of my being out there. It was therapeutic for Darrell. I could almost tell that a different countenance would overtake him when we played catch. His shoulders would relax, his eyes would sparkle, and a faint smile crossed his lips.

The whole experience was gripping. I grew and learned things about life that I hadn't known at that point. But the reason I was sent there—so I could become a confidant to Darrell—actually had a different outcome.

I had always had a good relationship with Darrell, who was by nature kind of a quiet and private guy. After I spent that week with him, he saw me not as the person to put an arm around and take over to the corner and share something. Rather he saw me instead as the guy who looked into his soul in those very private and revealing moments at the rehab center. He saw me as the guy who learned of the dysfunction that had occurred in his life. He looked at me as the guy who saw his inadequacies as a human being.

While we all have inadequacies, he saw me as the one who knew his too well. I had been invited behind the curtain. I had seen too much. I'd gone to a place where most bosses don't have a right to be.

Sadly, it was as if the good relationship that Darrell and I once had was sealed off—gone forever.

When Darrell returned from rehab, there was a stunning and heart-warming example of how the entire community of Kansas City forgave Darrell for his transgressions and welcomed him back. Just about every tree in Kansas City had a yellow ribbon tied around it to welcome Darrell home. They treated and supported him like a fallen hero, not a drug addict. They loved him for the way he played and smiled and for his contribution to our team and his courage to fight this addiction.

The good people of Kansas City said, in effect, Okay, this guy stumbled and fell. He made a horrible mistake. We don't endorse it and we don't like it because that's not the way we live. But we are also willing to forgive him and give him our support. We're going to provide him an environment in which he can recover.

Darrell did, in fact, reclaim his playing career and was the World Series MVP in 1982. For two decades, during and after his time as an active player, he was a role model of the highest order. Then around the year 2000, he became addicted again, this time to alcohol.

In 2002, some twenty-two years after I shared that emotional week with him in that Arizona detox center, sadly, Darrell Porter died of a heart problem that was attributed to his drug and alcohol abuse.

So, yes, I have been confronted with a number of team management or crisis management situations where various decisions had to be made, leadership exercised, and plans of action put in place. Sadly, a few of those have been downright gut-wrenching and personal.

AS CRISES GO, I CAN'T IMAGINE ONE ANY MORE UNUSUAL OR AS DIS-tracting for our entire organization, top to bottom, than the one that visited us Christmas 1999. What came down our chimney two days early was a public relations nightmare of the first order. That was the day *Sports Illustrated* hit the stands with its infamous profile of John Rocker, our flamboyant and blossoming closer.

In the piece, he said many terrible and damaging things about other people—comments that are completely counter to my personal beliefs and the beliefs of this organization. So I wondered how I was going to be able to manage this particular crisis. John Rocker might have said these things on his own and they might have been his words, but, un-fortunately, he was in effect wearing our organization name across his chest when he spoke.

Big John Rocker, from Macon, Georgia. Had an arm like a cannon and a head like a cannonball.

Rocker was quoted extensively in the piece, spewing vitriol at all New Yorkers and just about every minority and ethnic group on the planet. John's scattergun attack hardly spared anyone. He intimated he would retire before playing for a New York team. "Imagine having to take the 7 train to [Shea Stadium] looking like you're in Beirut next to some kid with purple hair, next to some queer with AIDS, right next to some dude who got out of jail for the fourth time, right next to some 20-year-old mom with four kids." The biggest thing John didn't like about New York, he said, was "all the foreigners. . . . How the hell did they get in this country?"

The reaction was instant and widespread, severely calling into ques-tion not only John's IQ, but the temerity of the entire Atlanta Braves organization for employing such a societal misfit. Overnight, this be-came Public Opinion Issue No. 1 in America.

Here was a guy like Man Mountain Dean, built with a tiny waist, broad shoulders, triangular muscular body, thick neck. A tremendous talent, John came flying through our farm system and burst into the Show with a bang. One of the first games, if not the first game, he pitched in Atlanta, the Cubs' Mark Grace was the hitter and Rocker was throwing 100 mph-plus. His first pitch was right at the earhole of Mark's batting helmet. It seemed as if all of Grace's body parts became disconnected. The helmet went one way, the bat went another, one foot that way, the other leg this way, one arm went down, the other arm went up. Down on his back with a crash went Grace, barely managing to avoid this shoulder-fired rocket streaking for his head.

How that ball didn't hit him in the head is one of the marvels of modern physics. But, neither did Mark hit the next three bastard curveballs that Rocker threw. Game over. No chance. "Bastard curveball" is one of several names in baseball for a virtually unhittable curve that breaks so sharply it qualifies as yet another marvel of physics. Yakker. Bowel-locker. Yellow hammer. Take your pick.

John Rocker was dominating. What a career he had before him!

Then came the fateful magazine interview.

Initially, as John shared with me, this interview, ostensibly, was going to be a personality piece about John's life off the field. It became a ripe opportunity for this particular sportswriter, Jeff Pearlman, to have an entrée to this colorful personality and, while there, write anything and everything John said. Whether John was irritated at the way a driver in front of him was driving. Whether he was agitated that the toll booth arm was slow in lifting. Whatever it was. John laid his soul bare to this guy not consciously, but through his obscenity-laced natural actions and reactions. John went on to talk about his view of the now infamous No. 7 train in New York and denigrated the people who ride that subway train and in that city. He verbally mowed down everyone—immigrants, gays, unwed mothers, welfare recipients, you name it. Bad stuff.

It set off a major public explosion. I, as the general manager, and Stan Kasten, as the president, quickly became consumed in damage control. We began by calling Rocker in for a meeting at the stadium the week between Christmas and New Year's.

We started out having him confirm that he had, indeed, said the things that were attributed to him in the magazine piece. Stan's theory was that John had embraced a niche, like outrageous basketball player Dennis Rodman did for a few years. John already was being booed at Shea Stadium after thumbing his nose at New Yorkers while handling the Mets in the '99 playoffs. We advanced, four games to two, over the Mets, who managed just one unearned run against John in that series. Racing in from the bullpen in his flamboyant, snorting style, John appeared in all six games, recording nine strikeouts, two saves, and dissed the Mets fans throughout. Thus, John stamped himself as "Mr. Anti–New York City." You can't buy publicity like that, Stan reasoned, and to the rest of America it's cool that you're Mr. Anti–New York. But if that was what John was indeed trying to do, he rode it off the rails. Just went way, way off the tracks.

Stan tried to make John see the problem from Stan's own personal perspective as a New York child of two Holocaust survivors, both of whose families were put to death during the war. "You can't teach me about racism," Stan told him. "We all grow up understanding what the Statue of Liberty is about—'give me your tired, your poor, your huddled masses.' When you talk about all these bleeping immigrants, do you think you were descended from Adam, who was born in South Georgia? C'mon! You're talking about my parents and probably your great-grandparents!"

We did the civics lesson. We explained that we represent an important company in America, an important communications company. We work hard at our image. We are very civic-minded and do good things in the community. Now virtually all of that had been wiped out by John's rant.

We also assured him we felt he wasn't a racist at heart. We knew he had been a good teammate all through the minors with players of every background. We knew some of our African-American players had even stayed at his home and had dinner with his family in Macon. But now, we told him, we had to figure a way to mitigate this mess he had created.

By then, we had talked nearly an hour and, for the first time, he seemed to appreciate what we were up against and what we were trying to do on his behalf.

"When I walked in here," he said, "I thought you guys were coming to bury me."

There were plenty who would have volunteered for that honor, believe me. Their names were on a stack of little pink telephone message slips that grew by the hour. We were trying to help. This was a young guy who was a dominant closer, who we thought would be dominant for years. As a baseball player, we certainly valued him highly. This was precisely my predicament. As a pitcher, this guy was a superior talent. On the other hand, I had equally strong concerns whether this guy was any longer right for our team and franchise.

It was important that our organization address this issue and yet we still had to do our business. We knew John was a big-time player who could help our team. That was also very important. It was challenging to deal with the community pressure and still do what had to be done for our franchise and our team.

Commissioner Bud Selig and our club jointly banned Rocker from spring training and suspended him for the first month of the regular season. The penalty was reduced to fourteen days by an arbitrator after the players union appealed the suspension. Just before reporting for spring training, John penned an apology to his teammates and fans that ran on the front page of the Atlanta paper. On his first day at spring camp, two months after the *SI* article appeared, we held a press conference in the field house next to our ballpark at Disney World, attended by dozens of national baseball writers. The bleachers were packed with members of the print and electronic media. John took no questions and instead read a statement, which wasn't judged to be very heartfelt because it was believed by many to have been written by his agents, the Hendricks brothers.

Back in Atlanta, Stan and I met at least once a week with some offended group—whether it was the gay and lesbian coalition, black preachers of Atlanta, Asian-American coalition—all of the groups offended by John's comments. Each group wanted to let us know on an ongoing basis how they felt about what he said. We had to continually explain to them that, yes, this guy worked for us, but we don't tell him how to think. We don't tell people what to say. We don't tell people how candid to be in the presence of a writer who might want to advantage himself on your words, although we have had media experts speak to our team from time to time on this issue.

But the fact of the matter is that John said these things. The Atlanta Braves didn't say them. It was real damage control that we had to manage.

Besides, we, too, were deeply offended by what Rocker said. As good citizens of the world and people who live in this multicultural city and work in the multicultural business of baseball, we were aghast.

John was irritated, agitated, and angry by the fact that some guy with a tape recorder took advantage of his trust. The writer led John to believe he merely wanted to spend a day with him and see what life was like with a wild left-handed relief pitcher.

But in our view, that fact didn't excuse the words that John spoke, which were a reflection of how he felt. If you are a professional athlete, you should have at least the minimum intellectual capacity to understand what is appropriate to say and not to say in any scenario, whether a guy tells you one thing about an interview and sets you up for something entirely different.

Also, if you truly have those thoughts, if you feel that way about people, then sooner or later they are going to come out. There was no victimization in terms of John Rocker. He made a horrible, horrible judgment that reflected on him so badly that people decided this is a horrible man.

Making it worse, John was not truly contrite about it, but instead was focused on what he considered the betrayal by the writer. John obviously believed those shocking things he said, and he—and *we*—had to suffer the consequences. There were threats of protests and boycotts of our games, by virtually every kind of activist group of any stripe. Everyone was calling for his head. They didn't just want his release or trade; they wanted him eliminated.

That spring, we hired the Cook Ross Group, a consulting company from Washington, D.C., that specializes in cultural diversity to help us through this difficult circumstance. My brother Jerry, who does work in this field, recommended them to me. On their staff was Mike Singletary, the very admirable former NFL linebacker and Hall of Famer, who came to Disney to speak to our team and our staff on the matter of diversity sensitivity. Mike is a well-known, highly regarded, highly respected athlete who really gets your attention when he speaks.

People who were there for Mike's presentation—staffers and players—were impressed by Mike and by the message he brought. He could relate as a black athlete. He had lived with this whole racial tension thing when he played. He understood it. But he also expanded the topic to more than just racial diversity to include *human* diversity. It was all about working with and understanding people, especially in the sports environment where you must depend on diverse teammates to help you succeed.

One of the several issues that came out of all this, in addition to heightening our organizational awareness of diversity, was to make us aware that perhaps there were some reasons for John to have said the things he said and to have shown the hostility he displayed. And we should look into that. So we began to discuss that internally, not as it related to that one incident or that one player, but as it might relate to other issues and players. It definitely opened our eyes and made us more conscious of the need to ask, Why did this happen? How can we prevent it from happening again by enlightening our players and ourselves? With our diversity planning and education, we believed we could.

There was a notable relationship that was a glowing by-product of that diversity training. Pitcher Terry Mulholland and infielder Bobby Bonilla sat next to each other when we were having those seminars in Orlando. And to hear them tell it, it was a marvelous epiphany. They had played against each other for a decade or more and despised each other, because of what other people told them about each other and what they thought of each other from afar. That spring training was the first time they had been teammates.

As a result of some of the drills and some of the structured activities that our players did as part of that diversity training program, Terry and Bobby Bo communicated and interacted like never before. They discovered how likable each was and how wrong it was for them to have had the opinions they harbored of each other. It was a wonderfully warm and poignant development that came out of this difficult and detestable situation involving John Rocker.

Otherwise, that was a trying time for us. It required not only managing technical or economic change in our industry, but managing perception changes of an organization that had been built into a classic, proud, dignified championship entity. We were determined that all of our fans in Atlanta be assured we were taking this problem seriously and dealing with it.

As an organization, we were getting unfairly criticized because we happened to be John's employer. That same thing doesn't always happen when a guy who works for IBM has a DUI. Or an individual who works for Xerox is cuffed for tax evasion. The story is not written about IBM or Xerox or whatever the company may be. However, with a professional sports team, there is that joined-at-the-hip perception/connection. Because the Braves didn't release John Rocker by nightfall, many people were angry as hell at the Braves.

There were people who wanted his head on a platter the next day.

And probably still do. But their anger at him was somehow quickly redirected to us because he happened to be our employee.

A significant challenge of managing crisis and leadership in this particular issue was dealing with the broader problem of the community agitation. Dealing with the sociological issues. Hey, we're baseball executives. We're sports executives. We're not sociologists. We're not psychologists. We're not philosophers. We're not social workers.

But we had to become all of those because we had the responsibility to serve in those capacities as we were trying to deal with the very legitimate anger and emotional circumstances of the people John offended. We had to show them that we did have a legitimate concern for the abuse they felt they suffered. And we did think what he said was inappropriate and wrong, no matter what the reason, or what the circumstances around his allowing himself to say it.

We had a responsibility to help manage the emotions of our community, on behalf of our organization.

One of the things we did was to invite a representative of each of the offended groups to a lengthy meeting in our large conference room at Turner Field. It came to be known as the "Big 12 Meeting" for the approximate number of groups represented. We informed John he would have to attend the meeting and face these people. His first reaction was that he would sit in for five minutes or so but we told him that wouldn't suffice. He would have to sit in there and be contrite while he listened to the hurt and anger of each group.

We assuaged the Big 12 reps and assured them we were equally offended by what John had said. But after all of this reaching out and subsequent damage control, Stan and I knew that in our heart of hearts, we would have to get rid of John Rocker.

Shortly after the story broke, we also had a session with several of our star players who live in Atlanta year-round. They met with me and Stan in our smaller conference room off Stan's office.

They were upset by the firestorm Rocker had created and were clearly fine with our trading him. He was a young hotheaded guy. That didn't work in our kind of clubhouse. They didn't want the team hurt and they felt it was important that John be contrite and do everything he needed to do to correct the record. If he needed to take sensitivity training, then that's what he should do. He definitely needed something. They were completely fed up with his antics.

This whole incident made our clubhouse unsettled for a long time. When John found his way back into the clubhouse after the suspensions, the environment there was edgy and chilly. Every time John stepped into the locker room, the temperature dropped 20 degrees.

Our players were still his teammates so some were more supportive of him than others, though not many. All of them had now been drawn into this controversy and had to answer questions about John Rocker's words everywhere they went, and that was irritating. They felt like they were walking on eggshells when John was among them.

Even worse, we already had a real intense rivalry going with the Mets, but it had been a respectful rivalry. Thanks in large part to John, it had taken on a bizarre and ugly aura. Our locker room isn't that kind of locker room. Bobby Cox's teams treat opponents like professionals, with respect—while trying to kick their butts.

That season, we weren't scheduled into New York to play the Mets in Shea Stadium until June 30, so this wasn't going to go away until then. It was an intense six months, the worst we had had, with piles of letters still streaming into our offices from both sides of the issue every day.

When we did go into New York that first time, the Commissioner's Office took the lead on handling security. Kevin Hallinan, the security director for Major League Baseball, did a really great job. We also carried our own security personnel on every trip we took thereafter for the duration of that season. Occasionally, we still do that, but only on a selected basis.

I'll be honest: I had more than a little trepidation about going back into Shea Stadium. The prior October, my wife and I practically had to wear hard hats during playoff games there. We had beer poured on us and gum thrown at us way before John Rocker spoke a word about New York. The visiting GM and club executives sit out in the stands during playoff games. In the regular season, a suite up in the press box is provided to us that is not as accessible to rowdy fans who decide they want to scream profanity at you or throw things at you. In the post-season, we sit in the stands, and we're open targets.

The environment in that ballpark has often been pretty testy. But nothing like the Return of Rocker.

The fans threw everything at him—bottles, batteries, golf balls, you name it. It was a very dicey situation. Some teammates and coaches tried to make light of the situation. Pitching coach Leo Mazzone would joke about the dangers of going out to the mound to confer with Rocker. During one of those Shea games, Leo mused to Chipper Jones: "Look, if he gets in trouble, you go talk to him. I ain't coming out there."

At the hotel we had extremely heightened security. We had extraordinary police protection there and as we traveled by bus to the stadium. There was obviously extra police protection at the stadium. Rocker took on the aura of a professional wrestler. That's how it all seemed. He was cast in the role of John the Redneck.

The whole Rocker controversy was unsettling and, as Bobby Cox noted, a monumental hindrance to the workplace. Rocker was having an effect on a lot of people, not only on the team but all around us. Even in other cities, we had to have special security for him, taking him in squad cars to the hotels and the ballparks and then getting him up into the hotel through freight elevators.

We managed our way through it, letting everyone vent at us. Not fun. Not easy. But we got through it somehow. In fact, that summer, the *Wall Street Journal* ran a long story complimenting us on how we managed our organization through this crisis.

But ultimately, as I mentioned, for the good of the team, we had to move Rocker. We needed to restore order in our clubhouse. So we traded him to Cleveland.

I truly thought in another environment, he might get a new lease on life and could relax and be the natural pitcher he once was and have success again. I didn't think that would ever happen in Atlanta. There were too many raw edges here. Too many emotional scars. It would have been impossible for him to succeed here again.

John Hart, then GM of the Cleveland Indians, thought like me: that Rocker could be successful again in a totally different environment. I told John Hart that I believed this player had problems that were not fixable in Atlanta, but were fixable elsewhere. After the trade, Rocker had decent productivity in Cleveland for a while. But it was obvious the weight of this issue continued to grow and have an impact on him. Then, in addition, he developed physical problems and eventually had to have elbow surgery.

You can't be an effective baseball player at any level if your mind is not at ease. That's true especially for professional athletes, who are in a highly intense environment. You must have your senses and wits about you, and have complete control and command of them or you're not going to succeed. And Rocker didn't have that control anymore. Every day he was fighting through the agitation and aggravation, all of which was self-afflicted. It had become impossible for him to take the mound and be a successful pitcher.

In reality, this applies to any profession. You can't be a schoolteacher or a house painter or a truck driver or a stockbroker and do it well, or as well as you had done it before, if your mind is tied in knots. If your brain is not at ease.

Certainly, John's wasn't during this tumultuous time in his life. And in these trying times in the life of this organization, we, too, had to deal with the tumult.

Flash-forward to the winter following the 2004 season. John Rocker pitched in winter ball without a contract and Joe Sambito, who had become John's agent, called around to teams fishing for interest. He called my assistant, Frank Wren, who relayed the message to me. I told him to tell Joe thanks, but no thanks.

Actually, it was Leo Mazzone, our pitching coach, who called me first. John asked Leo to help him with his delivery. Leo did, was impressed with the way John was throwing, and called me. "I think we can fix him," Leo ventured.

"Leo," I said, "you can fix him, but it will have to be for someone else. It won't be for us. We just can't do that anymore. It simply won't work here."

I just knew it would create some level of discomfort both in the clubhouse and in the community. That is the reality of the situation and I always try to manage the circumstances around reality. Having John Rocker return would not have been good for our team, so we simply were not going to do it.

FOUR YEARS AFTER *L'AFFAIRE ROCKER* WE HAD ANOTHER CRISIS THAT, though not quite as national in scope, had some of the same aspects of heartfelt, but unwarranted blame being heaped upon the Atlanta Braves for the actions of a player.

Rafael Furcal, our exceptional young shortstop, was stopped by police for driving erratically one evening during the final month of the 2004 season. When an officer administered a Breathalyzer, it was determined that Furcal was driving while under the influence. It was his second DUI arrest within four years, which put him in violation a number of ways, including driving without a valid license.

We were called and made aware of the situation. It was devastating to us to learn a key member of the team and a guy who was being relied upon for the team's success was now entwined in a personal circumstance that was embarrassing to him and the organization. We didn't know what was going to happen. We didn't know if we were going to have Raffy available to us in the postseason. He was already in jail. Was he going to stay in jail?

As part of our preparation for our course in this particular crisis, I made a call to Frank Coonelly in the Commissioner's Office and asked what latitude we had, if any, with respect to discipline from a club standpoint. I was told, quite frankly, we had none. While this matter was still in the courts, double jeopardy is not allowed. We were told we didn't have the authority to discipline, based on our labor relations agreement. The Braves were absolutely prohibited from initiating any club penalty until the issue was fully adjudicated by the courts.

In the legal proceedings, Raffy was represented by a lawyer named Bubba Head, a nationally renowned DUI attorney. The judge convicted Furcal, but made a ruling that, in essence, delayed his penalty of jail time, mandatory rehab program, and community service time until *after* we were no longer involved in postseason play. Raffy would have to report to the Cobb County Jail and begin his incarceration immediately after the Braves' season ended, either through elimination or ultimate victory in the World Series.

Understandably, there was some public outcry against the judge and even against the Braves for this accommodation. But the truth is, we didn't have a thing to do with it. We didn't make any request of the court to go easy on Raffy. We were simply his employer, and we were ready to abide by the judge's ruling.

Furcal was penalized severely by the court—and we thought properly so.

After Furcal was initially released from jail the day after his arrest, he arrived at the ballpark around four o'clock. What we did in an effort to "manage" this crisis was conduct a meeting with him in Bobby Cox's office in the clubhouse. We had a game, but Raffy was not going to play because he had been in jail overnight.

Bobby sat in for part of the meeting because I wanted to have a witness to what I said. Bobby had already met with him and told him how sorry he was that this had happened. He wanted Raffy to know he was part of our "family" and that we would do all we could to help him and support him through this tough time. Good managers and caring organizations do that for their people.

At the same time I was offering our organizational support, I also had to make crystal clear our deep disappointment. I explained to him how embarrassing his actions were not only for him and his family back in the Dominican Republic, but for our great organization as well. "This classy, highly respected Atlanta Braves organization is now tainted by the fact," I said, "that we have one of our star players arrested for a DUI not for the first time, but for a *second* time." I went on further to say that he should know that the federal laws of this land, with the new immigration guidelines as a result of 9/11, put his career in great peril. His ability to get into this country to continue to pursue his baseball career would be in serious jeopardy if this should happen one more time. His actions were disappointing and inexcusable.

As I was told, the federal laws decree that if someone is an immigrant and has not become a citizen—which Raffy had not—and is on a work visa and broke the law, he could be deported and never allowed back in the United States again.

That would make it real tough for him to play shortstop for the Atlanta Braves.

Unlike Rocker, Raffy was thoroughly and genuinely contrite. Apologetic and remorseful. And to his credit, from the time he entered jail to this day, to my knowledge, he has followed the judgment of the court, did his twenty-one-day jail time when he got up at five o'clock in the morning and worked in the jail's laundry room, did his community service, and went to his mandatory rehab meetings. Even when he went back to the Dominican that winter, he would fly to Atlanta every Monday to attend his rehab classes.

Although his penalty was delayed during our participation in the first round of the playoffs against Houston, Raffy was basically on house arrest. He was required to use a portable, sophisticated Breathalyzer that transmitted the test results and personal ID verification from Houston back to the police in Atlanta. It became the duty of my assistant GM, Frank Wren, to oversee this procedure.

The device, about the size of a portable typewriter, features a video phone and a tube into which the subject blows his breath. The recorded data and images are then transmitted by a special phone connection to a control center. The gadget didn't work through the hotel's switch-board, so we had installed a separate line to his hotel room.

Before we departed for Houston, Raffy had hit a walk-off, game-winning home run as we defeated the Astros, 4–2, in extra innings of Game 2 in Atlanta. That squared the series at a game apiece and we were off to Houston for the next two games. But within hours after his dramatic home run, Raffy was in his hotel room in Houston, with Frank helping to administer that long-distance Breathalyzer test at about midnight. They called in, followed the voice prompts, then Raffy blew into the tube as a photo was transmitted to verify that he was the person taking the test. He had been warned that if he tested positive—even from alcohol traces from mouthwash or other products—he would immediately go to jail.

At 2:00 A.M., just as Frank was going to sleep, he received a call from Raffy's probation officer in Atlanta. Big problem. The test had not been received. As it turned out, the special phone line had been wired wrong and the machine didn't function properly. Raffy had only a half-hour to report to a Houston police station to perform a conven-tional Breathalyzer test. A Houston police officer working with MLB picked up Frank and Raffy and quickly took them downtown to a holding tank for the test, which Raffy passed.

Phone technicians solved the problem with the phone line in Raffy's room. So for the next two games, he had just one hour after the final out to return to his room and take another long-distance test. The system randomly called the device outside of the hours we were at the stadium and when it rang, Raffy had to be the one to answer it.

When they returned to the hotel in the middle of that first night Frank recalled walking back into the hotel at 4:00 A.M. "Raffy couldn't have apologized more profusely to me. 'I'm so sorry I put you through all this,' he said. He was great," Frank said. "I was proud of him for the way he handled it and appreciated that he understood how he affected everyone in our organization."

Hopefully, Raffy has now finally learned his lesson and clearly understands that this circumstance relating to DUIs and the immigration laws of our land are just like baseball—three strikes and you are out!

We hope beyond anything there will not be another strike as it relates to this kind of behavior by Raffy. He is a wonderful guy. He's well liked, well respected, but he made a horrible personal choice on how to behave. He paid the consequences.

I RECEIVED QUITE A FEW E-MAILS AND LETTERS FROM FANS AND OTHER members of the public. This was a very emotional issue and I understood that. Many of these came from people who had had a family member victimized by a drunk driver. If you are the parent or the sibling of someone who is killed or maimed by a driver arrested for DUI, I could certainly empathize with how you felt.

Some were mad at the Braves because, again, our name was on the front of the shirt Raffy wore at work. Sometimes when people are frustrated by the individual actions of a person who works for a baseball team, the immediate connection is made that we are responsible for those individual, personal actions. The players work for us. Ergo, we ought to be able to tell them to behave and use good judgment.

There was not much I could say to assuage their anger at Furcal. I couldn't diminish their frustation that he happened to work for us and so therefore we had some responsibility in their eyes. I truly felt for them and their grief. They sent pictures of grave sites, or photos of the victim from their family. It was sad. Very, very sad.

I get angry when I read of drunk driving and vehicular homicide. I get very angry. Those who know me know I'm very much a law-and-order person. I don't like people who commit crimes excusing it because they weren't in control of their actions because they were on drugs or they had too much to drink—because they were impaired. I feel you are responsible for your personal actions in any and all circumstances. So I tried as best I could to understand how these letter writers felt. Perhaps I don't have the same deep feelings because, thank

God, I haven't had to suffer as these people have. But I did feel sorry for them, though there was nothing I could say or do.

Normally, I respond to most every letter, call, or e-mail. In this case, however, I decided there was nothing I could say. I couldn't dismiss their pain and anguish. I couldn't rationalize what happened. There was nothing I could offer to these people in the way of a good response. I just had to understand their anguish and accept their anger.

I wrestled with that. I didn't have what I thought was the kind of response that would be appropriate. The fact that this player who happens to work for us broke the law is another matter. The judge made the decision of how and when to mete out the penalty and we had nothing to do with it.

I sat at my desk and tried to craft a few responses to the letters, but I finally decided it would not be doing the right thing. I didn't know what I could say without, in some way, hurting or offending these people who sent the letters.

This was an adult human being who made a terrible personal mistake in judgment. Thank God no one was injured as a result of his actions.

ALTHOUGH RAFAEL FURCAL'S SITUATION HARDLY FLEW UNDER THE radar, it was overshadowed to some degree on the national level in 2004 by the blossoming scourge of steroid use in athletics that has become both a real and public relations problem, particularly for baseball.

What bothers me about this whole steroids issue is the unfair criticism leveled at Commissioner Bud Selig by a wide swath of the media. So many of them took the position (a) that he ought to have known what was going on with regard to steroid use in baseball back in the late '90s when attention was brought to performance-enhancement drugs by Mark McGwire's admission of the use of androstenedione, or (b) that he did know something about it and he and every owner and every executive in the game turned their backs.

I dispute those positions. I dispute them wholeheartedly.

I say that because we did not have a testing mechanism available to us. Everyone remotely familiar with baseball was acutely aware of the fact that player testing is a collectively bargained issue. It could not be unilaterally imposed by the Commissioner's Office or Major League Baseball on the players without the players union willingly accepting a testing program for any kind of substance use or abuse. The commissioner's hands were tied without the cooperation of the Major League Baseball Players Association—and he did not have it.

And the position that the Players Association took was that the rights of personal privacy were far more important in their view than a testing program that would (a) determine if someone was abusing performance-enhancing drugs, (b) penalize him for doing it, (c) help him get the medical help he needed to provide important health and safety considerations, and (d) protect and defend the integrity of the great game of baseball.

None of that could be done in the major leagues without a collectively bargained agreement with the union, which the commissioner could not get. There was steadfast refusal on the union's part for the testing of anything. Now, contrast that to the program that the Commissioner's Office instituted in the minor leagues, where players could be tested at any time for any reason, randomly, for any substance, and, if found abusing a substance, penalized and counseled accordingly. The number of occurrences in the minor leagues has dropped precipitously since that program was instituted. Testing really does work.

I'm convinced the same thing would happen in the major leagues were a similar program in place.

Unfortunately, it was only when the infamous BALCO incident came to light and its grand jury testimony became the centerpiece of this whole steroid situation that national attention was drawn to the issue. Consequently, the embarrassment was raised to such a height that the president of the United States mentioned it as a huge problem in his State of the Union address at the outset of 2004.

Other political leaders threatened that if Major League Baseball didn't tend to their own house and correct the horrible circumstance of steroid use, they were going to involve themselves and propose federal legislation that would demand that baseball test players for steroids and other substances. It was only then that the union became willing to sit down with the Commissioner's Office and carve out the most meaningful testing program of major league baseball players that has ever existed.

Now, does this new plan cover all of the elements that everybody would want? Does it go as deep as some may want? Does it satisfy to the nth degree all the skeptics of the program would demand?

No. It doesn't.

But what is important to realize is that it is the first time in the history of a collectively bargained agreement in baseball that the basic agreement had been reopened during the midst of the contract and new guidelines crafted to address the need for an honest, meaningful testing mechanism.

The revelations that came out of the BALCO investigation got it rolling and it didn't just include baseball players. That disturbing saga included athletes from many other sports. But there were some highly recognized baseball names that were caught in the net of the BALCO investigation by the federal government. It was after that investigation became public when legislators became engaged and outraged with this whole matter. They properly reasoned this had a very bad influence on the children of this country as they watched their sports heroes connected to illegal, inappropriate, and dangerous performance enhancement drugs.

It was raised to such an attention level in this nation—not by the association that represents the players' health and well-being—but by a congressional investigation. That's sad.

What is good about it is that the union saw fit, after all of that, to sit down and, in essence, acknowledge a problem that needs to be dealt with, and agreed to cooperate with the commissioner and Major League

Baseball to craft a program that would provide for testing, penalties, and fines. And, beginning with the 2005 season, we have such a program. It may have some shortcomings, but it's the best we've ever had in the major leagues—a great first step.

My assumption is that if it weren't for this public outcry created by the BALCO probe, senators, congressmen, and the president of the United States, I'm not so sure the union would have been willing to permit any sort of testing. After all, the union had never been willing to have any meaningful testing before this—ever.

In a 2003 *Sports Illustrated* survey of major league players, 40.7 percent thought the drug testing policy in place at that time was adequate. Only 36.5 percent wanted something more stringent. And, remarkably, 7.6 percent said even that very limited testing policy should be *abolished.*

Thankfully, the leaders in our clubhouse have taken an admirable stance on the issue of the use and abuse of drugs and steroids. Pitcher John Smoltz, in particular, has been outspokenly in favor of stronger steroid testing.

"The main thing for me," John stated, "is that we eliminate from the fans' standpoint of them thinking, 'Yeah, he hit 50 home runs. What's he using?' And I'll take it a step further. I'm so upset because it's had a trickle-down effect to the youth, that they believe it's the only way to get better. I'm so upset that people will do whatever they need to do, and not care about the consequences, just to get ahead. Yeah, there's a lot of money to be made in the game. But I'm a big believer in what goes around comes around, and eventually you pay the consequences in some way.

"People talk about what steroids have done to the game. I'll tell you one good thing it's done. It's given more credence to guys like Hank Aaron who stood above the crowd. When they accomplished something, you didn't hear anything later that tarnished it. Unfortunately, that's what is happening now."

Many players and union officials have tried to downplay the

performance-enhancing aspects of steroids. Yeah, okay, steroids may not help you hit a 95-mph fastball, because you still have to have God-given hand-eye coordination and reflexes, courage and quickness. But they can help you hit it farther. If you can hit it harder and farther, you can have better statistics and command a higher salary.

If you are 6-foot-7, 220 pounds, have shoulders the width of a small condo, and you can throw a ball 95 miles an hour, performance enhancement drugs may allow you to throw it a *100* miles an hour. That's wrong. That's an unfair advantage.

So while I don't disagree with the fact that it takes ability to hit a baseball or to pitch at the major league level, I absolutely believe that if your body is artificially made stronger by a performance-enhancing drug, you have an unnatural and unfair advantage over players who don't use such substances.

You have created for yourself an unfair competitive advantage.

HANK AARON IS A GENTLEMAN. HANK IS A COMPETITOR. HANK IS THE greatest home run hitter of all time. I watched Hank as I grew up as a child of baseball and watched his remarkable physical accomplishment: the all-time home run leader in major league baseball history. I had to rely on the information provided by the media in those days, but I never once heard anything, nor read anything, even suggesting that he used a performance-enhancing substance. He was an au naturel home run hitter.

But his nature is to give every other person the benefit of the doubt. I don't want to speak for Hank Aaron. But in my mind, I can honestly say there's going to be doubt within me if some modern-age player who is suspected, to one degree or another, of using performance-enhancing drugs—whoever that may be—surpasses Hank's all-time home run record. Should that occur, that record ought not be viewed in kind against Hank Aaron's record.

Perhaps a mark or designation has to be created.

But it's just not that simple. How do you decide who is saddled with the scarlet letter? As are many issues like this with many levels of complexity, I don't know the answer to how we decide which level of substance abuse puts you over the line. Maybe somebody tried steroids for a year and hit 45 homers and decided it wasn't good for his health or life expectancy and wants to be around for his wife and kids. Maybe that somebody stopped using those substances and went on to hit 700 more home runs. Now, does that guy qualify for an asterisk, or do you need to be a proven user for two years? Three years? Or should there simply be a zero tolerance policy?

I'm not trying to be Solomon here in my judgment. But in fairness to the guys who got it done without performance-enhancing supplements, there needs to be some distinction.

Then again, someone may ask me, "How do you know, John, whether guys in those past years did something else to artificially raise their level of attention, raise their level of alertness?" Maybe there were things guys did back then as beneficial as what the modern-day muscle enhancers might use. I doubt it, but I just don't know. I don't have sufficient facts to make a firm judgment. I'm just saying, in my opinion, there ought to be some way to make a distinction between the players who used drugs from the ones who didn't. A good, strong testing program could have eliminated this problem and this debate.

I would prefer to draw that line with cold, hard factual evidence that steroids were used. If it is proven beyond a shadow of doubt that a player or several players used steroids and established new records, then forget the scarlet letters. Eliminate those records altogether. Testing then and testing now would provide the truth and completely eliminate all doubts.

Decades ago, a hypothetical asterisk was assigned to Roger Maris's name because he put up his single-season home run record while playing more games, 162, than did Babe Ruth, 154.

But the question of using an asterisk is even unfair for me to comment on because there has been no way for me or this organization or this industry to gather any definitive evidence since we were prohibited from testing players on major league rosters.

And none of us had any expertise about steroids in terms of its physical manifestation, in terms of what impact it has on a guy's physicality, the impact it has on a player's psychology, its impact on emotional stability, its dermatological impact, how it affects skull size. Now we've all been fast-tracked on our education regarding steroids.

The medical people in baseball meet all the time and conduct forums and have discussions about all manner of medical and physical issues. Obviously, nutritional supplements have been a topic of great discussion and we've all become more aware of those. And, sadly, we're all becoming more aware, in this modern era of baseball, of performance-enhancing drugs. Whatever it may be, whether andro or streroids or creatine.

We've all become more educated about them because of that heightened awareness. More factual information is starting to be gathered.

One thing about our modern society is that accessing information is so quick. With the click of a button on a computer, we can tap into mountains of medical research. We've all had to become more knowledgeable of circumstances regarding these issues than we were before. I try constantly to be as knowledgeable and as up to date as I possibly can.

But having knowledge of an issue or a subject doesn't make me an expert. It prepares me to have an opinion that is more informed, more valid. A more educated opinion. While it doesn't make me an expert, I can offer a stronger opinion. I can provide expert testimony about how to build and lead organizations and how to construct teams and how to utilize scouts, but I can't speak as an expert on drugs and supplements. There are experts in those areas available to offer their views—and they have.

Because we couldn't test before 2005, I have no basis in fact that any of our Braves players were using steroids. If someone were to ask me if I have any knowledge of a player using steroids, I'd say no. Because we had no legitimate way of gaining such knowledge. When someone asked me if there were any Braves I thought *might* have used performance-enhancing drugs, I said I suspected a few and even directly confronted one with my suspicions.

In fact, Stan Kasten and I were determined to get a face-to-face with the suspected player. We went to the clubhouse together at a time we knew there wouldn't be much traffic and we made it a point to be in there when this player was the only player in that part of the clubhouse.

With what little we knew then of steroids and their implications and their manifestations in a player's psychology and physiology, we suspected this one particular player might be using steroids.

So in the clubhouse, with no one else around, Stan and I approached him and asked the question: "Are you using steroids?"

"Absolutely not," he said. He laughed at us and stuck out his arms. "Look at these skinny little arms. No, I don't do steroids."

He didn't have a steroid physique then, but he had these bouts of irrational behavior.

Basically, that was the end of it, because we had no grounds to go beyond that. There was no testing program allowed. Our hands were tied behind us as management. We could only walk away and shake our heads and say, "That's too bad."

Too bad that we couldn't test and validate if that player was using a performance-enhancing drug, or perhaps some other drug. Who knows? Could we get him on the right track? Could we save this guy's life?

We had little choice other than to take that one player's word. There was no retaliation against him. I've always felt this demonstrated the shortsightedness on the part of the players union. Their position was that they were trying to protect the "rights of privacy" of their players. Even if that were true, we also know they are always trying to protect the money-earning potential and the growth of player salaries.

Call me a cynic if you like, but that's how I feel.

*   *   *

IN 1982, FOLLOWING MY FIRST YEAR AS GM OF THE ROYALS, I MADE A big deal with San Francisco. We acquired Vida Blue, one of the very best pitchers in baseball at that time, along with outfielder Jerry Martin for pitcher Atlee Hammaker and minor-leaguers.

The deal was never an issue. It made sense to both clubs. The story behind the deal was the negative impact it had on the Royals' pristine image due to the drug scandal that erupted with Vida Blue in the middle of it.

As a federal drug investigation ultimately determined, Vida was the one who introduced this horrible pox of drugs upon our highly respected organization in Kansas City. Its web became so wide it entrapped some really good people and players. Among them was Vida himself, Martin, and two of our top players: Willie Aikens and Willie Wilson. It destroyed a couple of careers and caused pain and anguish and personal suffering to those and many others. Several of our players were indicted on charges of the use and trafficking of cocaine. I publicly characterized it as "a kick in the organizational groin."

The trade was made in the off-season and the drug allegations exploded into the public light during that subsequent season when the federal drug investigation was disclosed.

My personal assessment was I had made a mistake in completing this deal because I didn't do my due diligence in knowing more about Blue's character, moral makeup, and involvement with drugs at that time. This horrible event gravely impacted our fine organization. But we were not running from it, nor going to wallow in self-pity. We chose instead to be honest and forthright with the media and our fans about what had happened. I updated the media virtually every day as this terrible story unfolded.

We were going to clean up our major league team and properly fix the problem. And we did. That was my leadership responsibility. We had to take this raging bull of embarrassment and humiliation by the horns, wrestle it to the ground, and defeat it. And we did. Those actions were a reflection, in some sense, of our leadership by saying,

"This is a horrible set of circumstances that has beset this grand organization. We don't deserve this. This is not our image. This is as far removed from our image as possible. Kansas City *Royals* with a *drug scandal?* We will not stand for this!"

I also felt I may not have been fully informed by the Giants' front office, which might have withheld the knowledge that Blue had a drug problem when we made the trade. Until my friend Al Rosen became GM of the Giants in 1985, I kept a Giants batting helmet on the credenza in my office as a constant reminder not to do any deals with them.

We eliminated the person we found out to be the perpetrator of this drug culture that was brought into our clubhouse—Vida Blue. Jerry Martin was also dismissed. I felt bad about Jerry. He had a young family and I liked him a lot. He just got caught up in a horrible addiction and paid for it. He's a good man and back on track. I'm glad.

We had never had problems before with the other two guys. Never had reason to suspect trouble. They served jail time. As I write this, Willie Aikens, sadly, remains in the federal penitentiary in Atlanta, serving a twenty-year sentence for later drug missteps.

The other leadership element of this—and a good story—is that the Royals' kindly owner, Ewing Kauffman, called me to his office at Marion Laboratories. I'll never forget this. He sat me down, just the two of us in his office. He said, "John, the reason we made you general manager is we have all the faith and confidence in your ability to operate this organization effectively, making good decisions and showing leadership. And you've done that. I do not want you (this is the important part) to pull in your horns, because your aggressiveness in making deals—and having the confidence to make deals—is what separates you from the others."

And he added, slowly for emphasis, "Do . . . not . . . let . . . this . . . circumstance . . . cause you to lose confidence."

Isn't that great? I somehow resisted the urge to leap across his desk and hug him.

I mean, you'd think if an owner is calling you to his office after an event like this, he's going to say you're a dumb sonuvagun and you really disappointed us and we now have no faith in you and we're going to move you into another job. Or, out the door.

But the opposite happened. Ewing Kauffman, what a man, what a leader.

It was a great life's lesson and leadership lesson that was palpable. I lived it. It was beating in my chest then and still does today. Just imagine—here I was in only my second year as a general manager and this embarrassing event occurs to this grand and glorious and first-class organization with which I had been entrusted. It shocked knowledgeable sportswriters and other media people throughout the country. It embarrassed us beyond words. And the owner calls me in and says *this?*

It's a lesson I have tried to apply in each of the many times I have been on the other side of that desk. Almost on a yearly basis, when someone fails or has fallen short of our expectations of them, or of a circumstance they were managing, or a personnel issue that they were in control of that didn't turn out well, I try to make it a point to say, "You're good at what you do. Work your way through it. We are confident that this is a temporary negative situation that you're going to deal with in a winning way. It won't change how we feel about you and it shouldn't change how you feel about your ability to do your job."

Then, if it happens a second time, that old saw applies—fool me once, shame on you; fool me twice, shame on me. Then we reevaluate. And we take the appropriate action.

Shortly after joining the Braves in the early '90s, I had another encounter with a player with a drug addiction. Outfielder Otis Nixon was arrested and charged with cocaine possession.

I was in my hotel room in San Francisco late in the 1991 season as we were getting ready to begin the playoffs. Otis, who was a prime outfield defender and offensive catalyst for us, was taken from us because of his illegal activities involving drugs. We lost him for those playoffs and part of the next season.

It's a sad and vicious cycle. He worked his way out of it and worked for us for a while after his playing career as an instructor. What a great guy he is, and it's sad that this insidious addiction won't let go easily.

Former All-Star third baseman Ken Caminiti, toward the end of his brief time with us in 2001, had similar problems. Shortly after we released him, he came up missing and was gone for three days. Ken was found in a motel room in south Atlanta. No one had heard from him. No one knew where he was. Sadly, it was his involvement with drugs that ultimately cost Ken his life a few years later. What an awful tragedy.

So, yes, I have been presented with a number of crisis situations where various decisions have to be made and various degrees of leadership exercised and plans of action had to be put in place. A few that were gut-wrenching and downright personal. No one ever said leadership would be easy.

10

Giving Back

ONE OF THE GREAT JOYS OF MY POSITION IS HAVING THE opportunity to speak to various businesses and civic groups throughout the Southeast, sharing my business and team-building philosophies and leadership principles. My audiences are typically eager and interested to hear how we went about building winning teams on such a consistent basis for so many years and the leadership principles involved.

While it's important for me and interesting for them to have me share that information, at each and every one of those sessions I try always to impress upon the listeners the importance and significance of giving back to our communities.

I challenge them to consider seriously the great responsibility we all have beyond simply performing our jobs as successfully and faithfully as we must. The greater challenge is doing all we can individually and collectively to build a better neighborhood, a better community, a better society, and, yes, even a better world. We can begin that by doing all we can to raise our children properly.

Here's a story I like to share to illustrate that point: A small boy walks into the room where his dad is reading a newspaper. The youngster tugs on his father's shirtsleeve and says, "Dad, I need to talk to you. Can you talk to me just for a minute?"

The man is consumed by what he is reading and hardly acknowledges his son. Without looking up, he waves the boy away. Only after the lad persists, does he gain his father's attention. "Dad, I really do need to talk to you," he repeats. At that moment, the father had turned to a large picture of the globe in the newspaper. He proceeds to tear the photo into a hundred little pieces and hands the pile of scraps to the boy, saying, "Here, when you put this picture of the globe back together, I'll talk to you." The child departs, barely able to carry all the pieces of paper in his hands. The father figures he'll have his peace and quiet for most of the day.

Remarkably, within just a few minutes, his son is back holding up the picture of the globe, Scotch tape everywhere. "Here, Dad, I've put the picture back together. Will you talk to me now?"

Astonished, the father blurts: "That's impossible! How did you do that so fast?"

"Well," the boy says, "I didn't put the picture of the globe together. But on the other side was a picture of a small boy and his dog. And I put *that* picture together."

The moral of the story is clear; if we take care in putting our children together properly, the world will take care of itself.

I think it is imperative to remind ourselves that while we have these responsibilities of our jobs that may be substantial and important, what is far more critical is how we contribute to this world in which we live. The essence of this part of my presentation is that I simply urge everyone in the audience to have a lively concern for the well-being of others. We can't demand that people live their lives a certain way, but I believe it is imperative that we cause them to think about it.

For me, personally, aside from helping my wife, Karen, raise our children properly, I had the opportunity to impact lives directly during my four years as a teacher. Not only did I have a direct requirement to educate my students, I also had the responsibility of teaching them to be good, productive citizens. To prepare them to make appropriate choices when the tough challenges of life confronted them. It was so rewarding for me when my eighth-grade students would return to talk about their high school experiences, their lives in general, their achievements and their challenges. No matter what their level of academic ability, I always encouraged them to do their best, work as hard as they could, and have fun in their lives. With respect to my own children, Gina and Jonathan, I tried to be as involved as I could in their school and church activities.

Additionally, I have always tried to become involved in worthwhile, meaningful programs in my community. In Kansas City, I served on the board and hosted a fund-raising golf tournament for the Whole Person organization, which assists disabled, physically challenged people—primarily adults—who need help and financial support finding living quarters that are handicapped-accessible.

Since I've been in Atlanta, I have served on the boards of two charitable programs. One is Camp Sunshine, which is an amazing organization that provides opportunities for children with cancer and includes twenty-four-hour on-site medical and psychosocial support. Bereavement groups are also offered for families that have lost a child to illness. Each summer, with the support and love of a phenomenal staff of caring volunteers including nurses and doctors, these very special kids have the opportunity to enjoy canoeing, swimming, arts and crafts, and other typical camp activities. They share a cabin with other children suffering from the physical and emotional ravages of cancer and cancer treatment. For this precious week, they bond with other children in their same predicament, to smile, laugh, enjoy life, create friendships, and engage in fun and "normal" kids' activities.

Our daughter, Gina, is a volunteer cabin counselor at Camp Sunshine. In 2003, I had the honor of serving as the capital campaign chairman, raising funds to build Camp Sunshine House, where we are able to provide many more services.

My other board position is with YES! Atlanta. YES is an acronym for Youth Experiencing Success. This is an organization that focuses on Atlanta's at-risk youth, most of whom have found their way into the juvenile court system, dropped out of school, and are primed to become part of the criminal element. YES! Atlanta has a wonderful mentoring program for these kids. Volunteers from all facets of our professional community serve as "committed partners," spending time trying to guide these young people back on track, save their lives, and make them productive, contributing citizens. Annually, I host the John Schuerholz YES! Atlanta Golf Tournament, which raises most of the operating budget for the group.

"BRAVES WIN! BRAVES WIN! BRAVES WIN!"

Skip Caray's words still ring loudly and sweetly in my ears

When Marquis Grissom glided under the lazy fly ball in left center field and caressed the last out of the 1995 World Series, Caray, our play-by-play announcer, used his trademark exultation on that moment when the Atlanta Braves became the first and only world champion professional sports team in the city's history.

What a thrilling and proud moment that was for me and our entire organization.

That remarkable accomplishment, the crown jewel in an unprecedented, unbelievable 14-year run of consecutive division championships, began for me in 1990 when I decided to resign my post as general manager of the Kansas City Royals and accept the executive VP/general manager position in Atlanta.

"Braves win!" intones so much more than just the '95 Series triumph, however. It signifies many of the various aspects of the organization during my time in Atlanta—the aspects that go into our annual quest for championship excellence and the successful hurdling of so many barriers that the changing times keep erecting in the path of any sports executive, particularly those leading Major League Baseball clubs.

And while Caray's *"Braves win!"* exhortation on that 1995 October evening in old Fulton County Stadium signaled that we had achieved our ultimate goal, I flash back to another autumn evening, in 1992, in a dramatic playoff series with the Pittsburgh Pirates. When Sid Bream slid across the plate on a two-out, bottom-of-the-ninth base hit by

Francisco Cabrera to take the seventh game, Caray shouted those same sweet words, *"Braves win!"* I thought back about Bream being a part of that special moment and Rafael Belliard, our little, slick-fielding short-stop, being a part of that, and so many of the changes we had to make in the early years of the reconstruction of this team and how this organization came together so well in my very first couple of years in Atlanta.

It signaled dealing with those changes, managing those changes, and effectively blending those changes into good working parts for a successful team composition. And we've been challenged to do that almost continually in baseball over the past fifteen years, particularly with the Braves.

We've had to deal with significant changes from the explosion of player salaries, the growth and increased involvement of player agents, the Internet and the daily bloggers who demand that we general managers, as team spokesmen, be prepared to answer all questions at all times, over and over and over in this fast-paced, give-me-the-information-now society in which we live.

We've had to deal with the changes of division play and wild card teams and the playoff format going from the old format where the winner of the American League played the winner of the National League to this new postseason tournament. Now there is even less assurance that the first seed in this tournament—the team with the best record over the 162-game regular season—will prevail and become world champions.

"Braves win!" is also the banner cry in celebration of the hard work done in a far more traditional manner than those trendy methods and theories proffered in recent years. In addition to traditional statistical analysis, our continuing success is more affirmation of good, intuitive scouting, player development, and homegrown players. It is affirmation of doing things the old-fashioned winning way: working hard and earning the spoils. No fancy equations. No bizarre analyses. Just good, solid baseball people doing their jobs.

It has been scouts scouting well, finding that high school player, the international player, or that college player who fits the prescribed Braves mold. It has been player development people working endless hours upon endless hours developing the tools and the skills and competitive spirit of these young men. In what we call organizational meetings—where we gather everyone from our scouting and player development departments—I always addressed this group at the outset of these meetings and often remind them of the analogy that characterizes the synergy that must exist between scouting and player development: We rely on our scouts to provide us with the finest raw material, much like a classic piece of Italian marble. In turn, we rely on the player development staff to pick up the hammer and chisel of player development and craft in the fashion of an artisan the finest finished product from this prime raw marble. The point being that the interrelationship between scouting and player development is so crucial that neither one can succeed unless the other does. Scouts must find the young players with unrefined skills, and the minor league managers and instructors must hone those skills to major league caliber.

"Braves win!" is a real signal cry that here is an organization that, during my years as GM, has dedicated itself to the traditional principles of baseball, worked with those principles in a successful way, and, consequently, ran off this remarkable, never-before-accomplished string of 14 consecutive division titles. I'm very proud of that.

It's also an affirmation of the business and management principles that we have developed and utilized over time and adhere to in uncompromising fashion.

"Braves win!" is about what I consider the most important element in my career and whatever success I have enjoyed, and that is *"Braves win!"* with GOOD PEOPLE. *"Braves win!"* occurred during my leadership years by recognizing and motivating those good people, continuing to educate good people, celebrating the good work they do, and by acting upon the sound recommendations they made. And honoring them by listening to their judgments, listening to their evaluations, listening to their recommendations, and, most importantly, basing my decisions on them.

That's been my leadership style as a GM—surround myself with good, honest people and rely on them. Period. I consider myself a great delegator, but I delegate with supreme confidence because I am asking people who are very talented and in whose judgment I have great faith. I rely on them and trust in them and give them an honest sense of empowerment.

Obviously, I have no magical or mystical powers in decision-making. I am an active and attentive listener. I attempt always to ask probing and challenging questions and in the end use my innate decision-making ability to serve as the final filter. I always attempt to be forward thinking and to utilize ingenuity.

Our staff continually makes good recommendations because, I believe, they know I listen to them. They know what they say really matters. They know the work they do is valued. They are the essential element to this great administrative and organizational team we've constructed. We *need* them and we *rely* upon them.

"Braves win!" is a message to our fans, who were properly skeptical at first in 1991, not knowing what this new kid on the block might be doing with their team. Me, the most recent in a long series of changes and promises the Braves had made to their fans.

"Braves win!" was a cry out to our fans, saying, in effect, "This is for you. This is for your support. Because you came, because you support us, because you began to believe in what we were doing, because you gave us your trust and allowed us the capability of being aggressive in our operations."

This is for all our fans of all ages and walks of life. And for the many, many letters from the grandmothers in California and Wyoming and Montana and western Georgia and South Carolina and Alabama and New England who in 1991 said to me, "Thank you. I'm so happy that *my boys* finally won!"

I've had so many people tell me how much more enjoyable the lives of their elderly relatives have been with the success of the Braves. How they listen to our games and watch on cable TV and follow the Braves. It provides at least a sliver of joy and happiness in their lives.

"Braves win! Braves win!" is a much appreciated validation of the principles and policies that I have adopted, nurtured, and implemented both with the uniformed personnel and the club's administration throughout my tenure as general manager. It has given credence to the traditional baseball style of human scouting and dedicated player development people—rewarding their considered judgments and years of experience as the impetus for our success rather than some trendy statistical formula for roster building.

It rewards the leadership concept of supporting the staff, providing them with a vision and with clear goals, and infusing them with the self-confidence and pride to execute that blueprint at a championship level. It smoothes over the missteps, the disappointments, the crises that we overcome together.

It also validates our clubhouse concept of team-oriented players who conduct and present themselves in an appealing professional manner. It speaks volumes about the personal support and backing I have received from my family and from those who have entrusted their baseball operations to a former junior high teacher with a dream.

"Braves win! Braves win!" is a special legacy created by all of the button-popping proud individuals on and off the field who have pulled together to create the uncommonly consistent beacon of success that the Atlanta Braves have come to represent.

I am both humbled and gratified beyond words to know that I was given the opportunity to play a key role in guiding, learning from, and working alongside all of those championship people in the adventure of this remarkable accomplishment.

"Braves win! Braves win! Braves win!"

Afterword

The 2005 Season

What a year, 2005: an exciting, challenging, remarkable, gut-wrenching, rewarding season!

Though it ended with an unbelievable 18-inning, heartbreaking playoff loss to the Houston Astros, it nevertheless substantiated our strong, positive attitude toward our team and our hopes for the 2006 season. Our 90 regular-season wins and major league–record 14th consecutive division title were significant on their own merits. But when considering the myriad challenges we faced and met with respect to the midseason reconstruction of our roster, those achievements are even more remarkable.

Serious injuries cost us starting pitchers Tim Hudson, Mike Hampton, and John Thomson for various portions of the year, as well as our reliable star and cornerstone offensive player, Chipper Jones. A disappointing season by acquired closer Dan Kolb, a nagging, season-long injury to Brian Jordan and the unsuccessful Raul Mondesi experiment compounded our challenges to field another division champion–caliber team.

In the face of these serious issues, we found ourselves in mid-June in fourth place, *five-and-one-half games* out of the National League East lead, and constrained by our team payroll limits. We had no choice but to rely on young, inexperienced players to plug these many holes and help us get back to our winning ways. We decided that because of our familiarity with their abilities and our in-depth knowledge of their competitive spirit, we were going to challenge our young minor league players. And did they respond!

Kyle Davies, Ryan Langerhans, and Kelly Johnson, joined soon thereafter by Jeff Francoeur and Brian McCann, together with Pete Orr, Wilson Betemit, Joey Devine, and others added later in the season, rose to the extreme challenge. In unprecedented fashion, we utilized an unthinkable total of 17 rookies in the regular season to make up *11½ games* in baseball's toughest top-to-bottom division to extend our record string of division titles to 14. The clincher came against Colorado, 12–3, on September 27. More remarkably, we included eight of those rookies on our postseason roster, establishing a new major league mark.

The lifeblood of our organization these past 15 glorious seasons—our scouting and player development system—proved more than ever to be a constant, significant ingredient to our success. And in the salvaging of our 2005 season, they signaled loud and clear to the entire baseball world that the Atlanta Braves pipeline of young, talented players was as full and productive as ever.

That clinching September 27 evening became an insightful high tide of champagne euphoria, a celebration that outstripped any of the 13 pennant-clinchers that had preceded it. I knew this would be a special celebration given the makeup of this team. And, indeed, it was especially satisfying, joyful, and youthful.

Predictably, all the rookies were wildly ecstatic while spraying bubbly on one another, coaches, and staffers. The veterans were swept up in this outpouring of joy and exuberance as well.

You sometimes hear the words "jaded" and "laissez faire" attached to some of our veteran stars. But there in that locker room, I delighted at the sight of Chipper Jones and Andruw Jones and John Smoltz and Julio Franco in the frenetic middle of the happy, juvenile-like melee wearing smiles wider than I've ever seen. There was nothing indifferent about Chipper's giggling bearhug takedown of rookie sensation Jeff Francouer, who scrambled to his feet in mock vengeance, laughing and vowing to get even.

Bobby Cox, too, was in the middle of the fest, wearing goggles to protect his ailing eyes from the stinging shower of champagne as he embraced and congratulated everyone.

Family members were allowed into what is normally a team-only sanctuary for champagne-soaked hugs and special-moment snapshots with teammates, wives, kids, and even media members.

Special division-championship sweatshirts and caps had been handed out as the players frolicked in through the dugout tunnel to uncork their glee. Giles, our demonstrative spark plug, quickly became such a drenched target of teammates he had to peel off his soaked shirt. After giving me a bare-chested hug, he grabbed another shirt and leaped atop a table to announce how dry his shirt was. On cue, a half-dozen teammates drowned him in a foamy white tsunami of champagne spray. When the bubbly was exhausted, someone found a couple of cases of beer, which they popped open and continued pouring over one another's happy heads.

And amid the celebratory din, they even paused to exhibit the deep-seated team spirit that had so characterized these '05 Braves. Led by several vets, the whole team was assembled around a table at one end of the clubhouse to record a raucous camcorder message/tribute to "Hammy," starting pitcher Mike Hampton, whose contributions had been cut short by a season-ending surgery. Amid this emotional high, they didn't forget a teammate.

Poignantly, our superb shortstop Raffy Furcal sat quietly but grinning broadly as he took in the madcap scene from a stool at the edge of the clubhouse, toasting his teammates with a soft drink. Raffy, admirably contrite about his past misstep, was celebrating in his own non-alcohlic style.

When the celebration waned, I made my way from the clubhouse to a nearby suite where many on our administrative staff were sharing the moment. As I entered, Derek Schiller, our senior vice president of sales and marketing, shouted for quiet and called for everyone to hold aloft their glasses to toast me and our accomplishment. It was a special, moving moment, and I struggled for a response but was most appreciative of the gesture.

Twelve days later, our magical season came to a gut-wrenching end with the stinging pain of that epic 18-inning loss in Houston in the final game of our NL Division Series. Behind a determined outing by Tim Hudson, we held a 5-run lead in the eighth inning and we were surely headed back to Atlanta for the deciding game in the best-of-five series the next night. But the surreal took over. In a bizarre series of events—a missed call here, a missed step there, an opposite-field, grand slam homer by Lance Berkman into Minute Maid Park's extremely short left field box seats off previously perfect closer Kyle Farnsworth, another homer literally one inch above the yellow home run line in left center with two outs in the ninth—and we waded into nine historic extra innings of excruciating anxiety. Inning after inning, we left runners in scoring position, stranding a total of 18 in the game as our hitters went an unthinkable 1-for-18 with runners in scoring position. Just 2-for-18 and we would have been playing in Atlanta the next night, with a chance to advance to the next round, and the noisy fan support would have been our own.

Though that early October Sunday turned out to be a beautiful day for baseball in Houston, the Astros chose to close the retractable roof to maximize the home-fan noise. On the field before the game, I approached Bob Watson of the commissioner's office and asked why, if a team had admitted publicly they would gain a competitive advantage by closing the roof on a perfect day, it would be permitted to do that. After all, we wouldn't be permitted to let our infield grow shaggy if we had a sinkerball pitcher on the mound, or saturate the base paths if the opponent had a fast lineup. Bob shrugged and said he didn't have an answer.

As that fateful game unfolded, and frustrations mounted through all those extra innings, the mood in the luxury suite I shared with several other Braves executives became one of bewilderment and disbelief. At one point Mike Plant, our vice president of business operations and member of the United States Olympic Committee, leaned over to me and wryly declared: "When this is over, I'm gonna need counseling—no matter how it comes out!"

In the bottom of the 18th, the longest postseason game in baseball history ended suddenly, with Houston rookie Chris Burke's solo homer barely into that same short porch in left—ironically caught by the same fan who had also collected Berkman's slam in the eighth. Our suite emptied quickly, but I stayed behind for perhaps half an hour with my wife, Karen, and my assistant, Frank Wren, reflecting on the surreal afternoon before finally making my way down to the equally dazed pall in our clubhouse.

As athletes always do, our players found the courage and the strength to shake one another's hand and congratulate each other for a hard-fought season and overcoming so much. I bumped into Tim Hudson and congratulated him for the warrior-like effort he had given that day. If there was a silver lining on this day, it was Hudson's performance that signaled to all of us he was poised to become the ace of our staff. We had to have that game, and he was determined he was going to win it. In winning Game Two, John Smoltz had exhibited those same traits—guile, guts, and sheer will power—despite pitching with a very sore shoulder. John could not have pitched Game Five, and it was doubtful that he could have pitched in the next round.

After boarding our chartered flight home, I sat down for a moment alongside Bobby Cox and offered my congratulations to him for a great exciting year and said what an exceptional job he had done through all the changes and injuries we endured. "We should have won that game a zillion times over," he said, wincing. "I really wanted to play at least one more game back in Atlanta to thank the fans for their support and give them the chance to see their team at least one more time—the team they had fallen in love with and enjoyed so much."

Over the next couple of days, the sour memories of that 18-inning exit began to be replaced by the upbeat visions of our immediate future. I began to reflect on the spirit of our young players taking hold of this franchise. I felt a sense of strong optimism about the 2006 season and years beyond. The reasons widely given that we should not have even been *in* the playoffs, let alone go deep in the postseason, are the very reasons we feel so good about our near-term future. By all logic, that unprecedented crop of "Baby Braves" will only improve now that they have a season of experience in the most challenging of circumstances. And if there's such a thing as a law of averages, our pitching staff won't be decimated by the unfathomable rash of injuries we had to endure in 2005.

That disappointment in Houston quickly gave way to the conviction that we'll be making room for more of those pennants across the Turner Field left field facade.

Confidence in the steady, guiding hand of Bobby Cox, the veteran leadership of Chipper and Andruw and Smoltzie, and the talent and relentless energy of our emerging young players signaled to us all and to the baseball community that for many seasons to come, this team and this organization are truly Built to Win.

The 2006 Season

We knew that sooner or later the streak would end. No one expected us to continue winning our division forever—although, to many baseball observers, fourteen consecutive titles was as close to forever as there is in baseball. On September 18, 2006, the Mets officially won the NL East Division. Our remarkable run had ended.

As we moved closer to that inevitable ending, I was often asked how I felt about it. Well, I said, I was as proud as I could be of our entire Braves organization, especially the many dedicated professionals throughout our system who made our historical, record-setting streak possible. I also believed that the improbable streak would be viewed even more positively when baseball historians do their examination of these fantastic fourteen seasons.

Ironically, when the streak came to an end, the light of intense scrutiny shined even more brightly and the focus was even sharper. Our fourteen consecutive titles were rightly viewed by sage baseball people for what they truly were: phenomenal!

One after the other weighed in with accolades about our accomplishment:

OMAR MINAYA: "What they've done is more than impressive. If they were to give a Pulitzer Prize in baseball, Bobby Cox and John Schuerholz and that whole organization deserve it."

BILLY WAGNER: "It's unbelievable, to have the run that they've had for so long, to constantly be chased and to win. When I was in Philly, and before that when I was in Houston, we knew we were going to play Atlanta in the playoffs. They established that tradition, and that's what every organization wants to achieve."

MIKE LOPRESTI, *USA Today* writer: "Fourteen straight titles. Only Russian pairs skaters and Tiger Woods are supposed to have runs like that."

Again, it's ironic that this great feat seemed to enjoy more celebration and acclaim at its end than it did during its life.

In 2006 the Mets were no doubt stronger than in past seasons, the Phillies were tough, and the Marlins had a talented young roster, all of which combined to create a tough and competitive division. The strength of those teams and our own roster weaknesses, injuries, and a horrendous June record of 6 and 21 led to our disappointing third-place finish. The previous year, when our team was floundering mightily, we had made the dramatic decision to virtually restructure our roster with youngsters from our own rich farm system. No fewer than eighteen rookies were called to our major league team that year, and they palyed a major role in our mid-season turnaround and our fourteenth consecutive division title.

Depleting our farm system of so much quality talent at that time left us without that same level of in-house talent to salvage our 2006 season. That and a rash of bizarre injuries, especially among our pitching staff, were the main reasons our streak ended. Never once, though, did our players or Bobby and his coaches give up the fight. They battled hard to the very end of the 2006 season. They even capped it off by knocking the Houston Astros out of the NL Central race on the very last day of the season, ensuring that the St. Louis Cardinals won the NL Central championship. And, of course, the Cardinals went on to be World Champions in 2006.

Our season ended and so did our remarkable streak. Sure, we were frustrated and disappointed, but in our clubhouse that day, I saw something else in our players and staff: a sense of heightened appreciation of our great feat, as well as a sense of personal intensity and motivation to renew that legacy. A look of commitment to regain that NL East division title was etched on every face.

That same level of frustration and disappointment prompted us to begin our important offseason evaluation and "game-planning" much earlier than we've been accustomed. We know well what went wrong and how we need to fix it. The high level of intensity and commitment that showed in the eyes of our players that night is fueling our drive to construct a 2007 team that will allow us a chance to win our division and hopefully achieve the ultimate goal of another World Championship.

—John Schuerholz, November 2006

The Unprecedented Streak

1991—94-68, Won NL West by 1 game, NL champs

Schuerholz Year One. Braves become first team in MLB history to reach World Series just one season after posting worst record in baseball. Overtook Dodgers with strong second half to win division. Set Atlanta records for wins and home attendance, 2.1 million. Tom Glavine wins Cy Young Award, Bobby Cox named NL Manager of the Year, and Schuerholz name UPI NL Executive of the Year. Steve Avery was MVP of NLCS with 16.1 straight scoreless innings. Lost Series in seven games to Twins.

Key Schuerholz Move: Acquired free agent 3B Terry Pendleton, who led NL in hitting at .319 and won NL MVP award. Also shored up defense with acquisitions Pendleton, OF Otis Nixon, SS Rafael Belliard, and 1B Sid Bream.

1992—98-64, Won NL West by 8 games, NL champs

Braves become first team to win back-to-back NL pennants in 14 years. In last place in late May, Braves overtook Giants with franchise record-tying 13-game win streak in July. Tom Glavine won 20 games second year in a row and Braves led NL in ERA at 3.14. John Smoltz leads league with 215 strikeouts. Terry Pendleton has another solid year at .311 with 105 RBI. Lost to Toronto in baseball's first international World Series.

Key Schuerholz Move: Acquired speedy Deion Sanders—actually picked up in 1991 but he saw limited playing time that year—who hit .533 and stole five bases in Series.

1993—104-58, Won NL West by 1 game

Braves set all-time franchise record with 3.88 million home attendance. Overcoming 10-game July deficit, overtook Giants to win division on the last day of the season and become first team ever to win NL West three straight years. Fred McGriff, Ron Gant, and David Justice give Braves first trio of 100+ RBI men in 23 seasons. Braves led the league in homers (168) and ERA (3.14) for second year in a row. Greg Maddux (20-6) wins Cy Young Award and Tom Glavine (22-6) is first NL pitcher in 25 years to win 20 or more games in three straight seasons. Jeff Blauser (.305) is first Braves shortstop to hit over .300 in 45 years.

Key Schuerholz Move: Outmaneuvered Yankees to sign Greg Maddux in the preseason, but midseason trade for Fred McGriff was key. McGriff hit two homers first night as Braves stadium caught fire and Braves caught fire behind him for torrid second-half run to wipe out Giants' 10-game July lead.

1994—68-46 (Player strike ends season August 12)

After league realignment, Braves open NL East with seven-game win streak. Bobby Cox becomes 41st MLB manager to win 1,000 games with June win over Cincinnati. Greg Maddux starts All-Star Game and Fred McGriff wins MVP for the game with three-run homer in ninth inning to tie the game, won by NL in 10th. McGriff was leading the team in homers (34), average (.318), and RBI (94) when season was halted August 12 by player strike. Greg Maddux wins third Cy Young Award.

1995—90-54, Won NL East by 21 games, NL and World Series champs

Braves win their first World Series title in 38 years. Greg Maddux wins his unprecedented fourth straight Cy Young Award, going 19-2 with 1.63 ERA, and Mark Wohlers emerges as dominant closer with 25 saves. Clutch-hitting Braves won 25 games in last-at-bat, including 18 over the final half of the season. Promising young third baseman named Chipper Jones is runner-up Rookie of the Year with 23 homers. Recorded first-ever four-game sweep of Reds in NLCS before defeating Cleveland in six for Series title. Tom Glavine spins one-hitter over eight innings and David Justice's solo homer provides only run in 1–0 finale.

Key Schuerholz Move: Trade with Montreal netted OF Marquis Grissom, who had a career-high 207 hits and 23 homers in '95 and would win his fourth straight Gold Glove Award in '96.

1996—96-66, Won NL East by 8 games, NL champs

Braves make their fourth World Series appearance in five years, but lose to Yankees in six. Playing their final season in Atlanta-Fulton County Stadium, Braves took the NL East lead on May 19 and were never headed as they cruised to eight-game division title. Team hits a lusty .270 with 197 homers. Mark Wohlers rings up club record 39 saves. Promising center fielder Andruw Jones, 19, makes major league debut in mid-August, hits a homer in his second game, and ripped homers in his first two Series at-bats in the opener against Yankees. In previous year, his homer against Colorado in the NLDS had made him the youngest in MLB history to homer in the postseason.

Key Schuerholz Move: Late-season trading brings P Denny Neagle, who would win 20 games, including four shutouts, in '97. Acquired reliever Kerry Ligtenberg in bizarre trade with independent minor league Minneapolis Loons in exchange for two dozen bats and six dozen balls. Two years later, in '98, Ligtenberg would become first NL rookie in a dozen years to post 30 saves.

1997—101-61, Won NL East by 9 games

Braves won a MLB-high 101 games and an unprecedented sixth straight division title, breaking the old mark of five in a row by the 1949–53 New York Yankees and 1971–75 Oakland A's. By winning 12 of their first 13 games, Braves took sole possession of first place on April 14 and kept it throughout the season. Pitchers led MLB with 3.18 ERA and 17 shutouts. Mark Wohlers became first Brave to notch consecutive seasons with 30+ saves, striking out 92 in 69.1 innings of relief. Braves hitters launched 12 grand slams, including three by Chipper Jones, who became the first Brave in 37 years with back-to-back 100 RBI seasons. Little Rafael Belliard hit his first home run in 10 years. Braves swept Houston in the Division Series, but lost in six games to Florida Marlins in the NLCS, marking the first time since '93 that a team other than the Braves represented the NL in the World Series.

Key Schuerholz Move: Forced to trade OF David Justice to free up money to re-sign P Greg Maddux, acquired OF Kenny Lofton in the deal. Lofton led Braves in average (.333) and stolen bases (27).

1998—106-56, Won NL East by 18 games

Braves set a franchise record with 106 wins and 215 homers. Became only third team in MLB history to produce four players with 30+ homers. Javy Lopez and Chipper Jones each hit 34 homers. Andruw Jones becomes youngest 20-20 player in MLB history with 31 homers and 27 stolen bases. Pitching staff paced both leagues with 24 complete games, 23 shutouts, and 1,232 strikeouts. Tom Glavine goes 20-6 with career-low 2.47 ERA to win Cy Young Award. Greg Maddux led league with 2.22 ERA and notched his 200th career victory. After division runaway and three-game sweep of Cubs in Division Series, lost NLCS in six games to Padres.

Key Schuerholz Move: Acquired free agent 1B Andres Galarraga, who led team with 44 homers and 121 RBI.

1999—103-59, Won NL East by 6.5 games, NL champs

Braves overcome loss of several key players, including 1B Andres Galarraga, who is diagnosed with lymphoma during spring training, closer Kerry Ligtenberg, who is lost for the season with an elbow ligament injury, and catcher Javy Lopez, who had an ACL tear in July after hitting .317 in first half. The team blew open a tight race with the Mets by taking five of six games from the New Yorkers in late September. Chipper Jones's four-HR barrage in one of those series led to his NL MVP selection. Braves set franchise record by scoring 840 runs. P Kevin Millwood upstaged Braves' "Big Three" by posting 18-7 record with NL second-ranked 2.68 ERA. John Rocker stepped in as Braves' third closer in as many seasons with 38 saves and 104 strikeouts in 72.1 innings. Beat Astros in Division Series and Mets in NLCS, but are swept 4–0 by Yankees in World Series.

Key Schuerholz Moves: Winter free agent grab OF Brian Jordan led team with career-high 115 RBI. Trade acquisition 2B Brett Boone contributes 20 homers in first year as a Brave. Trade acquisition P Mike Remlinger becomes unsung hero with 10-1 record and 2.37 ERA as middle reliever.

2000—95-67, Won NL East by 1 game

Stretch division championship streak to nine despite losing John Smoltz in the spring for entire season to shoulder surgery. Season highlighted by Braves' modern franchise record 15-game winning streak, longest in NL in 49 years. Team ran off 10-3 stretch in late September to clinch title over Mets. Chipper Jones followed his MVP season with fine .311, 36-111 production. SS Rafael Furcal, 19, is NL Rookie of the Year after hitting .295 and stealing 40 bases. 1B Andres Galarraga is Comeback Player of the Year with 28 homers and 100 RBI after missing '99 season with cancer bout. CF Andruw Jones makes All-Star Game for first time. Tom Glavine is second in Cy Young voting after 21-9 record and 241 innings pitched. Pitchers faltered as Cards swept Division Series.

Key Schuerholz Move: Winter trade acquisition IF Quilvio Veras is off to hot start with .309 average and 25 steals before being lost three games into the second half with an ACL knee injury.

2001—88-74, Won NL East by 2 games

Braves become the first team in all professional sports to claim a 10th straight division title by fighting off the Phillies in a race that went down to the final three days of the season. Once again, the team overcame a rash of injuries. Three-quarters of the starting infield had to be replaced by the start of September. P John Burkett becomes one of the biggest surprises in MLB, finishing third in the NL with 3.04 ERA and earning a spot on the NL All-Star team. Transformed as a closer, John Smoltz rebounds from surgeries with 10 saves in 11 opportunities, giving hint to his dominance as a closer over the coming three seasons. After sweeping Houston in the first round of the playoffs, Braves lose NLCS to Arizona.

Key Schuerholz Move: Traded away John Rocker and his massive PR distraction to Cleveland.

2002—101-59, Won East by 19 games

Braves breeze to division title by huge margin after overcoming their worst April (12-15) in the Schuerholz era. Pitching staff leads MLB in ERA (3.13) for the ninth time in 12 seasons. John Smoltz, in his first full year as a closer, sets NL record with 55 saves. Braves won the final 49 games in which Smoltz appeared. Mike Remlinger has another outstanding season in middle relief, posting a 1.99 ERA in 73 appearances. Greg Maddux (16-6) becomes first pitcher in MLB history besides Cy Young to ring up 15 consecutive 15-win seasons. Chipper Jones drives in 100 runs for the seventh straight season while making the unselfish transition to left field to make room for slick-fielding 3B Vinny Castilla. Andruw Jones leads team with 35 homers and wins his seventh straight Gold Glove Award. Braves lose to Giants in Division Series.

Key Schuerholz Move: OF Gary Sheffield, acquired in a trade with the Dodgers, launches two seasons of high-octane power hitting. After early-season injury, Sheffield rebounds to stroke 25 homers and .307 in 135 games. He reaches base in 52 straight games for franchise record.

2003—101-61, Won NL East by 10 games

Despite loss of starting pitchers Tom Glavine and Kevin Millwood, Braves once again confound the soothsayers by winning the division in a walk. The team rewrites franchise records with 907 runs, 235 homers, and 1,608 hits. Braves are never out of lead after May 2. C Javy Lopez, with 43 homers, leads procession of six Braves with 20 or more home runs. Bobby Cox is named NL Manager of the Year for second season in a row. Gary Sheffield sets franchise record with 132 RBI. Braves lose to Cubs, three games to two, in Division Series.

Key Schuerholz Moves: Again having to jettison a front-line player (this time Kevin Millwood) to make room for Greg Maddux money,

Schuerholz salvages minor league C Johnny Estrada in the deal. A year later, Estrada makes the NL All-Star team as a rookie and leads Braves with .314 average. Also acquired P Mike Hampton and P Russ Ortiz to plug the rotation vacancies. Ortiz leads NL with 21 wins and Hampton later develops into star-quality starter.

2004—96-66, Won NL East by 10 games

After losing Sheffield, Maddux, Lopez, and Castilla, Braves still won't go away, coasting to division title by 10 games after falling as low as fourth midseason. Starting June 26, Braves would win 47 of next 62 games, taking over first place in the process. Bobby Cox is selected NL Manager of the Year a third straight season. On September 29, he becomes ninth manager in MLB history to win 2,000 career games. Ageless 1B Julio Franco's .309 average was the highest ever by a player who opened the season at least 43 years old. John Smoltz becomes the fifth pitcher in MLB history to post three straight 40+ save seasons. Astros defeat Braves three games to two in Division Series.

Key Schuerholz Moves: P Jared Wright, fished out of scrap heap on waivers near the end of the '03 season, posts solid 15-8 season. P John Thomson, signed as a free agent, becomes solid starter and was a key down the stretch with 5-0 and 1.77 ERA over final eight starts. OF J. D. Drew, acquired in a trade with St. Louis, led team with 31 homers and 158 hits.

2005—90-72, Won NL East by 2 games

After losing stars Jared Wright and J. D. Drew to free agency, the Doubting Thomases were out in full voice. When the Braves fell to fourth place in June, 5½ games behind, and had three starting pitchers plus Chipper Jones and Johnny Estrada out with injuries, the pennant string was on life support. The bullpen was unreliable, and reclaimed veteran outfielders Raul Mondesi and Brian Jordan were unproductive.

Index

Enter the Baby Braves, an infusion of minor leaguers led by *SI* cover-boy Jeff Francoeur, who, along with vets CF Andruw Jones (51 homers, 128 RBI), 2B Marcus Giles (.291, 104 runs), and Rafael Furcal (46 stolen bases, 100 runs), picked up the slack in a second-half surge to the team's 14th straight division title. Reincarnated veteran starter John Smoltz spiked the critics of his bullpen-to-rotation return with a solid 14-7 record despite six blown saves by the bullpen and four starts with run support of 2 runs or less.

Key Schuerholz Moves: Acquired Jorge Sosa from Tampa Bay in the spring for middle relief and possible spot starting duty. When the starters went down, Sosa exceeded all expectations by posting a sterling 13-3 record as a starter. A July 31 trade with Detroit brought fireballer Kyle Farnsworth, who solved the glaring closer void with 10 saves in 10 opportunities over the final weeks of the stretch run.